Bayesian Analysis and
Uncertainty in
Economic Theory

BAYESIAN ANALYSIS AND UNCERTAINTY IN ECONOMIC THEORY

RICHARD M. CYERT
MORRIS H. DeGROOT

Carnegie Mellon University

ROWMAN & LITTLEFIELD
PUBLISHERS

ROWMAN & LITTLEFIELD

Published in the United States of America in 1987
by Rowman & Littlefield, Publishers
(a division of Littlefield, Adams & Company)
81 Adams Drive, Totowa, New Jersey 07512

Library of Congress Cataloging-in-Publication Data

Cyert, Richard Michael
  Bayesian analysis and uncertainty in economic theory.

  (Rowman & Littlefield probability and statistics series)
  Bibliography: p. 189
  Includes index.
  1. Economics—Statistical methods. I. DeGroot,
Morris H. II. Title. III. Series.
HB137.C93 1986   330'.01'51   85-18414
ISBN 0-8476-7471-1

87 88 89 / 10 9 8 7 6 5 4 3 2 1
Printed in the United States of America

To our wives,
Margaret S. Cyert and Marilyn D. DeGroot,
whose indifference to this work was
deeply appreciated by us.

Contents

Preface

We began this research with the objective of applying Bayesian methods of analysis to various aspects of economic theory. We were attracted to the Bayesian approach because it seemed the best analytic framework available for dealing with decision making under uncertainty, and the research presented in this book has only served to strengthen our belief in the appropriateness and usefulness of this methodology. More specifically, we believe that the concept of organizational learning is fundamental to decision making under uncertainty in economics and that the Bayesian framework is the most appropriate for developing that concept.

The central and unifying theme of this book is decision making under uncertainty in microeconomic theory. Our fundamental aim is to explore the ways in which firms and households make decisions and to develop models that have a strong empirical connection. Thus, we have attempted to contribute to economic theory by formalizing models of the actual process of decision making under uncertainty. Bayesian methodology provides the appropriate vehicle for this formalization.

We recognize that the topic of decision making under uncertainty is a wide one, and one that is actively being studied from many different perspectives. In particular, we applaud the work done by many economists in attempting to model oligopolies through the use of supergames and games of incomplete information. We are concerned, however, that the expectational assumptions of game theory, including dynamic "supergames" with imperfect information, have a weak empirical basis. The ongoing development of game theory through the use of more sophisticated mathematical models, we believe, is at best tangential to the actual process of decision making under uncertainty. Hence, we have largely eschewed this topic and its literature in favor of the Bayesian approach that is more relevant to our objective.

Advocates of game theory may still wonder why we have not emphasized Bayesian game theory. From our perspective, Bayesian game theory refers to models and processes in which the firms or other decision makers represent their uncertainties about their rivals and other aspects of their environment by their *actual* subjective probability distributions, unconstrained by any ad hoc expectational or equilibrium assumptions. In the framework of this definition, as described in Chapter 2, Bayesian game theory is clearly in an incipient stage. It is a promising but as yet undeveloped methodology.

The use of subjective probability in decision making under uncertainty is still relatively uncommon and not well understood in economics. One obvious confirmation of this assertion is the popularity of rational-expectations models, which enable economists to construct dynamic models in which there is a well-defined formula for the expectations to be used. Some type of expectation lies at the base of every dynamic model in economics, and the rational-expectations approach eases the problem of the specification of expectations, despite the typical lack of any empirical justification. Although we show in Chapter 13 that our approach can be used in some contexts to develop a process by which the rational-expectations equilibrium is attained, it is more often true that our approach is to be contrasted with rational expectations. We have utilized a decision-making process that we think has empirical validity. Therein, for us, lies the beauty of the work and its potential usefulness.

Because this book has evolved from a series of articles, we are sensitive (perhaps even defensive) about its cohesiveness. We have rewritten large segments of a number of the articles and, in particular, have developed a unified notation. In addition, new material has been included throughout the book.

Because our central and pervasive topic is decision making under uncertainty, we have included our work on adaptive utility. In adaptive utility models, firms and consumers must learn about and refine their own tastes and preferences, as well as learn about their environment, by making decisions under uncertainty and evaluating their experiences. We think the concept of adaptive utility has empirical relevance and great potential for theory. We have emphasized the cohesiveness of all our material by liberal cross-referencing throughout the book. It may be true that a few chapters are expendable in the sense that our points could be made even if they were omitted, but each chapter adds something new and the chapters are all connected by our general theme.

It is impossible to list the names of colleagues to whom we are indebted because the list is so extensive. We have received a large number of comments over the years that have resulted in improvements of our work, and this book incorporates those comments.

We are pleased with the great increase of activity in the area of Bayesian analysis applied to economic theory since we first published on this topic. We believe, however, that much remains to be done in this area. Our hopes for this book are that it will prove to be the stimulus that induces additional work and that it will make a contribution to economics and statistics, two fields about which we both care.

Richard M. Cyert
Morris H. DeGroot

Carnegie Mellon University
Pittsburgh, Pennsylvania
    January 1987

Acknowledgments

We owe a significant debt to our colleague Herbert A. Simon, to the late Leonard J. Savage, and to George J. Stigler, all of whom have influenced us at various times in our lives. None of them would agree with everything in the book, but we hope there are some parts that reflect their influence.

The continuous support of the National Science Foundation over the life of this research is deeply appreciated.

We thank Charles A. Holt for permitting us to adapt material from the articles of which he was a coauthor.

We also thank the publishers of the following articles for permission to adapt portions of them in this book:

"Bayesian analysis and duopoly theory," *Journal of Political Economy* **78** (1970). Reprinted with revisions in *Studies in Bayesian Econometrics and Statistics,* ed. S. E. Fienberg and A. Zellner. North-Holland Publishing Co. (1975).

"Multiperiod decision models with alternating choice as a solution to the duopoly problem," *Quarterly Journal of Economics* **84** (1970).

"Interfirm learning and the kinked demand curve," *Journal of Economic Theory* **3** (1971).

"An analysis of cooperation and learning in a duopoly context," *American Economic Review* **63** (1973).

"Rational expectations and Bayesian analysis," *Journal of Political Economy* **82** (1974).

"Adaptive utility," *Adaptive Economic Models,* ed. R. H. Day and T. Groves. Academic Press (1975). Reprinted in *Expected Utility and the Allais Paradox,* ed. M. Allais and O. Hagen. D. Reidel Publishing Co. (1979).

"Sequential strategies in dual control problems," *Theory and Decision* **8** (1977).

"Sequential investment decisions with Bayesian learning," *Management Science* **24** (1978) (with C. A. Holt).

"Capital allocation within a firm," *Behavioral Science* **24** (1979) (with C. A. Holt).

"Learning applied to utility functions," *Bayesian Analysis in Econometrics and Statistics*, ed. A. Zellner. North-Holland Publishing Co. (1980).

"The maximization process under uncertainty," *Advances in Information Processing in Organizations, Volume 1*, ed. P. D. Larkey and L. S. Sproull. JAI Press (1984).

Bayesian Analysis and
Uncertainty in
Economic Theory

1

Introduction

This book chronicles our efforts to grapple with ways of introducing uncertainty into economic theory, and then dealing directly with that uncertainty. Most previous attempts to deal with uncertainty have been designed to finesse the problem. Uncertainty is put into the problem, and an assumption is then made that allows the problem to be turned into one of certainty. Economists in particular have shown a talent for bringing every problem back to a world of certainty where all solutions are known or can be easily found.

This is not to say that economists have not worked on uncertainty. Chapter 3 cites some of the vast amount of work that has been undertaken. Cournot (1897), however, typifies the way in which uncertainty is introduced and then taken out by assumption. He posed a situation in which two firms sell mineral water from the same spring and have no costs. Assume a linear demand curve,

$$p = a - b(q + r). \tag{1}$$

Then firm 1's total revenue (profit) is

$$pq = aq - bq^2 - bqr. \tag{2}$$

Firm 1 maximizes profit by choosing a value of q such that

$$\frac{d(pq)}{dq} = a - 2bq - br - bq\frac{dr}{dq} = 0 \tag{3}$$

Similarly, firm 2 maximizes profit by choosing a value of r such that

$$\frac{d(pr)}{dr} = a - 2br - bq - br\frac{dq}{dr} = 0 \tag{4}$$

Cournot handled the uncertainty contained in the derivatives $dr/(dq)$ in (3) and $dq/(dr)$ in (4) by assuming that each was zero. That is, he assumed that neither rival would change output as a result of a change

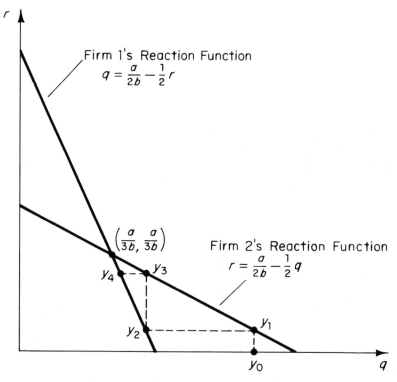

Figure 1.1 Cournot reaction functions

in the other's output. The model is then easily solved and the equilibrium value is found to be $a/(3b)$. The Cournot model generates a dynamic process that is illustrated in figure 1.1. If the process begins at the point y_0, then the reaction function of firm 2 leads to the point y_1 at the next stage. The reaction function of firm 1 then leads to y_2 and, in turn, the points $y_3, y_4, \ldots$ are reached successively. The process reaches equilibrium asymptotically even though each producer continues to make an erroneous assumption about the rival. Each time that one firm makes a change, it does so with the expectation that its rival will keep output constant. There is no learning mechanism for either firm built into the model. We refer to this model as inconsistent because the firms base their decisions on incorrect assumptions. Thus, through this inappropriate use of market information, the firms can reach an equilibrium even though they have the wrong model.

Other variations of this approach can clearly be made. One can assume values other than zero for the derivatives in (3) and (4), and a different equilibrium will be found. Stackelberg (1952) developed a series of different models by assuming the possibility of one firm being a leader and the other a follower. The follower continues to expect a zero change in output by the leader, whereas the leader is assumed to know the reaction function of the follower. An unstable situation results when both firms attempt to be leaders (Cohen and Cyert 1975, pp. 240–43).

An understanding of the way decisions are made under conditions of uncertainty is necessary if the behavior of economic units is to be explained (Simon 1957). There has been quite widespread recognition of this fact in recent years, but an inadequate amount of attention has been given to an understanding of the nature of uncertainty itself. In this chapter, we shall try to clarify the meaning of decision making under uncertainty. We shall then try to abstract some of the empirical generalizations derived from observation of decision making under uncertainty and develop a general model which may be useful for describing the decision-making process. In a broad sense, it will be a general prototype of the models we will develop for more specific purposes in this book.

Nature of Uncertainty

Knight (1920) distinguished between risk and uncertainty on the basis of the existence of numerical probabilities. He defined a state of uncertainty as existing for an event when no numerical probability of the event occurring can be assigned. In contrast, a state of risk exists when a numerical probability can be assigned. From the Bayesian point of view (see chapter 2) every event can be assigned a subjective probability by the decision maker. Since we take a Bayesian approach in this book, we make no distinction of the kind Knight made. We shall use the term "uncertainty" to describe any situation in which an event has a probability other than one or zero of occurring. Decision making under uncertainty refers to situations in which the outcome of the decision is not precisely predictable.

The decision situations that are usually included under the rubric of uncertainty are those in which the model contains parameters with unknown values, random error terms, or both. In order to understand the nature of decision making under uncertainty, it is useful to examine the role that learning can play in each of these decision situations. Learning takes place, of course, through additional observations. The simplest and most straightforward situation is one in which only a single parameter, such as the mean of some distribution of responses, is unknown. The standard problem of estimating the mean of a normal distribution when the variance is known is a typical example.

In general, the decision maker may have some control over the observations that can be obtained. Suppose a monopolist is operating in a situation with an unknown demand curve and wants to find the price that will maximize profit. A variety of decision rules might be used regarding the price that is set in each period of a sequential process. For example, price can be increased as long as profit is increasing and decreased when profit turns down. The actual increase or decrease is determined by the decision maker in order to optimize the trade-off between obtaining information about the unknown demand curve for use in future periods and profit in the immediate period.

This example could be contrasted with a model in which the demand at each price is equal to a known value *m* plus a random error term with a mean equal to zero. If the error terms are independent from period to period and each has a completely specified distribution, then the monopolist is unable to learn about the demand curve from any of the pricing decisions made. The monopolist can calculate the optimal price for maximizing expected profit and would have no reason to deviate from this price regardless of observed demands.

When *m* is unknown or the random error has a distribution that itself involves some unknown parameters, then learning is possible and decision rules of the kind described above for setting prices can be used. As the number of observations increases, the monopolist learns more about the demand curve but usually can never know it with certainty.

Sequential Approach to Decision Making

We believe the sequential approach just described characterizes most decisions in the real world made under conditions of uncertainty. Since in this book we will develop theoretical models with empirical relevance, it is useful to examine further the way in which the sequential decision-making process is actually used. This approach involves a division of the decision into parts, frequently just two, with the first decision designed to gather information with which to make the second decision. This approach is common to all firms that sell a product that has style and color variations. Firms in such cases do not make a single output decision as is assumed in static economic theory, but rather a sequence of output decisions. Each decision leads to additional information about the demand parameters, and uncertainty is decreased.

A good example of the sequential approach can be found in the ordering procedure of department stores (Cyert and March 1963). The store divides its order decisions into two stages—the advance (initial) order and reorders. The size of the advance order depends on the prior distribution of sales. The reorders are the final stage and are based on the sales of the various types of merchandise from the advance order. In this discussion we will consider how one of the departments in the store determines the advance order.

The particular department to be considered has four seasons—Easter, summer, fall, and Christmas. Prior to each season, a sample of the kinds of goods that would be available during the season is offered for sale. On the basis of the sales of these goods, the department makes decisions on the types of goods it should order for the season. It determines the amount of its advance order by estimating the total sales for the season and then taking a fraction of that total. The estimated total sales for a season are based on certain rules of thumb that depend heavily on the previous year's experience. The fraction applied to the total sales for the advance order is a function of the variability in sales experienced in the past.

As in the hypothetical example of the monopolist, the store must make a trade-off between information and immediate profit. Larger advance orders yield more information but create a greater risk to profit if the goods are not sold.

However, advance orders generally offer some additional advantages to the department over reorders. Greater selection is possible (some goods may not be available later), and some concessions may be offered by the producer, such as credit terms and extra services. The department exploits these advantages by ordering a substantial fraction of its anticipated sales in advance, but an attempt is made to limit the advance order fraction to an output that could be sold profitably even if the demand curve shifted downward.

As can be seen from this example, the sequential decision-making process is a practical one. It is also interesting from a theoretical standpoint and, therefore, forms the basis for all the models discussed in this book.

Future Chapters

This book presents a variety of decision-making models in a variety of decision-making contexts. Chapter 2 contains a review of the basic ideas of the Bayesian approach to decision theory. It includes a discussion of utility functions, subjective probability, statistical decision problems, sequential methods, and backward induction. In chapter 3 we present a control-theory model of the firm, in which the firm sets performance targets and selects control actions period by period to minimize deviations below the targets.

Chapter 4 begins a sequence of five chapters dealing with duopoly and oligopoly. Chapter 4 is an introduction to the use of Bayesian analysis and multiperiod problems in duopoly markets. In chapter 5 we extend the use of multiperiod models by assuming that the two firms in a duopoly make decisions in alternating periods. We develop mutually optimal reaction functions that give insight into the nature of various equilibrium positions that have been discussed in the literature. In chapter 6 we build a model that utilizes quantitative measures of cooperation between the firms. In this model the firms are able to move from a path leading to a noncooperative equilibrium to a path leading to a cooperative solution.

The kinked demand curve, which has a controversial position in oligopoly theory, is treated by Bayesian sequential methods in chapter 7. The resulting model explains why the behavior predicted by the kink sometimes holds and sometimes does not. In chapter 8 we apply the methods developed in chapters 5 and 6 to linear-quadratic stochastic control problems involving two decision makers. This chapter constitutes a helpful summary of our work on duopoly, but it may be omitted without any loss of continuity.

Chapters 9 and 10 contain models for handling the uncertainty that individuals have about their own utility functions. The models are applied to the standard income allocation problem and to a marketing problem in which a firm makes a trial offer to consumers.

Chapter 11 considers the optimal sequential process for making an investment decision for a project that consists of a number of modules. Chapter 12 deals with a number of decisions involving the allocation of resources for capital expenditures by large, multidivisional firms. The results of the analysis in this chapter reinforce the liquidity theory of investment. The models in chapter 13 demonstrate the process by which the equilibrium assumed by the rational-expectations hypothesis is attained, a process which is explicated by the use of Bayesian learning. In chapter 14 we address the criticism that Bayesian analysis is not a good description of the actual decision-making process and end the book with our view of its significant contributions.

2

Bayesian Decision Theory

In this chapter we shall present a review of decision theory based on the Bayesian approach to statistical inference and decision making. Decision theory deals with the development of methods and techniques that are appropriate for making decisions in an optimal fashion. In fact, statistics itself is sometimes described as the science of decision making under uncertainty. Although decision theory may not encompass the entire field of statistics, the importance of decision theory has steadily grown during the past 30 years as virtually all the classical problems of statistical inference, and many new problems as well, have been formulated in decision-theoretic terms.

The Bayesian approach is characterized by the fundamental assumption that any uncertainty that is present in a decision problem regarding the values of specific variables or quantities can be expressed in terms of a joint probability distribution for those values. In general, this distribution will be subjective in nature, in the sense that it will represent an individual economist's or decision maker's information and beliefs about the unknown values of these quantities. A useful reference for most of the material in this chapter is DeGroot (1970).

Parameters, Decisions, and Consequences

Consider a problem in which a decision maker (DM) must choose a decision from some class of available decisions, and suppose that the consequences of this decision depend on the unknown value θ of some *parameter* Θ. We use the term parameter here in a general sense, to represent any variable or quantity whose value is unknown to the DM but is relevant to his or her decision. Some authors refer to Θ as the "unknown state of nature" or "state of the world." The set Ω of all possible values of Θ is called the *parameter space*. Further, the *decision space D* is defined to be the set of all possible decisions d that the DM might make in a given problem.

For each value of $\theta \in \Omega$ and each possible decision $d \in D$, let $\gamma(\theta,d)$ denote the consequence to the DM if he or she chooses decision d when the parameter has value θ. Let C denote the set of all consequences that might result from all possible pairings of θ and d. At this level of generality, the set C is quite arbitrary. It might be a set of possible monetary gains or losses, a set of different commodity bundles, or a set of different levels of satisfaction that might result from purchasing and eating different meals at various restaurants. If Θ has a specified probability distribution, then the choice of any particular decision d will induce a probability distribution of $\gamma(\Theta,d)$ on the set C of possible consequences. Hence the DM's choice among the decisions in D is tantamount to a choice among various probability distributions on the set C.

Utility

The DM will typically have preferences among the consequences in C which in turn will result in his or her having preferences among the different possible probability distributions on C. In other words, if the DM could have a consequence from C generated by a random process in accordance with some specified probability distribution, he or she would generally have a preference as to which distribution was used.

Let U denote a real-valued function on the set C—that is, a function that assigns a real number to each consequence in C. Also, for any probability distribution P on the set C, let $E(U|P)$ denote the expectation of U with respect to the distribution P. Then under certain conditions regarding the coherence of the DM's preferences among probability distributions, it can be shown that there exists such a function U with the following property: For any two distributions P_1 and P_2, P_1 is not preferred to P_2 if and only if $E(U|P_1) \leq E(U|P_2)$.

A function U with this property is called a *utility function,* and the value that U assigns to any particular consequence is called the *utility* of that consequence. The *expected utility hypothesis,* as we have just described, states that the DM will prefer a probability distribution P for which $E(U|P)$ is as large as possible. In other words, the DM will prefer a distribution for which the expected utility of the resulting consequence is a maximum.

The four basic assumptions regarding the coherence of the DM's preferences that guarantee the existence of a utility function will now be described. For any two probability distributions P_1 and P_2 on the set of consequences C, we shall write $P_1 \leq P_2$ if P_1 is not preferred to P_2; $P_1 < P_2$ if P_2 is strictly preferred to P_1; and $P_1 \sim P_2$ if the DM is indifferent between P_1 and P_2.

Assumption U_1: For any two distributions P_1 and P_2, exactly one of the following three relations must hold: $P_1 < P_2$, $P_2 < P_1$, $P_1 \sim P_2$.

Assumption U_2: If P_1, P_2, and P_3 are distributions such that $P_1 \leq P_2$ and $P_2 \leq P_3$, then $P_1 \leq P_3$.

Together, these two assumptions state that the DM can order all the possible probability distributions on C in a complete, transitive ordering, with the possibility that he or she may be indifferent among some distributions. Because of Assumption U_2, the transitivity assumption, it is not possible for the DM to have cyclical preferences in the sense that he or she prefers P_2 to P_1 and P_3 to P_2, but also P_1 to P_3.

Next, for any two distributions P and Q, and any number α such that $0 < \alpha < 1$, we shall let $\alpha P + (1 - \alpha)Q$ denote the distribution which assigns the probability $\alpha P(A) + (1 - \alpha)Q(A)$ to each subset of consequences $A \subset C$.

Assumption U_3: For any distributions P_1, P_2, and P, and any number α such that $0 < \alpha < 1$, $\alpha P_1 + (1 - \alpha)P < \alpha P_2 + (1 - \alpha)P$ if and only if $P_1 < P_2$.

This assumption, which is often referred to as the independence assumption or the sure-thing principle, is the most controversial of the assumptions regarding utility theory. One consequence of this assumption is that if P_2 is preferred to P_1, then the mixture distribution $\alpha P_2 + (1 - \alpha)P$ will be preferred to the mixture distribution $\alpha P_1 + (1 - \alpha)P$ *regardless* of the nature of the distribution P with which both P_1 and P_2 are being mixed. A famous example constructed by Allais (1953) demonstrates that the preferences of skilled decision makers may violate Assumption U_3 in practical problems, and there have been interesting efforts to develop a theory of utility without Assumption U_3 (for example, Machina 1982).

Assumption U_4: For any distributions P_1, P_2, and P such that $P_1 < P < P_2$, there exist numbers α and β ($0 < \alpha < 1$ and $0 < \beta < 1$) such that $P < \alpha P_1 + (1 - \alpha)P_2$ and $P > \beta P_1 + (1 - \beta)P_2$.

This assumption states, in essence, that each distribution P has a finite, rather than an infinite, utility. The number α in Assumption U_4 is usually close to 0 and β close to 1. Thus, in words, the assumption states that if P_2 is preferred to P then, no matter how terrible the distribution P_1 may be, it is possible to assign a small enough probability α to P_1 so that $\alpha P_1 + (1 - \alpha)P_2$ is still preferred to P. Similarly, if P is preferred to P_1 then, no matter how wonderful the distribution P_2 may be, it is possible to assign a large enough probability β to P_1 so that P is still preferred to $\beta P_1 + (1 - \beta)P_2$.

The existence of a utility function follows from these four assumptions, together with a few other mathematical conditions guaranteeing the measurability of certain functions, the continuity of certain preferences, and the existence of certain expectations (DeGroot 1970, chapter 7). It should be noted that there is more than one utility function that could be used in a given problem. If U is a utility function, then

$$V = aU + b,$$

where a and b are constants ($a > 0$) is also a utility function. The reason is that for any two distributions P_1 and P_2,

$$E(U|P_1) \le E(U|P_2)$$

if and only if

$$E(V|P_1) \le E(V|P_2).$$

Hence, both U and V represent the DM's preferences equally well. In practice, this arbitrariness is exploited and removed by choosing two particular consequences and assigning to them the utilities 0 and 1, or 0 and 100, or some other convenient pair of reference values.

Components of a Decision Problem

We now return to the original decision problem. For each value of $\theta \in \Omega$ and each decision $d \in D$, let $U(\theta,d)$ denote the utility of the consequence $\gamma(\theta,d)$. We may think of $U(\theta,d)$ as the utility of choosing decision d when the parameter Θ has the value θ. Now assume that Θ has a specified probability distribution ξ. Then in accordance with the expected utility hypothesis, the DM will choose a decision d for which the expected utility $E(U|\xi,d)$ is a maximum. Such a decision is called an *optimal decision* or a *Bayes decision* with respect to the distribution ξ.

In many decision problems, it has become standard to specify the negative of the utility function, rather than the utility function itself, and to call this function the *loss function*. Thus the *loss* $L(\theta,d)$ is the *disutility* to the DM of choosing decision d when the parameter has the value θ. An optimal or *Bayes decision* with respect to the distribution ξ will be a decision d for which the expected loss $E(L|\xi,d)$ is a minimum.

Thus the components of a decision problem are a parameter space Ω, a decision space D, and a loss function $L(\theta,d)$. For any given distribution ξ of Θ, the expected loss $E(L|\xi,d)$ is called the *risk* $R(\xi,d)$ of the decision d. The risk of the Bayes decision—that is, the minimum $R_0(\xi)$ of $R(\xi,d)$ over all decisions $d \in D$—is called the *Bayes risk*.

Comparison of Bayesian and Classical Approaches to Decision Theory

In the original formulation of decision theory, as developed by Wald (1950), the parameter Θ was not necessarily assigned a probability distribution in every decision problem. Wald and many other decision theorists base their development on a classical or frequency concept of probability in which a probability can be assigned to an event only if this probability can be interpreted as the relative frequency of occurrence of the event in an infinite sequence—although perhaps only a hypothetical or conceptual infinite sequence—of trials. In this view, Θ is often a parameter with a fixed but unknown value θ to which these frequentist concepts do not apply.

In such problems the basic object of study becomes the loss function $L(\theta,d)$, regarded as a function of $\theta \in \Omega$ for each $d \in D$, and the comparison of two or more decisions is based on a comparison of their loss functions. A decision d is said to be *dominated* by another decision d^* if $L(\theta,d^*) \leq L(\theta,d)$ for all $\theta \in \Omega$ with strict inequality for at least one value of θ. A decision d is said to be *admissible* if it is not dominated by any other decision in D. A set of decisions $D_0 \subset D$ is said to be *complete* if every decision outside D_0 is dominated by some decision in D_0.

Thus, when trying to choose a decision in a particular problem, the DM can restrict himself or herself to considering only the decisions in a complete class D_0. For this reason, the smallest such class, called a *minimal complete class,* is of interest. In many decision problems, but by no means all, the class of all admissible decisions is a minimal complete class.

Under this approach some further criteria must be brought to bear to help the DM choose a single decision from a complete class D_0. The most commonly proposed criterion is the *minimax* rule: Choose a decision d_0 such that

$$\sup_{\theta \in \Omega} L(\theta,d_0) = \inf_{d \in D} \sup_{\theta \in \Omega} L(\theta,d). \tag{1}$$

A decision d_0 that satisfies this relation is called a *minimax decision.* In words, a minimax decision is one for which the maximum possible loss over all possible values of Θ is as small as possible. The minimax decision is clearly based on a worst-case analysis in which the DM tries to protect himself or herself as much as possible against the worst loss that can possibly occur.

Another approach to choosing a single decision from D_0 is for the DM to assign a weight function $w(\theta)$ over the values in Ω and to choose a decision d_0 that minimizes

$$\int_{\theta\in\Omega} L(\theta,d)w(\theta)d\theta. \tag{2}$$

If Ω contains only a finite or countable number of points, the integral in (2) is replaced by a sum. In our opinion, the only reasonable basis for assigning a particular weight function w is that it reflects the relative likelihood of the different values in Ω being the true value of Θ. In other words, w should be taken to be a probability distribution assigned to Θ that reflects these relative likelihoods. These considerations bring us back to the Bayesian approach to decision theory that we will follow in this book, in which it is assumed that such a probability distribution can always be assigned.

Subjective Probability

In some decision problems, the probability distribution ξ that the DM assigns to Θ will be based on a large amount of historical data or on theoretical frequency considerations. In such problems, the distribution ξ will be "objective" in the sense that any other DM who faced the same problem would assign the same distribution. In most decision problems, however, the distribution ξ will be a "subjective" distribution that is based, at least in part, on the DM's personal information and beliefs about what the value of Θ is likely to be.

The existence of *subjective probabilities* is based on the assumption that certain conditions are satisfied regarding the coherence of the DM's judgments about the relative likelihoods of various values of Θ. When these conditions are satisfied, it can be shown that there exists a unique probability distribution P on the set Ω that satisfies all the mathematical properties of probability and has the additional property that, for any two subsets $A \subset \Omega$ and $B \subset \Omega$, $P(A) \leq P(B)$ if and only if the DM does not believe that the value of Θ is more likely to lie in A than in B. In accordance with the common terminology of probability, it will be convenient to speak of an *event* $A \subset \Omega$ rather than a subset $A \subset \Omega$. In this terminology, if the value of Θ lies in the subset A, then we say that the event A has occurred.

The three basic assumptions regarding the coherence of the DM's judgments that guarantee the existence of a probability distribution P over all events $A \subset \Omega$ will now be described. For any two events A and B, we shall write $A \leq B$ if A is not regarded as more likely than B; $A < B$ if B is regarded as more likely than A; and $A \sim B$ if A and B are regarded as equally likely. The symbol ϕ denotes the empty set (the null event).

Assumption P_1: For any two events A and B, exactly one of the following three relations must hold: $A < B$, $B < A$, $A \sim B$.

Assumption P_2: If A_1, A_2, B_1 and B_2 are any four events such that $A_1 \cap A_2 = B_1 \cap B_2 = \phi$, $A_1 \leq B_1$, and $A_2 \leq B_2$, then $A_1 \cup A_2 \leq B_1 \cup B_2$. If, in addition, either $A_1 < B_1$ or $A_2 < B_2$, then $A_1 \cup A_2 < B_1 \cup B_2$.

It can be shown that these two assumptions together imply the transitivity of judgments: If $A \leq B$ and $B \leq C$, then $A \leq C$. Thus, the assumptions imply that there is a complete, transitive ordering of all events with respect to their relative likelihoods, with the possibility that some events may be judged to be equally likely. These assumptions also go a long way toward guaranteeing the additivity of the probabilities of disjoint events, which is a necessary property of any probability function P.

The next assumption states that no event is less likely than the null event ϕ, and the certain event Ω is strictly more likely than ϕ.

Assumption P_3: If A is any event, than $\phi \leq A$. Furthermore, $\phi < \Omega$.

The existence of a unique probability distribution P that agrees with the DM's judgments of relative likelihood follows from these three assumptions, together with a few other mathematical conditions that guarantee the continuity of certain probabilities and ensure that the space in which we are working is rich enough so that the probability of each event can be located as a unique point in the interval [0, 1] (DeGroot 1970, chapter 6).

Some decision theorists feel that there are different types of probability and that subjective probabilities are of a different type from *logical, frequency,* or *physical probabilities*. On the other hand, it can be argued that subjective probability is the only type of probability that can be put on a sound foundation and the only type of probability that exists. In this book we take the position that all probabilities are subjective; some are more "objective" than others only because larger groups of DM's would assign the same values for these probabilities based on their experience.

Together, the concepts of subjective probability and utility provide a unified theory of decision making. The DM's subjective probabilities represent his or her knowledge and beliefs, and the DM's utilities represent his or her tastes and preferences. Expert DM's are careful to maintain the distinction between these concepts, and do not confuse the value that they wish Θ would have with the value that they think Θ is likely to have. In other words, the DM does not let utilities influence the subjective assignment of probabilities, and vice versa. The DM then chooses a decision that maximizes subjective expected utility or, equivalently, minimizes subjective expected loss.

Decision Analysis

Many problems of decision making, such as deciding where to locate a new airport, are extremely complicated, and it is often not immediately clear how to apply the concepts of decision theory that have just been described. The process of aiding the DM in applying these concepts in a particular problem is called *decision analysis*. In recent years techniques of decision analysis have been developed that are intended to aid the DM in (a) identifying all the relevant dimensions of the parameter Θ, (b) specifying the spaces Ω and D of all possible parameter values θ and decisions d, and especially (c) specifying the DM's probabilities and utilities (Raiffa 1968; Keeney and Raiffa 1976; Decision Analysis Group, SRI International 1977).

Various procedures are available, including computer programs, for the elicitation of a DM's subjective probabilities. A probability distribution on Ω must be determined on the basis of the DM's responses when questioned about the relative likelihoods of different events. Some type of statistical procedure is usually needed to fit a distribution because few persons exhibit the degree of coherence necessary to specify a unique distribution (Kadane et al. 1980; Lindley, Tversky, and Brown 1979). Similarly, procedures are available for fitting a utility function on the basis of the DM's responses when questioned about preferences among different probability distributions that might yield a consequence from the set C (Becker, DeGroot, and Marschak 1964; Novick and Lindley 1979).

Statistical Decision Problems

In many decision problems, the DM has the opportunity, before choosing a decision in D, of observing the value of a random variable or random vector X that is related to the parameter Θ. The observation of X provides information that may be helpful to the DM in making a good decision. We shall assume that the conditional distribution of X given $\Theta = \theta$ can be specified for every value of $\theta \in \Omega$. A problem of this type is called a *statistical decision problem*.

Thus the components of a statistical decision problem are a parameter space Ω, a decision space D, a loss function L, and a family of conditional densities $f(x|\theta)$ of an observation X whose value will be available to the DM when he or she makes a decision. The conditional densities $f(x|\theta)$ might be of either the discrete or the continuous type. In a statistical decision problem, the probability distribution of Θ is called its *prior distribution* because it is the distribution of Θ before X has been observed. The conditional distribution of Θ given the observed value $X = x$ is then called the *posterior distribution* of Θ.

Suppose that Θ has the prior density $\xi(\theta)$, which again could be of either the discrete or the continuous type. Then for any given value $X = x$, the posterior density $\xi(\theta|x)$ of Θ can be found from the following basic result, known as Bayes' theorem:

$$\xi(\theta|x) = \frac{f(x|\theta)\xi(\theta)}{\int_\Omega f(x|\theta')\xi(\theta')d\theta'}. \tag{3}$$

This expression for $\xi(\theta|x)$ is written using an integral, as though $\xi(\theta)$ is a probability density function (p.d.f.). If it is actually a discrete probability function, the integral in (3) should be replaced by a sum. Throughout this chapter we shall write expressions with integral signs, as if $\xi(\theta)$ or $f(x|\theta)$ were p.d.f.'s, but all these expressions will apply equally well to discrete distributions by replacing the integrals with sums.

A *decision function* is a rule that specifies a decision $\delta(x) \in D$ that will be chosen for each possible observed value x of X. The *risk* $R(\xi,\delta)$ of a decision function with respect to the prior distribution ξ is the expected loss

$$R(\xi,\delta) = E\{L[\theta,\delta(X)]\} \tag{4}$$

$$= \int_\Omega \int_x L[\theta,\delta(x)]f(x|\theta)\xi(\theta)dxd\theta.$$

We recall that a decision function $\delta^*(x)$ for which the risk $R(\xi,\delta)$ is a minimum is called a *Bayes decision function* with respect to ξ, and its risk $R(\xi,\delta^*)$ is called the *Bayes risk*.

A Bayes decision function is easily described. After the value x has been observed, the DM simply chooses a Bayes decision $\delta^*(x)$ with respect to the posterior distribution $\xi(\theta|x)$ rather than the prior distribution $\xi(\theta)$. Thus, if the DM has no control over whether or not the observation X will be obtained, he or she need not specify the entire Bayes decision function in advance. The DM can wait until the observed value x is known, and then simply choose a Bayes decision $\delta^*(x)$ with respect to the posterior distribution. At this stage of the decision-making process, the DM is not interested in the risk $R(\xi,\delta)$, which is an average over all possible observations, but in the posterior risk

$$\int_\Omega L[\theta,\delta^*(x)]\xi(\theta|x)d\theta, \tag{5}$$

which is the risk from the decision he or she is actually making.

On the other hand, if the DM must decide whether or not to obtain the observation X at some specified cost, or must choose among different possible observations or different possible sample sizes, at varying costs, then he or she must consider the Bayes risk $R(\xi,\delta^*)$. In these situations, the DM must compare the reduction in risk that can be obtained from an observation X with the cost of observing X.

It can be shown that information is never harmful in the following sense. In every statistical decision problem, for every possible observation X, the Bayes risk $R(\xi,\delta^*)$ is never greater than the Bayes risk $R_0(\xi)$ that could be obtained by immediately choosing a decision $d \in D$ without observing X. Thus, if an observation X is offered without cost, it can never hurt the DM to observe its value, and it will typically be helpful in the sense that it will reduce the Bayes risk.

It should be emphasized that the reduction in Bayes risk from the observation X, as represented by the inequality $R(\xi,\delta^*) \leq R_0(\xi)$, means that the overall average risk $R(\xi,\delta^*)$ from observing X is not greater than the risk $R_0(\xi)$ that could be attained by an immediate decision. It is possible that for certain values of x, the posterior risk given by (3) is actually larger than $R_0(\xi)$, even if the observation is costless. If one of these values of x is observed, the DM will find that the posterior risk from a Bayes decision $\delta^*(x)$ is larger than the risk $R_0(\xi)$ that he or she would have suffered by making a decision without observing X. Should the DM regret making the observation, or even "forget" that it was made and just revert to the original decision?

The answer to this question is, of course, no. If the posterior risk is larger than $R_0(\xi)$, the reason is usually that the posterior density $\xi(\theta|x)$ is more spread out and less concentrated than the prior density $\xi(\theta)$. This means that the DM was relatively certain that he or she knew the value of Θ and concentrated the prior density around that value. The Bayes risk from an immediate decision was, therefore, small *with respect to that prior density*. If the observed value x indicates that Θ may be far from the favored value, the posterior density will be more spread out and the DM will be less certain than originally about the value of Θ. Although the posterior risk of the Bayes decision $\delta^*(x)$ will be relatively large, the posterior risk from the original Bayes decision would be even larger with respect to the posterior density, which represents the DM's current state of knowledge. Thus the DM benefits from the observation because having concentrated the prior density around a possibly incorrect value of Θ might have led to a bad decision. Further observations, when available, would ultimately lead the posterior density to become more and more concentrated around the correct value.

Conjugate Families of Prior Distributions

Consider a problem in which the observation vector $X = (X_1, \ldots, X_n)$ is a random sample from one of the standard distributions that are used in statistics such as a Bernoulli, Poisson, normal, exponential, or uniform distribution. If the distribution depends on a parameter Θ, it is convenient to have another standard family of prior distributions that can be used to represent the DM's prior information. One convenient property of such a family is that it be *closed under sampling;* that is, if the prior distribution of Θ belongs to the family, then for any sample size n and any values of the observations in the sample, the posterior distribution will also belong to the family. A family with this property is also called a *conjugate family of prior distributions.*

For a conjugate family of distributions to be useful it must be small enough so that it can itself be described by just a few parameters (or *hyperparameters,* as they are called, in order to distinguish these parameters of the conjugate family from the parameter Θ). On the other hand, it must be rich enough to permit the DM to find within the family a distribution that will adequately represent the prior distribution. Thus both the family of *all* probability distributions on Ω and the family containing just a single degenerate distribution that concentrates all its probability on one particular value in Ω are always conjugate families in every problem, but one family is much too large and the other is much too small to be useful.

We shall now describe the conjugate families that have proven to be useful for sampling from Bernoulli and normal distributions. A sequence of random variables $X_1, \ldots, X_n$ is said to form a sequence of *Bernoulli trials* with parameter Θ if these variables are independent and identically distributed, each can take only the values 0 and 1, and for $i = 1, \ldots, n$,

$$\Pr(X_i = 1) = \Theta, \; \Pr(X_i = 0) = 1-\Theta. \tag{6}$$

The most commonly used conjugate family of distributions for Θ is the family of *beta distributions,* defined as follows:

The parameter Θ is said to have a beta distribution with hyperparameters α and β ($\alpha > 0$ and $\beta > 0$) if the p.d.f. of Θ is of the form

$$\xi(\theta) = \frac{\Gamma(\alpha + \beta)}{\Gamma(\alpha)\Gamma(\beta)} \theta^{\alpha-1}(1 - \theta)^{\beta-1} \qquad \text{for } 0 < \theta < 1, \tag{7}$$

and $\xi(\theta) = 0$ for θ outside the interval $0 < \theta < 1$. The notation $\Gamma(u)$ in (7) represents the gamma function evaluated at the point u.

The basic result can now be stated as follows:

Proposition 1: Suppose that $X_1, \ldots, X_n$ form a sequence of Bernoulli trials with unknown parameter Θ, and suppose that the prior distribution of Θ is a beta distribution with hyperparameters α and β. Then the posterior distribution of Θ given the observed values $x_1, \ldots, x_n$ is again a beta distribution with hyperparameters $\alpha + \Sigma_{i=1}^{n} x_i$ and $\beta + n - \Sigma_{i=1}^{n} x_i$.

It is said that a random variable X has a *normal distribution* with mean m and precision h if X has a distribution of continuous type for which the p.d.f. is given by

$$f(x) = \left(\frac{h}{2\pi}\right)^{1/2} \exp\left[-\frac{h}{2}(x - m)^2\right] \qquad \text{for } -\infty < x < \infty. \qquad (8)$$

It should be noted that the precision h in (8) is the reciprocal of the variance. Any normal distribution is characterized by its mean m and its variance $\sigma^2 = 1/h$, and is often denoted $N(m, \sigma^2)$. We shall now present the basic result for sampling from a normal distribution when the precision is known:

Proposition 2: Suppose that $X_1, \ldots, X_n$ form a random sample from a normal distribution with unknown mean Θ and known precision h, and suppose that the prior distribution of Θ is a normal distribution with mean μ and precision τ. Then the posterior distribution of Θ given the observed values $x_1, \ldots, x_n$ is again a normal distribution with mean

$$\mu = \frac{\tau\mu + h\sum_{i=1}^{n} x_i}{\tau + nh} \qquad (9)$$

and precision $\tau + nh$.

In order to state the corresponding result when both the mean Θ and the precision H are unknown, we need to introduce the family of *gamma distributions*.

It is said that a random variable H has a gamma distribution with parameters α and β ($\alpha > 0$ and $\beta > 0$) if H has a distribution of continuous type for which the p.d.f. is given by

$$\xi(h) = \frac{\beta^\alpha}{\Gamma(\alpha)} h^{\alpha-1} e^{-\beta h} \qquad \text{for } h > 0 \qquad (10)$$

and $\xi(h) = 0$ for $h \leq 0$.

We can now present the basic result regarding conjugate prior distributions for Θ and H:

Proposition 3: Suppose that $X_1, \ldots, X_n$ form a random sample from a normal distribution with both unknown mean Θ and unknown precision H, and suppose that the joint prior distribution of Θ and H is as follows: The conditional distribution of Θ given $H = h$ is a normal distribution with mean μ and precision τh, where τ is a positive constant, and the marginal distribution of H is a gamma distribution with parameters α and β. Then the posterior joint distribution of Θ and H given the observed values $x_1, \ldots, x_n$ is as follows: The conditional distribution of Θ given

$H = h$ is again a normal distribution with mean

$$\frac{\tau\mu + \sum_{i=1}^{n} x_i}{\tau + n} \tag{11}$$

and precision $(\tau + n)h$, and the marginal distribution of H is again a gamma distribution with parameters $\alpha + (1/2)n$ and

$$\beta + \frac{1}{2}\sum_{i=1}^{n}(x_i - \bar{x})^2 + \frac{\tau n(\bar{x} - \mu)^2}{2(\tau + n)}. \tag{12}$$

Standard conjugate families of prior distributions for samples from a variety of distributions other than the Bernoulli and normal distributions, including the other distributions mentioned at the beginning of this section, are given by DeGroot (1970, chapter 9).

Improper Prior Distributions

In some problems, the prior information of the DM about the parameter Θ is vague relative to the information about Θ that will be obtained by observing X. Because of the vagueness of the prior information, it may be difficult for the DM to select a particular distribution from the conjugate family to represent the prior distribution. Also, because the DM will soon acquire relatively precise information about Θ from the observation X, it will typically not be worthwhile for the DM to spend much time making a careful determination of the prior distribution. In this type of situation it may be convenient to use a standard prior distribution that is suitable as an approximate representation of vague prior information.

The standard prior distribution that is used is often an *improper distribution* in the sense that it is represented by a nonnegative density $\xi(\theta)$ for which the integral over the entire space Ω is infinite rather than 1. For example, suppose that the DM is going to draw a random sample $X_1, \ldots, X_n$ from a normal distribution with unknown mean Θ and known precision h, and that the DM has only vague prior information about Θ. To use a prior distribution for Θ from the conjugate family, the DM must specify a normal distribution for Θ with a small precision (a large variance). Rather than try to select particular values for the mean and precision of the prior normal distribution, it is common practice to represent this prior distribution by a uniform, or constant, density over the entire real line, even though this density does not represent a proper probability distribution. In a sense that will now be described, this uniform density can be thought of as the limit of a proper normal prior distribution as the precision of that normal distribution approaches zero.

Although a uniform density over the entire real line represents an improper distribution, it is often possible to develop a proper posterior distribution for Θ by formally inserting the uniform density into Bayes' theorem—that is, taking $\xi(\theta) = c$, a constant, in (3) and carrying out the calculation for the posterior density. When Bayes' theorem is applied in this way for the observed values $x_1, \ldots, x_n$ of the normal random sample, it is found that the posterior distribution of Θ is a proper normal distribution with mean $\bar{x}$ and precision nh.

This result can be compared with the posterior distribution of Θ that was presented in Proposition 2 based on a conjugate normal prior distribution with mean μ and precision τ. It can be seen that the posterior distribution derived from the uniform prior density is the limit of the posterior distribution derived from the normal prior distribution as the precision τ of that prior distribution approaches zero.

When a random sample $X_1, \ldots, X_n$ is to be drawn from a normal distribution for which both the mean Θ and the precision H are unknown, and about which the DM has only vague information, it is common to represent the joint prior distribution of Θ and H by the joint density

$$\xi(\theta,h) = \frac{1}{h} \qquad \text{for } -\infty < \theta < \infty, h > 0. \tag{13}$$

This density again represents an improper prior distribution in which Θ and H are independent and Θ and $\log H$ each have uniform densities over the entire real line. For $n \geq 2$, a proper posterior distribution is obtained from the formal application of Bayes' theorem that is the same as the limiting posterior distribution that was presented in Proposition 3 based on a conjugate joint prior distribution when we let $\tau \to 0$, $\alpha \to -1/2$, and $\beta \to 0$.

Improper prior distributions must always be used with utmost caution, since they do not satisfy the rules of probability. Although the posterior density $\xi(\theta|x)$ may represent a proper probability distribution, the conditional densities $f(x|\theta)$ and $\xi(\theta|x)$ will typically be mutually incompatible because they did not arise from a proper probability model. In certain circumstances, especially when the parameter Θ is a vector of high dimension, decisions based on posterior distributions derived from improper prior distributions can be unreasonable.

Estimation and Tests of Hypotheses

The standard estimation problems of statistical inference can be formulated as decision problems. For example, consider a real-valued parameter Θ that is to be estimated. The parameter space Ω in a problem like this is usually an interval of the real line, possibly an unbounded interval or the entire line. Since the decision to be chosen is an estimate of Θ, the decision space D is the same interval as Ω itself.

The most widely used loss function in problems involving the estimation of a real parameter is the *squared error loss*

$$L(\theta,d) = (\theta - d)^2. \tag{14}$$

A Bayes estimate of Θ for this loss function is a number d for which the *mean squared error* $E[(\Theta - d)^2]$ is a minimum. It can be shown that the Bayes estimate is the mean of the posterior distribution of Θ, and the posterior risk is the variance of that posterior distribution, assuming that the mean and variance exist.

Another loss function that is often used in the estimation of a real parameter is the *absolute error loss*

$$L(\theta,d) = |\theta - d|. \tag{15}$$

A Bayes estimate for this loss function is a number d for which the *mean absolute error* $E(|\theta - d|)$ is a minimum. It can be shown for this function that the Bayes estimate is the median of the posterior distribution of Θ or, more precisely, *any* median of the posterior distribution of Θ, since the median need not be unique.

Both the loss functions (14) and (15) are of the general form

$$L(\theta,d) = \lambda(\theta)|\theta - d|^p, \tag{16}$$

where p is a positive number and $\lambda(\theta)$ is a positive function of θ. If $\lambda(\theta)$ is not constant, the loss in (16) depends not only on the magnitude of the error $|\theta - d|$ but on the value of θ as well. However, every loss function of the form (16) is still rather special, because overestimates and underestimates of the same magnitude yield the same loss. Loss functions that do not have this symmetric feature can also be introduced.

The standard problems of testing hypotheses can also be formulated as decision problems. In fact, every test of competing hypotheses is, at least theoretically, a problem with exactly two decisions: accept the null hypothesis H_0, which we shall call decision d_0, and accept the alternative hypothesis H_1 (or, equivalently, reject H_0), which we shall call decision d_1.

Loss functions appropriate to testing hypotheses can easily be developed. For example, suppose that Θ is a real-valued parameter and it is desired to test the hypotheses $H_0 : \Theta \leq \theta_0$ and $H_1: \Theta > \theta_0$, where θ_0 is a specified number. A typical loss function for this problem would have the following form:

$$
\begin{aligned}
L(\theta,d_0) &= 0 && \text{for } \theta \leq \theta_0, \\
L(\theta,d_0) &= \lambda_0(\theta) && \text{for } \theta > \theta_0, \\
L(\theta,d_1) &= \lambda_1(\theta) && \text{for } \theta \leq \theta_0, \\
L(\theta,d_1) &= 0 && \text{for } \theta > \theta_0,
\end{aligned}
\tag{17}
$$

where $\lambda_0(\theta)$ is positive and nondecreasing for $\theta > \theta_0$ and $\lambda_1(\theta)$ is positive and nonincreasing for $\theta < \theta_0$. The posterior p.d.f. of Θ can be calculated from any specified prior p.d.f. The Bayes test procedure would then choose the decision with the smaller posterior risk.

Special consideration is needed for testing hypotheses in which the dimension of the set of values of Θ that satisfy H_0 is smaller than the dimension of the whole parameter space Ω. A null hypothesis H_0 with this property is sometimes called *sharp*. For example, suppose again that Θ is a real-valued parameter and it is desired to test the hypotheses $H_0 : \Theta = \theta_0$ and $H_1: \Theta \neq \theta_0$. Under any prior p.d.f. that is assigned to Θ, the probability of H_0 will be zero since the probability of any single value of Θ is zero. Hence the posterior probability of H_0 after any observations will again be zero, and the Bayes decision is always to choose d_1 and reject H_0.

This decision is not entirely unreasonable in many problems, since the DM knows to begin with that the continuous parameter Θ is not *exactly* equal to θ_0, even though it may be very close. Therefore, H_0 cannot strictly be true, and it is appropriate to reject it immediately. Often, however, the DM wishes to accept H_0 if Θ is sufficiently close to θ_0. In such problems, the hypothesis H_0 should be widened to include a suitable interval around θ_0. The hypothesis H_0 would then have positive probability under the prior distribution, and a Bayes test procedure can be developed in the usual way.

Finally, there are some problems in which the DM actually does believe that the sharp null hypothesis $H_0 : \Theta = \theta_0$ might be true. For example, there might be a physical theory that leads to this particular value. One way to proceed in such problems is to assign an atom of positive probability p_0 to the point θ_0 and to spread the remaining probability $1 - p_0$ over the values $\theta \neq \theta_0$ in accordance with some p.d.f. $\xi(\theta)$. Test procedures based on this type of prior distribution require careful study, because they can exhibit some unusual features.

Sequential Decision Problems

In many statistical decision problems, the DM can obtain the observations $X_1, X_2, \ldots$ in a random sample one at a time. After each observation X_n the DM can calculate the posterior distribution for Θ based on the observed values of $X_1, \ldots, X_n$ and can decide whether to terminate the sampling process and choose a decision from D or to continue the sampling process and observe X_{n+1}. A problem of this type is called a *sequential decision problem*.

In most sequential decision problems there is either an explicit or an implicit cost associated with each observation. A procedure for deciding when to stop sampling and when to continue is called a stopping rule. The fundamental task of the DM in a sequential decision problem is to determine a stopping rule that will minimize some overall combination of loss from choosing a decision in D and sampling cost.

If X_1, X_2, ... form a sequential random sample from some distribution that depends on the parameter Θ, it is relatively easy for the DM to update the posterior distribution after each observation. This updating can be done one observation at a time: the posterior distribution after X_n has been observed serves as the prior distribution of Θ for X_{n+1}. The DM can simply use this current prior density for Θ, together with the conditional density of X_{n+1} given Θ, in Bayes' theorem (3) to obtain the posterior distribution after X_{n+1} has been observed.

For example, the posterior distribution given in Proposition 1 for Bernoulli trials with a beta prior distribution could be built up sequentially. Each Bernoulli trial X_i increases either the hyperparameter α or the hyperparameter β by one unit in the posterior distribution at that stage, according as $X_i = 1$ or $X_i = 0$. At the end of n trials, after n successive updatings of this type, we will have attained the posterior distribution given in Proposition 1. Similarly, the posterior distributions given in Propositions 2 and 3 for normally distributed observations could be built up sequentially by updating the posterior distribution after each observation X_i and letting this posterior distribution serve as the prior distribution for the next observation.

The standard problems of estimation and tests of hypotheses can be treated sequentially. Once the DM decides to stop sampling, the choice of decision from D is clear: the DM will simply choose the Bayes estimate or Bayes test procedure with respect to the posterior distribution of Θ. It is often assumed that there is constant cost per observation (although a varying cost is more realistic in most problems), and the DM must find a stopping rule that minimizes a linear combination of risk and expected sampling cost.

In order to determine whether it is optimal to continue sampling or to stop at any particular stage of a sequential process, it is necessary to compare (1) the risk from taking another observation and then continuing in an optimal way after that, with (2) the risk from stopping immediately without taking any further observations. If (1) is smaller than (2), then it is optimal to continue for at least one more observation. If (2) is smaller than (1), then it is optimal to stop sampling. Finally, if (1) and (2) happen to be equal, then it does not matter whether the DM stops or takes another observation and then continues in an optimal way, since the risk is the same from either decision.

This discussion implies that in order for the DM to be able to determine whether it is optimal to continue or stop at a given stage, he or she must know what the optimal procedure would be at any future stage. In turn, this suggests that in a problem in which there is a fixed finite maximum number of observations that can be taken, the optimal stopping rule can be developed by working backward from the final stage toward the beginning, one observation at a time. This method for determining the optimal procedure is called *backward induction*.

Thus, suppose that the maximum number of observations that can be taken is K; that is, sampling must be stopped after the Kth observation if it has not been stopped sooner. For each possible posterior distribution ξ of Θ that might be reached after $K - 1$ observations, we can determine whether it would be optimal to take one more observation and then stop sampling, or to stop without taking the final observation. To be specific, let $\rho_0(\xi)$ denote the risk from stopping without any further observations and let ξ' denote the new posterior distribution that results if one more observation is taken. Further, let c denote the cost of taking each observation, and assume that the total risk from any sequential procedure is equal to the risk from the Bayes decision that is made after sampling terminates plus the expected sampling cost. Then the total future risk from taking one more observation and then stopping is $c + E_\xi[\rho_0(\xi')]$, where the expectation is taken with respect to the predictive, or marginal, distribution of the next observation X when the distribution of Θ is ξ. Hence, the total future risk from the optimal procedure, when *at most* one more observation can be taken and the distribution of Θ is ξ, will be either $\rho_0(\xi)$ or $c + E_\xi[\rho_0(\xi')]$, whichever is smaller. If we denote the optimal total future risk $\rho_1(\xi)$, then as we have just stated,

$$\rho_1(\xi) = \min\{\rho_0(\xi), c + E_\xi[\rho_0(\xi')]\}. \tag{18}$$

Let us now move back one stage, to the time when at most two observations remain to be taken. Again let ξ denote the posterior distribution at this stage and ξ' denote the posterior distribution after one more observation has been taken. At this stage, the total future risk from taking another observation and then making an optimal decision as to whether the final observation should be taken is $c + E[\rho_1(\xi')]$. The risk from stopping without any further observations is again $\rho_0(\xi)$. Hence, if $\rho_2(\xi)$ denotes the optimal total future risk when at most two observations remain to be taken, then

$$\rho_2(\xi) = \min\{\rho_0(\xi), c + E_\xi[\rho_1(\xi')]\}. \tag{19}$$

In general, if $\rho_n(\xi)$ denotes the optimal total future risk when at most *n* observations remain to be taken and the distribution of Θ is ξ, then

$$\rho_n(\xi) = \min \{\rho_0(\xi), c + E[\rho_{n-1}(\xi')]\}. \tag{20}$$

The relation (20) is known as the *optimality equation* or the *dynamic programming equation*. These ideas were initially developed by Bellman (1957).

Starting from the function $\rho_0(\xi)$, which is typically specified by the conditions of the decision problem, we can successively determine, at least in principle, the functions $\rho_1(\xi)$, $\rho_2(\xi)$, ... , $\rho_K(\xi)$ by using the relations (18), (19), and, in general, (20). Thus, by this method of backward induction, we first determine the optimal procedure at the final stage of the process, then the optimal procedure at the next-to-final stage of the process, and by working backward in this way, we ultimately determine the optimal procedure at the first stage of the process. In general, the calculations become more and more complex with each step backward and it is typically necessary to resort to numerical methods.

Knowledge of the functions $\rho_0(\xi)$, $\rho_1(\xi)$, ... , $\rho_K(\xi)$ implies knowledge of the optimal stopping rule as the following discussion shows: Suppose that the prior distribution of Θ is ξ_0. Then the first observation X_1 should be taken only if $\rho_K(\xi_0) < \rho_0(\xi_0)$, because this inequality implies that there is a procedure with smaller total risk than stopping immediately. Now suppose that X_1 is observed and the posterior distribution is ξ_1. Then the second observation X_2 should be taken only if $\rho_{K-1}(\xi_1) < \rho_0(\xi_1)$, because again this inequality implies that there is a procedure with smaller total future risk than stopping immediately. The process continues in this way until a posterior distribution ξ_n is reached such that $\rho_{K-n}(\xi_n) = \rho_0(\xi_n)$. Sampling then terminates.

In many sequential decision problems, the DM must decide not only whether or not to continue sampling at each stage, but also which one of several different types of observations he should obtain at each stage, where the different types provide different amounts or different kinds of information and have different costs. These are problems in the *sequential design of experiments*. In general, the method of backward induction and the optimality equation are easily extended to accommodate these problems.

The theory of sequential analysis tends to formalize the approach used by decision makers in most practical problems. Rather than making an irrevocable decision at the beginning of a process, the DM will try to make flexible decisions that can be changed from period to period as new information is gained or conditions change (Simon 1959; Shapira and Venezia 1981). Changing one's decisions in each period of a sequential process does not necessarily indicate shortsightedness on the part of the DM in his or her planning. On the contrary, an optimal sequential decision rule that fully takes into account the long-term future and its uncertainties may call for changing decisions in each period in order to gain different kinds of information and to react to the information so gained.

Decision Problems Involving Two or More Decision Makers

An important aspect of many decision problems in economics is that they involve more than one decision maker. Some examples are problems in the theory of teams (Marschak and Radner 1972), problems of the type that we will be discussing throughout this book in which two or more firms in the same market must each make decisions about production or prices, and problems in which the lawyers for the two sides in a court trial must jointly select a jury (DeGroot and Kadane 1980).

All of these examples fall under the general heading of non-zero sum, multiperson games. However, the theory of games as originally introduced by von Neumann and Morgenstern (1947) and extensively developed during the past 35 years is largely based on minimax and other notions that are basically non-Bayesian. There have been some promising attempts to develop a Bayesian theory of games and multiagent decision theory (Harsanyi 1977; Prescott and Townsend 1980; Weerahandi and Zidek 1981, 1983; Kadane and Larkey 1982; and DeGroot and Kadane 1983), but this theory must still be regarded as being in an incipient stage. Kreps and Wilson (1982) and McLennan (1985) have presented interesting criteria for equilibrium in sequential games using Bayesian concepts. We shall not attempt to outline a general theory of Bayesian multiagent decision problems here. Rather we shall content ourselves with describing an appropriate development within the setting of each particular chapter as we proceed through this book.

3

Behavioral and Control
Theory of the Firm

The theory of the firm has been developed mainly under conditions of certainty and assumptions of complete knowledge. Everyone familiar with that theory must acknowledge the great contributions it has made to our understanding of the functioning of the price system in the resource allocation process. At the same time it must be recognized that firms operate under conditions of uncertainty, and that the theory of decision making under uncertainty has been well developed in the literature of statistics and economics (Zellner 1980; Fienberg and Zellner 1975; Boyer and Kihlstrom 1984).

Models incorporating uncertainty have been particularly fruitful in a number of areas. Some of these areas are oligopoly (Friedman 1977, 1983; Shubik 1959); statistical decision theory (DeGroot 1970; Raiffa and Schlaifer 1961; Savage 1954); rational expectations (Muth 1961; Lucas and Prescott 1971; Grossman 1975b); theory of teams (Marschak and Radner 1972; Harris and Raviv 1978); asset pricing models (Sharpe 1964; Fama 1977); job search (Stigler 1961, 1962; Lippman and McCall 1976; Benhabib and Bull 1983); limit pricing (Kamien and Schwartz 1971; Milgrom and Roberts 1982); and econometrics (Zellner 1971, 1985). These are only a few of the subjects in which uncertainty has been interjected and the references are only a small sample from the literature as can be seen from Balch, McFadden, and Wu (1974), Hirshleifer and Riley (1979), and Lippman and McCall (1981). Clearly economists are trying to incorporate uncertainty and, thereby, develop models with more empirical implications than are possible with the standard models assuming certainty.

In general, the models that have been cited involving decision making under uncertainty are based on the maximization of the expectation of an explicit function of profits. Since it is recognized that firms do not specify operational utility functions, the actual process by which firms make their decisions has remained something of a black box and has cast doubt on

27

the actual maximization assumption itself (Simon 1979). Conceptually, we know that there has to be some approximation to the marginal process developed in the certainty models, but the problem is to determine how this approximation is made. In this chapter, we will develop a theory of the firm that describes this process in general terms by incorporating the concept of decision making under uncertainty. (See Simon 1976 and 1978a for a discussion on the importance of process.)

A business firm essentially follows a sequential process in making decisions in an environment of uncertainty. It sets goals, makes decisions, gets feedback, evaluates the feedback, and makes additional decisions (Radner 1975). It is this sequential process for the business firm that we will analyze and model.

The Firm

The firm that we postulate is one that has a decentralized organizational structure. The basic unit in each firm is a division. Each division is a profit center and is usually managed as though it were an independent firm. The firm sells a number of different products and through its divisions will operate in a number of different market structures in which it may have different market shares (Chandler 1966; Williamson 1975, chapter 8; Caves 1980).

The manager of each division will usually be a vice-president, although this person's title may range from manager to president, depending on the size of the firm. The division vice-president will have the power to make pricing and output decisions as well as some capital expenditure decisions. Furthermore, the division vice-presidents, along with the chief executive officer of the firm, will constitute the management coalition of the firm, although this coalition may also contain other executives, depending on the nature of the business and the characteristics of the individuals involved (Cyert and March 1963).

The firm in our theory operates under conditions of uncertainty. Thus the chief executive officer and his or her managers must make decisions about events whose occurrence is uncertain. Uncertainty as we use it might be described by a stochastic model in which the probability distribution of the observable random variables depends on the unknown values of the various parameters. In the problems that we will study, the true values of the parameters cannot be learned with certainty. Thus, there will always be uncertainty facing the firm as it makes decisions because of both the stochastic nature of the variables to be observed and the unknown values of the parameters. The description of the firm that we have presented is appropriate for most corporations and, therefore, this theory is meant to be general.

Developing a Plan

The management of the firm attempts to develop a plan from which some specific operational steps will follow. In order to develop such a plan, the management must be concerned with three sets of conditions: (1) conditions inside the firm; (2) conditions in the industry and, in particular, in rival firms; and (3) conditions in the economy as a whole.

Let X_j denote a vector of observable variables that describes the state of the firm in month j, where j ranges over the period under study. The components of this vector are variables such as net sales, net profits, cash flow, wage levels, and labor conditions. These variables are considered by the firm as it develops its plan, and their actual values each month provide useful feedback to the firm.

As the plan is developed it is also necessary to consider variables that describe the state of the industry and, particularly, the state of the firm's competition. Let Y_j denote a vector of observable variables such as prices, profits, sales, plant closings, and new investments of competitors, and variables describing an industry's condition such as price indices, industry output, industry inventories, and capacity utilization.

Finally, let Z_j denote a vector of observable, external variables that describes the state of the economy as a whole and that could affect the firm's plan. This vector will typically include macro variables in the political, economic, and social spheres, such as the gross national product, the unemployment rate, the inflation rate, and interest rates. In addition, summary figures of housing starts, new railroad car orders, and the like, that might be vital for a particular firm could also be included.

Establishing Targets

In the planning process, management selects certain key variables, which we shall call target variables, whose actual values during the year reflect the progress of the firm (Holt, Modigliani, Muth, and Simon 1969). The management selects specific target values for these variables for the firm as a whole and for each of the divisions. The plan consists of these target values specified for the firm and each division on a monthly basis and, when appropriate, for the entire year. The target values are the goals for the firm. Since these goals are believed by management to have a reasonable probability of being attained, the plan can also be regarded as a prediction. In effect, a predictive distribution is established for the X, Y, and Z vectors for the year, which, in turn, induces a predictive distribution for the target variables. Based on this distribution, management with the approval of the board must select the specific values that will constitute the plan.

It is interesting to note that the approach of setting targets is related to the way in which the firm operates in the Soviet economy. There, however, the targets are given to the firm rather than developed by the firm's managers. The target variables are generally different, but the procedure for dealing with uncertainty is similar (see Grannick 1967; Bornstein 1978).

The target values established are a compromise generated by an interactive process between the board and the management. Management wants to have high prior probabilities of achieving any targets that it selects. The board of directors wants target values that show a significant rate of growth for the firm. Thus the management tries to establish lower targets and the board tries to establish higher targets.

Although the target variables may vary somewhat from firm to firm, we will specify some that are generally used in order to illustrate the theory. We shall consider six targets for the firm as a whole: (1) net earnings per share, (2) net dollar sales, (3) cash flow, (4) return on investment, (5) return on stockholders' equity, and (6) new orders received.

(1) *Net earnings per share* (EPS) is equal to the net profit divided by the number of shares outstanding and represents the profit target for the firm. This variable is important because management will be evaluated on the attainment or nonattainment of its target values, and executive compensation plans are frequently tied to the degree of attainment.

(2) *Net dollar sales* are important because of their relationship to market share. The firm in this theory does not know its demand curve with certainty and gains information about it through the trend of net sales. Net earnings in the future are a function of this trend, as is the long-run survival of the firm.

(3) *Cash flow* is equal to net profit plus depreciation and deferred taxes and is crucial to the firm since the ultimate measure of the success of the firm is the amount of cash it generates. The flow of cash gives the firm information about the need for short-term and long-term borrowing and thus becomes another indicator of the firm's overall well-being in the face of uncertainty.

(4) *Return on investment* represents the proportion of the money invested in the firm by owners and lenders that is being returned as profit. It gives information to the firm that is important as a measure of quality of performance, and in addition, its value is one criterion of whether the firm should stay in business or not.

(5) *Return on stockholders' equity* has many of the same characteristics as return on investment. By focusing on the return on stockholders' equity the firm's management recognizes its responsibilities to the owners.

(6) *New orders received* give a measure that, like net sales, enables the firm to determine how well it is doing with respect to the future. It

is a significant variable because it gives the firm information about changes in its demand curve.

The monthly target values for these six variables are important because they are related to the targets for the year. If the target value for a variable is attained each month, the firm will reach its target for the year. Thus, whenever the actual value for a variable is less than its target value in any month, the firm is concerned.

The division targets are essentially the same as those for the firm as a whole. However, the return on stockholders' equity does not make as much sense for the division as for the firm and is replaced by a target variable representing the ratio of net profit to sales. This variable gives the division a measure of the effectiveness of its pricing policy in producing profit since it shows the amount of profit per dollar of sales revenue.

Thus, the firm and its divisions establish a set of target values that serve to structure the environment of uncertainty surrounding the firm (Simon 1955). Once the plan is completed, the firm must choose specific strategies to attain the target values and then wait for feedback to see if changes in strategy are necessary.

Comparison of Actual and Target

Feedback on the firm's performance is obtained from the monthly financial statements for the divisions and the firm as a whole. Let W_j denote the vector of the actual values of the target variables achieved in month j, and let t_j denote the vector of corresponding target values. Each month the financial system generates the actual values W_j, and the comparison of W_j and t_j is made. If $W_j \geq t_j$ in the sense that each component of W_j is at least as large as the corresponding component of t_j, then the firm is meeting its targets. (However, we will discuss below conditions in which the firm might take action if it is exceeding its EPS target by a significant amount.)

If $W_j \ngeq t_j$, then some targets are not being met and the firm enters the analysis phase of the process. An explanation must be found for the deficiency of an actual value from its target, whether the target relates to a particular division or to the firm. This explanation must be presented in terms of the present and recent past values of the vectors X, Y, and Z. The search for an explanation depends on the relationship between the particular target variables being considered and the variables composing X, Y, and Z. If no satisfactory explanation is found, the firm takes no new actions but rather waits for more information during the following month. The process of searching for an explanation, which is essentially a matter of making inferences from the data X, Y, and Z, continues until an explanation is found with a high enough probability to warrant acceptance. Once an explanation is accepted, the firm enters the next phase of the process—namely, the control phase.

Control Actions

If the explanation indicates that the deficiency in the W_j values is due to random factors that are essentially transient in nature, no action will be taken. Frequently, however, even when the explanation lies in the components of Y_j and Z_j, the firm may be able to take internal actions designed to bring the values of W_j into control—that is, actions to make $W_j \geq t_j$ for future values of j.

Let U_j denote a vector whose components are the various control actions that might be used by the firm in month j. Clearly U_j has many components. Some actions affect the firm's interactions with the market, such as price changes, marketing policy changes, or mergers and acquisitions. Others relate to the contraction of the firm's operation, such as closing plants, selling a division, or reducing the labor force. Basically, the first set is designed to increase revenue and the second to reduce cost.

In the usual control models, a cost function drives the model, but that function is often chosen to have a canonical form—more for its mathematical convenience than its relationship to reality. The specification of the cost function for the control process in the theory of the firm has the same difficulties. Consider, for example, the total earnings-per-share target. Management chooses a particular target value for a variety of reasons. Some of these may be personal and relate to executive compensation plans; others may be professional, since the achievement of the goal is a measure of the quality of the management. Still others may involve the concept of responsibility to the shareholders. It is difficult, therefore, to give meaning to the notion of the cost of falling short of the target.

On the basis of the explanation for the target not being met, the management must decide what actions to take in order to make the actual values meet the targets in future periods. Two aspects of each action that must be considered by management are the length of time required to take the action and the length of time for the effects of the action to become apparent. As examples, we will describe five commonly used control actions: (1) price changes, (2) mergers and acquisitions, (3) contractions, (4) sale of some parts of the business, and (5) changes of management.

(1) *Price change* is, of course, the primary action that has generally been considered in economic theory. The firm, in considering this action, goes through the kind of reasoning that has generally been portrayed in

oligopoly theory and will be discussed in detail in the next four chapters. The reaction of competitors is of major concern. Of equal importance, however, is a judgment about the position of the demand curve based on the information flowing from net sales and new orders. The advantage of a successful price change is that it takes effect quickly and the firm, therefore, can be brought into control relatively soon.

(2) *Mergers and acquisitions* are part of a longer-run set of actions designed to make $W_j \geq t_j$. This form of control action is used when the explanation indicates a structural deficiency that results in the firm's inability to attain its targets.

(3) *Contraction* as a control action includes such activities as closing plants, reducing the labor force and, hence, the output, and eliminating certain products completely. These actions are taken, generally, when the firm believes it cannot affect the market and must respond by internal changes. The aim of the control is to reduce expenses proportionally more than revenue.

(4) *Selling parts of the firm* that are losing money is a common, longer-run type of control. Again this method tends to be used when the explanation indicates that fundamental problems in the structure of the firm are preventing it from attaining control. Frequently these segments of the business have been retained for a period of time while they are losing money because future prospects are bright. At some point the firm makes a decision to sell. That decision will be made when $W_j \ngeq t_j$ for a number of months, and the explanation leaves the firm with no other action that can be taken to make $W_j \geq t_j$.

(5) *Changing management* tends to be a last resort. Such action, obviously, follows an explanation that leads to the inference that management is at fault. Generally this action can take place immediately, and usually a replacement can be found within the organization. The management changes might be at any level in the firm where the unit involved could have a significant effect on the target variables of the firm. Thus this action, if successful, can have quick effects in making $W_j \geq t_j$.

These five control actions are only a subset of the total number of possible actions, but they are important, we believe, and the ones most frequently taken. The objective of management is to select a value of U_j that will make $W_j \geq t_j$. It must select appropriate levels of the available actions to achieve this objective with the least expected cost over the entire planning period.

We have discussed being out of control only in terms of some of the elements of W_j being less than the corresponding elements of t_j, but there are some control actions that may be taken when $W_j \geq t_j$. In particular, the firm is sensitive to the amount by which the actual EPS exceeds the target. The primary reason for this caution is that the management wants

to show steady growth. This objective is desired because steady growth
of a given percentage is an indication of good management and because
it is believed that the stock market places a high value on steady growth.
All other things being equal, management would prefer two years of steady
growth rather than one of great growth and one of relatively low growth.
The firm tries to reduce profits that will push it far beyond its EPS target
by putting more funds into contingency reserves of various kinds. A general contingency reserve is not allowed, but it is frequently possible to
reserve for plant damage or to develop reserves for unemployment insurance or workmen's compensation. Thus, rather than allow the actual
EPS to be significantly in excess of the target, the firm will increase its
reserves and reduce profits in a particular period.

The Control Model

We shall now present a general control model that incorporates the concepts and the notation that we have discussed in the previous sections.
Let X_0, Y_0, and Z_0 denote the values of the observable vectors X, Y,
and Z in the final month of the year before the one being studied, so
X_0, Y_0, and Z_0 are specified initial values for the given year. Also, for
$j = 0, 1, \ldots, 12$, let $V_j = (X_j, Y_j, Z_j)$ and let $X^j = (X_0, X_1, \ldots, X_j)$,
with similar definitions of Y^j, Z^j, and V^j.

The random vectors $(V_j; j = 1, \ldots, 12)$ evolve in accordance with a
controlled stochastic process that we assume can be represented by a system of equations having the following form:

$$V_{j+1} = f_j (V^j, U^{j+1}, \theta, e_j) \text{ for } j = 0, 1, \ldots, 11. \tag{1}$$

In (1), f_j is a vector-valued function, $U^j = (U_1, \ldots, U_j)$ and the value
of the control vector U_{j+1} is chosen after V_j has been observed but before
V_{j+1} is observed; θ is a parameter vector whose value is fixed throughout
the process but unknown; and $e_0, e_1, \ldots, e_{11}$ are unobservable random
error terms having a specified joint distribution. (Any unknown parameters in the joint distribution can be regarded as components of the vector
θ.) The parameter θ represents all of the economic variables that are relevant but unobservable. The observations in any month j will depend on
θ and the effects of the random shock e_j. (In an example below, θ represents possible changes in the demand function.)

The assumption that θ is a fixed vector throughout the entire process
is not restrictive. If the value of the parameter vector in (1) changes from
month to month, we can let θ_j denote the value in month j and let θ be
the vector $(\theta_0, \theta_1, \ldots, \theta_{11})$. In this case, f_j would depend only on the
jth component of θ. Similarly, if the value of θ changes from month to
month in accordance with some stochastic process, we can regard the

stochastic part of these changes as part of the random error process $(e_0, e_1, \ldots, e_{11})$ and regard any fixed unknown hyperparameters in this process as part of the vector θ.

It should be emphasized that the initial conditions of the process will typically be described by a much wider history of the process than merely the value V_0. It is assumed that this full set of initial conditions is known and fixed at the beginning of the year, and it is not included in the notation.

Some common special cases of the system (1) are worthy of mention. It is typically true that the state X_{j+1} of the firm in month $j+1$ will depend on the state Y_j of the industry and the state Z_j of the economy as a whole, as well as on the control U_{j+1} and the state X_j of the firm itself in month j. If the industry we are studying is oligopolistic, then the state of any one firm will affect conditions in the entire industry, and Y_{j+1} will also depend on all four vectors X_j, Y_j, Z_j, and U_{j+1}. On the other hand, in a competitive industry, since no single firm can affect the state of the industry as a whole, the value of Y_{j+1} will not be affected by X_j or U_{j+1}. In this case the first two components of the equation for V_{j+1} are of the form:

$$X_{j+1} = f_{1j} (V^j, U^{j+1}, \theta, e_j), \tag{2}$$

$$Y_{j+1} = f_{2j} (Y^j, Z^j, \theta, e_j). \tag{3}$$

Furthermore, it will typically be the case that the evolution of the economy as a whole will not depend on changes in any particular firm and can be studied without reference to any particular industry. Thus, we may write

$$Z_{j+1} = f_{3j} (Z^j, \theta, e_j). \tag{4}$$

There is no loss of generality in using the same error term e_j in (2), (3), and (4), since each of the vectors X_{j+1}, Y_{j+1}, and Z_{j+1} could conceivably depend on different components of the vector e_j. More realistically, however, it is likely that random shocks that affect the economy as a whole will also affect the industry, and those that affect the industry will also affect the firm. Hence, it is often possible to define the vector e_j so that all of its components appear in (2), all but the last j_2 components appear in (3), and all but the last $j_2 + j_3$ components appear in (4), where j_2 and j_3 are positive integers.

If we let $W^{12} = (W_1, \ldots, W_{12})$ and $t^{12} = (t_1, \ldots, t_{12})$, then there will be a total cost to the firm over the entire year of the form $C(W^{12}, t^{12}, U^{12})$. In other words, the total cost will result from realizing the monthly values $W_1, \ldots, W_{12}$ of the target variables when the corresponding monthly targets were $t_1, \ldots, t_{12}$ and from using the monthly controls $U_1, \ldots, U_{12}$. The problem facing the firm is to choose the values

$U_1, \ldots, U_{12}$ sequentially in order to minimize its expected total cost $E[C(W^{12}, t^{12}, U^{12})]$. It is assumed that the firm's utility function is a linear function of the total cost C.

In some problems, it is reasonable to regard the total cost over the year as the sum of monthly costs, and we can write

$$C(W^{12}, t^{12}, U^{12}) = \sum_{j=1}^{12} C_j(W_j, t_j, U_j).$$ (5)

Furthermore, the cost C_j itself can often be regarded as the sum of a cost C_{1j} due to missing the target in month j and a cost C_{2j} of the control action in month j. Thus,

$$C(W^{12}, t^{12}, U^{12}) = \sum_{j=1}^{12} [C_{1j}(W_j, t_j) + C_{2j}(U_j)].$$ (6)

Finally, C_{1j} may depend only on the difference between the observed and the target values of W_j, so we may write

$$C_{1j}(W_j, t_j) = C_{1j}^*(W_j - t_j).$$ (7)

It should be emphasized that the components of U_j are the values of the different control actions that are available to the firm in period j. Some of these components may be binary variables, where the value depends simply on whether or not that particular action was taken. Others, such as a price change, are more quantitative in nature. Still others, such as mergers or changes of management, are actions with a relatively more sophisticated set of possible values. In any event, the direct cost C_{2j} of using some of these actions may be taken to be 0. Moreover, it may be true that each of the costs C_{1j} is 0 for $j = 1, \ldots, 11$, and only the cost $C_{1,12}$ of missing the target at the end of the year is positive. In this case, only the target t_{12} is important. The monthly targets $t_1, \ldots, t_{11}$ are irrelevant and need not even be specified.

Since the effects of any of the actions may be uncertain, an optimal choice may be difficult. Indeed, it is this uncertainty about the effects of the different available control actions in any given month that character-izes the control problem facing the firm. In general, the effect on X_j and W_j of a particular vector U_j of controls will depend on the unknown value of the parameter θ. In other words, the particular control action that is appropriate in response to certain variables falling below their target val-ues will depend on the causes of this discrepancy. These causes can be thought of as being part of the unknown state of nature that the firm faces or, equivalently, part of the vector θ. The more certain the firm is about the causes of not meeting all its targets in a given month, the more certain it will be about the effects of the different control actions, and the more certain it will be about which action will be optimal. The parameter θ represents the unknown aspects of the market in which the firm is operating and of the economy as a whole.

For example, if a firm finds that its earnings in a given month have fallen below their target value, it might consider raising prices. Two major factors will enter its decision. First, a control action that changes the operation of the firm should be taken only if there has been some change in the conditions of the market or economy in which the firm operates. Such a change would be represented by the values of certain components of θ. Thus, the firm must first decide whether such changes have taken place. More precisely, on the basis of the observed values of (X_j, Y_j, Z_j) it must evaluate its probability for the different types of changes that might have taken place. Second, in the light of these probabilities, it must decide whether a price increase, some other particular control action, or no change from the previous month's operations is optimal. Typically, once the firm has observed particular configurations of (X_j, Y_j, Z_j) over a period of several months, it will become relatively certain about which action will be optimal.

The firm must be relatively certain of which action is optimal because the effects of choosing an inappropriate control can be severe. For example, the effect of increasing prices when market conditions do not warrant an increase will be to reduce earnings further.

For example, assume that the firm begins with a known normal distribution $N(\mu_0, \sigma^2)$ for its demand at a given price p_0. In any month, the demand curve could decrease in such a way that the demand at price p_0 follows a new normal distribution $N(\mu_1, \sigma^2)$, where μ_1 is also a known number ($\mu_1 < \mu_0$). If the firm knew that this change had occurred, and had to select a control action, it is assumed in this model that it would be optimal for the firm to lower the price to $p_1 < p_0$. To complete the description of the demand conditions, we assume that when the demand has the distribution $N(\mu_0, \sigma^2)$ at price p_0, it will have the distribution $N(\mu_0 + \Delta, \sigma^2)$ at price p_1, where $\Delta > 0$ is known. Furthermore, we assume that when the demand has the distribution $N(\mu_1, \sigma^2)$ at price p_0, it will have the distribution $N(\mu_1 + \Delta, \sigma^2)$ at price p_1. Thus, in each month there are two possible states of the world, $\theta_j = \mu_0$ or $\theta_j = \mu_1$, and two possible control actions for the firm $U_j = p_0$ or $U_j = p_1$. No action will be taken unless $W_j \neq t_j$.

When $\theta_j = \mu_i$ in a given month, the optimal price for the firm in that month is $U_j = p_i$ ($i=0,1$). If $\theta_j = \mu_0$, but the firm lowers its price to p_1, it will suffer a reduction in profit through a drop in revenue. If $\theta_j = \mu_1$, but the firm keeps its price at p_0, it will suffer a reduction in profit. Thus, the loss function in each month is described in Figure 3.1, where $a_j > 0$ and $b_j > 0$ are given constants. As the notation a_j and b_j implies, we allow the losses due to a wrong decision to vary, in general, from month to month.

For $j = 1, \ldots, 12$, we assume that $P(\theta_j = \mu_1 | \theta_{j-1} = \mu_0) = \delta_j$

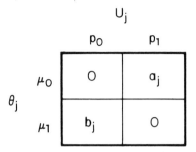

Figure 3.1. Matrix of Losses

and $P(\theta_j = \mu_0 | \theta_{j-1} = \mu_0) = 1 - \delta_j$. Furthermore, we shall assume that if $\theta_{j_0} = \mu_1$ for some month j_0, then $\theta_j = \mu_1$ for all months $j > j_0$. Thus, the parameter vector $\theta = (\theta_1, \ldots, \theta_{12})$ is of the general form $\theta = (\mu_0, \ldots, \mu_0, \mu_1, \ldots, \mu_1)$ and has only 13 possible values. These values depend on whether θ_j changes from μ_0 to μ_1 during the year and, if it does, on the month j in which the change occurs.

In each month j, the firm observes the demand D_j for which the distribution is either $N(\theta_j, \sigma^2)$ or $N(\theta_j + \Delta, \sigma^2)$, depending on whether the price is p_0 or p_1. It is assumed that $D_1, \ldots, D_{12}$ are conditionally independent given θ.

Suppose that at the beginning of the process $P(\theta_1 = \mu_1) = \pi_1$. In general, at the beginning of any month j, the firm will have a prior probability $\pi_j = P(\theta_j = \mu_1 | D_1, \ldots, D_{j-1})$. On the basis of this probability, the firm must choose either $U_j = p_0$ or $U_j = p_1$, and will then observe D_j. The posterior probability $\pi_j' = P(\theta_j = \mu_1 | D_1, \ldots, D_j)$ is given by

$$\pi_j' = \frac{\pi_j \phi\left(\dfrac{D_j - m_j - \mu_1}{\sigma}\right)}{\pi_j \phi\left(\dfrac{D_j - m_j - \mu_1}{\sigma}\right) + (1 - \pi_j)\phi\left(\dfrac{D_j - m_j - \mu_0}{\sigma}\right)}, \qquad (8)$$

where ϕ is the p.d.f. of the standard normal distribution and $m_j = 0$ or Δ according as $U_j = p_0$ or p_1. In turn, the prior probability for month $j + 1$ is

$$\pi_{j+1} = \pi_j' + \delta_{j+1}(1 - \pi_j'). \qquad (9)$$

Since the firm can change its price from p_i to p_{1-i} in any period, and since its choice of price affects neither θ nor the information that it receives about θ, it is not necessary for the firm to use backward induction to determine an optimal sequence of prices. The optimal price in any month will simply be the price that minimizes the firm's expected loss for that month. It follows from figure 3.1 that the optimal price in month j is p_0 if

$$b_j \pi_j < a_j(1 - \pi_j) \tag{10}$$

and p_1 otherwise.

In accordance with our control-theory approach, the firm will consider a price change only when a target value is not being met. If the relation (10) indicates to the firm that its price is not at the optimal value, then price will be changed. On the other hand, if (10) indicates that price is at the optimal value, then the firm concludes that its failure to meet the target is a temporary phenomenon due to random fluctuations, and no control action will be taken.

Summary

Our aim in this chapter has been to demonstrate how the firm actually behaves in making decisions when the environment contains uncertainty. We have stressed that the process emphasizes control mechanisms and consists of the following phases:

(1) *Predictions*. In this phase the firm examines the economy of the geographic areas in which it operates as well as the markets in which it does business. The end result is a set of economic predictions about the coming year.

(2) *Establishing targets*. On the basis of the predictions, the firm sets target values for the set of variables it deems critical for good performance.

(3) *Comparison of actual and target*. On a monthly basis the firm makes comparisons between its actual values and its target values to determine whether its plan is proceeding properly.

(4) *Analysis*. When the actual value is less than the target value, the firm makes an analysis to develop an explanation. This phase is essentially a hypothesis-testing exercise.

(5) *Control decision*. On the basis of the hypothesis accepted, the firm decides that a control action is necessary or that the situation is due completely to variables beyond its control and no action is necessary.

(6) *Selection of control*. If the firm decides that a control action is necessary, then the firm chooses the control that minimizes expected loss.

Since the process is sequential, it continues in this fashion until new targets are selected and then begins again.

We have looked inside the firm to gain greater insight into the decision-making process that is followed as the firm makes decisions that determine the quality of its performance. The essence of the process is the setting of targets as a way of developing a road map in an environment of uncertainty. Once the targets are set, the firm follows a sequential decision-making process that can be modeled by control theory.

4

Bayesian Analysis and Duopoly Theory

Duopoly theory has a long history in economics and a distinguished list of names associated with that history (Cournot 1897; Frisch 1951; Stackelberg 1952). Nevertheless, the problem has proved to be a frustrating one for economists. The obvious reason for the difficulty is the uncertainty that characterizes the problem. The specific uncertainty revolves around the interrelationship of the two firms and the fact that the decisions of one of them affect the other. Solutions have consisted of finding plausible (or implausible) behavioral assumptions that effectively eliminate the uncertainty. Economists have developed duopoly and oligopoly theory through the years by making different assumptions which produce models explaining some regularity believed to exist in duopoly or oligopoly markets (Bishop 1960).

The difficulty with these models is their nonadaptive character. In Cournot's model, for example, the firms continue to follow the same behavior each period, despite the fact that their assumption about the behavior of their rival is proved wrong in each decision period. In practice, however, even casual empiricism leads to the conclusion that firms adapt to their environment. They show a capacity to learn some aspects of the decision-making behavior of their rivals. At a minimum the firm recognizes the information base on which certain decisions of rivals are made. Thus the firm knows that cost changes affect all firms in the market and are highly likely to lead to price changes. Further, the firm has access to information through such sources as trade journals, industry conferences, business reports in the daily newspapers, and industry salesmen that enable it to develop expectations about the behavior rivals may exhibit (Shubik 1959, p. 277).

In this chapter we will discuss briefly the general framework of adaptive models for duopoly and will distinguish between models of simultaneous choice and models of alternating choice. We will then demonstrate how the expectations operator can be used in the analysis of both types of models, and we will examine the process of interfirm learning. Finally we will illustrate the use of formal Bayesian analysis in duopoly theory by two simple adaptive models.

Current Status of Duopoly

The current approach to duopoly owes a large debt to Cournot. The basic approach is one in which a firm makes an assumption about the way it expects a rival will respond to a change in the value of a decision variable (price or quantity) by the firm. This assumption, as we have seen in chapter 1, is usually expressed as a derivative, and Frisch (1951, p. 31) has given it the name "conjectural variations." Given conjectural variations for each rival, reaction functions for each firm can be derived. These reaction functions show the optimum response for each firm, given the value of a decision variable for the rival. The reaction functions have generally been based on a single-period maximization approach which leads to an equilibrium. Breaking with that tradition, Shubik (1959) studied long-run equilibria when each firm uses a multiperiod horizon for profit-maximizing decisions (see also Friedman 1968).

In both types of models, however, the firm can choose its reaction function only when its rival's reaction function is known. There is no provision in these duopoly models for the firm to learn over time the form of its rival's reaction function and then to adapt its decisions accordingly. In this chapter we use Bayesian methods to develop adaptive models.

There has also been ambiguity regarding the nature of the decision period in duopoly models. More specifically, there have been two different kinds of decision periods used in duopoly models. It can be assumed either that the firms make their decisions simultaneously or that the firms make their decision in different periods. The latter approach involves one firm making its decision first while the other firm maintains its position and reacts in the next period. It is, of course, not necessary for the same firm to be the leader each time.

When the decisions are made simultaneously, each firm must attempt to predict the values that the rival will set for the decision variables in the current period. A prediction function might include the actual values for decision variables for recent periods, profit figures, market-share data, changes in the decision variables over time, and other information such as announced plans of the firm.

When the decisions are made in alternating periods, the firm must attempt to predict the values that the rival will choose for the decision variables in the next period as a reaction to any values which the firm might choose for the variables in the current period. In other words, the firm must predict the reaction function of the rival, and it is this prediction that has typically been represented by a conjectural-variations term.

Of course it should be emphasized that in a multiperiod process, even when the decisions are made simultaneously in each period, a firm must consider its rival's reactions in future periods to the choices that are made in the current period. However, in any given period there is a basic difference: When choices are made simultaneously, the firm knows that its rival must choose values for its decision variables without knowledge of the values that are being chosen by the firm in that period. When choices are made in different periods, the firm knows that the rival will have knowledge of the values that the firm has chosen at the time that the rival must choose values for its decision variables. In later sections of this chapter we shall consider in greater detail single-period problems in which decisions are made simultaneously and multiperiod problems in which decisions are made alternately by the two firms.

Framework for Application of Adaptive Models

An adaptive model is one in which a firm can learn and, thereby, modify its previous behavior. This learning can take place with regard to other firms, the environment, or both. The important point in relation to conventional theory is that the firms in an adaptive model are not restricted to fixed reaction functions. In an adaptive model, for example, the firm is able to change its assumption about the way in which its rival will respond to any changes the firm will make in the decision variable. This means that for each decision period the firm can have a different value for the conjectural-variations term and, therefore, a different reaction function, chosen on the basis of the rival's decisions in earlier periods of the process.

For example, the firm may have a simple rule for shifting its conjectural-variations term, or equivalently, its reaction function, from period to period in accordance with its changing expectations of the rival's behavior. One approach is for the firm to assign subjective probabilities to various modes of behavior of the rival. The firm might use a given value for the conjectural-variations term over several periods. Then, when the weight of evidence leads to a substantial subjective probability in favor of one of the other modes of behavior, the firm might change the value of the conjectural-variations term accordingly.

Another class of adaptive models can be developed by weakening the usual assumption that the precise form of the demand curve is known. This approach has generally not been taken in duopoly theory, but it is possible to derive the interaction between firms through conjectures relating to the rival's perception of the demand curve. We have, in the models that follow, usually taken this approach, partly because of greater ease in exposition but primarily because of the greater simplicity in achieving analytic answers while demonstrating our Bayesian approach to the problems of duopoly. In some cases we have relied on behavioral rules that are different from those associated with economic models in the past. Various other behavioral rules might have been presented here, but the ones we have used serve our basic purpose of introducing the analytic treatment of learning and adaptive behavior in duopoly problems.

An Expectations Approach to Simultaneous-Choice Models

One difficulty in dealing with simultaneous-choice models by conventional methods is that the conjectural-variations approach is misleading. The problem arises because the firm must make a prediction about the value for the decision variable that the rival will set. Since both firms make their decisions at the same time, the problem cannot be one of conjecturing the reaction of the rival to the firm's decision. We propose in this section to demonstrate a method of approaching the problem that will better describe the process involved in simultaneous decision problems—the use of subjective expectations.

To illustrate the applications of subjective expectations, assume that firm 1 must choose a value for its output q, that firm 2 must choose a value for its output r, that the demand function is of the form $p = a - b(q + r)$, and that the firms have no costs. In the examples which we shall consider, it will be assumed that the value of b is fixed and known to both firms, but it will not be necessary to assume that the exact value of a is known to the firms. Indeed, we shall discuss examples in which the firms are uncertain about the value of a.

The profit of firm 1 is denoted by Q and is specified by the equation $Q = q[a - b(q + r)]$. It is assumed that utility function of the firm, as discussed in chapter 2, is a linear funciton of the profit Q. In this case, the firm maximizes its expected utility by maximizing its expected profit. The expected profit $E_1(Q)$ of firm 1 is

$$E_1(Q) = qE_1[a - b(q + r)] = qE_1(a) - bq^2 - bqE_1(r), \qquad (1)$$

where the expectations in equation (1) are firm 1's subjective expectations. The value of $E_1(Q)$ is maximized when

$$q = \frac{E_1(a) - bE_1(r)}{2b} \qquad (2)$$

Hence, this value represents the optimal choice for q in a one-period problem. The term $E_1(a)$ represents firm 1's expectation of external conditions. The term $E_1(r)$ represents firm 1's expectation of the value that firm 2 is going to choose. In order to aid firm 1 in evaluating $E_1(r)$, we can analyze this term further.

Firm 1 assumes that firm 2 will be going through the same reasoning as above, and that therefore, just as in equation (2), firm 2 will choose r in accordance with the equation

$$r = \frac{E_2(a) - bE_2(q)}{2b}.$$
(3)

When this value of r is substituted into (2), we obtain the following value for q:

$$q = \frac{E_1(a)}{2b} - \frac{E_1 E_2(a)}{4b} + \frac{E_1 E_2(q)}{4}.$$
(4)

In this equation, a term of the form $E_1 E_2(X)$ represents firm 1's expectation as to the value firm 2 expects for the unknown value of some variable X.

Next, if in the final term of (4) we replace q by the value given in (2), we get the following equation:

$$q = \frac{E_1(a)}{2b} - \frac{E_1 E_2(a)}{4b} + \frac{E_1 E_2 E_1(a)}{8b} - \frac{E_1 E_2 E_1(r)}{8}.$$
(5)

If we now replace r in the final term of equation (5) by the value given in (3), and if we continue making substitutions in this fashion, we will obtain the following infinite series:

$$q = \frac{E_1(a)}{2b} - \frac{E_1 E_2(a)}{4b} + \frac{E_1 E_2 E_1(a)}{8b} - \frac{E_1 E_2 E_1 E_2(a)}{16b} + \dots .$$
(6)

A similar expression can be derived for r. These expressions represent a formalization of the difficulties of infinite regress which characterize simultaneous-decision problems. These difficulties have been summarized by referring to this type of model as the "I think that you think that I think . . ." model. However, some special cases of interest can be developed in which this chain of regress can be broken and an equilibrium solution obtained.

Example 1: Suppose that both firms know the value of a and that each firm is aware of the other firm's knowledge. Then $a = E_1(a) = E_1 E_2(a) = \dots$ and, therefore,

$$q = \frac{a}{2b} - \frac{a}{4b} + \frac{a}{8b} - \frac{a}{16b} + \dots = \frac{a}{3b}.$$
(6a)

The same value will also hold, of course, for r. This result is of particular interest because the value $a/(3b)$ for the output is precisely the value for the output that prevails in the case of the Cournot model, as shown in chapter 1.

Example 1 demonstrates that the Cournot results can be obtained simply and directly from a model in which the firms make simultaneous decisions, where each firm has accurate expectations of the environment, and where each firm is aware of the other firm's knowledge. This analysis tends to make the equilibrium results of the Cournot model credible, since the assumptions given here are not unlike the assumptions economists frequently make. This is not to argue that the process in the Cournot model as conceived has any particular validity. Rather, this analysis demonstrates that the equilibrium position of the Cournot model can be reached by a model with reasonable assumptions.

Example 2: Suppose that firm 1 thinks that $a = a_1$, and that firm 2 thinks that $a = a_2$. Suppose that each firm is aware of the other's beliefs, but neither firm will change its own beliefs. Then $E_1(a) = a_1$, $E_1E_2(a) = a_2$, $E_1E_2E_1(a) = a_1$, $E_1E_2E_1E_2(a) = a_2$, ... Hence,

$$q = \frac{a_1}{2b} - \frac{a_2}{4b} + \frac{a_1}{8b} - \frac{a_2}{16b} + \ldots = \frac{2a_1 - a_2}{3b}. \tag{6b}$$

Example 3: Suppose that firm 1 knows that firm 2's estimate of a is $a = a_2$. Suppose that firm 1 believes also that firm 2 thinks that firm 1 has the same estimate a_2. In fact, however, firm 1's estimate is $a = a_1$. Then $E_1(a) = a_1$, and $E_1E_2(a) = E_1E_2E_1(a) = \ldots = a_2$. Therefore,

$$q = \frac{a_1}{2b} - \frac{a_2}{4b} + \frac{a_2}{8b} - \frac{a_2}{16b} + \ldots = \frac{3a_1 - a_2}{6b}. \tag{6c}$$

Example 4: Suppose that both firm 1 and firm 2 know the value of a. Suppose also that firm 1 believes that firm 2 is assuming, for some reason, that firm 1 will produce zero. Then $E_1(a) = E_1E_2(a) = a$, and $E_1E_2(q) = 0$. Therefore, by using equation (4) we obtain the relation

$$q = \frac{a}{2b} - \frac{a}{4b} + 0 = \frac{a}{4b}. \tag{6d}$$

This solution is of some special interest because it represents the monopoly output for one firm on the assumption that the firms share equally in the output. Thus, if each firm held the expectations described, they could be led to the monopoly solution even though the expectations were incorrect. This solution provides an alternative to the mutual-restraint approach of Chamberlin (1946 pp. 46–51). It is obvious from (4) that a variety of combinations of values of $E_1(a)$, $E_1E_2(a)$, and $E_1E_2(q)$ could lead to the value of $a/(4b)$ for q. An analogous expression exists for r.

This monopoly solution can be derived much more simply in problems in which the firms make their choices alternately rather than simultaneously. Such problems will now be considered. For other extensions, see Fried (1984).

Expectations and Alternating Decisions

In this section we shall again consider a model in which the demand function is of the form $p = a - b(q + r)$ and the profit Q of firm 1 is specified by the equation $Q = q[a - b(q + r)]$. However, we shall now assume that firm 1 must choose a value of q before firm 2 chooses a value of r, and that firm 2 will be aware of the value of q when it chooses r. In such a problem, firm 1 must choose q on the basis of the reaction it expects from firm 2 to each possible value of q. In other words, firm 1's expectation $E_1(r)$ will now be some function $\phi(q)$ of the value it chooses for q. Firm 1 will then choose q to maximize its expected profit $E_1(Q)$ as given by equation (1), with $E_1(r) = \phi(q)$. The function $\phi(q)$ is the expected reaction function, and the derivative $d\phi/dq$ is essentially the conjectural-variations term of the Cournot model.

Example 5: Suppose that the value of a is known, and that firm 1 expects firm 2 to choose its output r to equal the output q of firm 1. Then it is easily found from (1) that $E_1(Q)$ is maximized when $q = a/(4b)$, which is again the monopoly solution.

Example 6: Suppose that both firms know the value of a, and suppose that firm 1 expects firm 2 to choose r after it has learned the value of q in order to maximize its own profit $R = r[a - b(q + r)]$. Thus, firm 1 expects firm 2 to choose r according to the relation

$$E_1(r) = (a - bq)/(2b).$$

It then follows from (1) that the value of q which maximizes $E_1(Q)$ is $q = a/(2b)$.

Finally, suppose that each firm must choose its output in each period of a multiperiod process, and also that the value of a may vary from period to period in accordance with a stochastic process for which the probability distributions are not completely known. Then in each period firm 1 will gain information about this process by observing the value of a for that period, and it will gain information about firm 2's knowledge and behavior by observing the output of firm 2 in the given period. On the basis of this information, firm 1 will revise the relevant expectations for the next period.

Furthermore, when the process involves more than one period, firm 1 will not necessarily choose its output in any given period to maximize its expected profit in that period without regard to expected profits in future periods. In choosing its output in a given period, firm 1 must also consider the following three consequences: (1) the information which that choice will reveal to firm 2, (2) the information which that choice will elicit from firm 2, and (3) the expected profit which will be attainable in future periods as a result of this additional information. Models constructed with these concepts involve learning by firms (Ferguson and Pfouts 1962). Therefore, it seems desirable to make a brief diversion to examine the concept of learning as it might apply to firms.

Firm Learning

In duopoly theory learning concerns the behavior of rivals. More specifically, it is learning that enables a firm to predict how a rival will respond in the next decision period to an action that the firm takes in this period or to predict the value that a rival will set for its decision variable during a given period of simultaneous decision making. Our concept of learning involves the following three assumptions: (1) The entrepreneur (manager) of the firm starts with a prior probability that the rival is going to behave in a particular way with respect to the firm's decision making. (2) The manager observes the actual behavior of the rival in making a decision either in response or simultaneously. (3) The manager incorporates the results of this experience by modifying the original prior probability, and the process is then repeated. The utilization of the observation of the rival's behavior to set new prior probabilities is an act of learning by our definition, and the differences between the original and the new probabilities can be used to define a measure of the amount of learning. Such measures are the basis for the Bayesian approach to information theory (Goel and DeGroot 1979; Goel 1983).

Learning theory, the development of models explaining the process by which individuals learn, is an area of vigorous activity in psychology (Anderson 1980). Much is known about the learning process in individuals, and this knowledge has been embedded in both mathematical and computer models. There is, however, no well-established set of propositions that can be immediately transferred to firms.

It would be foolish to assume that the learning process in business firms is the same as that observed in individuals. Nevertheless, it is obvious that firms exhibit adaptive behavior over time, and such behavior is considered learning (Day and Groves 1975). As a first approach, it is useful to deal with this adaptive behavior at the aggregate level of the firm without referring to the individual members of the firm. The learning that takes place within the firm can be viewed as falling into two categories. First is the adaptation in the internal processes of the firm with respect to such factors as goals, attention rules, and search processes. The second relates to interfirm learning and is the area directly relevant to the problem of this chapter. More specifically, the problem is to exhibit the process by which firms are able to follow the Bayesian process in making decisions in an oligopolistic market (Harpaz, Lee, and Winkler 1982). In economic theory the approach followed has been one in which the firm is assumed to know nothing about its rivals and to be unable to learn, or it knows everything and the collusive solution is appropriate.

In our models firms make decisions and take actions in the market and then are able to learn from their experience. The learning process takes place in the first instance through observation of the reactions of the firm's rivals to its actions, and the storing of this information (Grossman and Stiglitz 1976; DeGroot 1980). These actions then become the basis for the computation of the new probabilities for the firm. These probabilities represent the firm's estimates, on the basis of its learning, of the reactions of its rivals for particular actions of the firm in the next decision period. Thus one aspect of learning as used here is the ability to develop enough knowledge of rivals to enable predictions of their behavior to be made. Increases in learning imply improvements in the accuracy of the predictions.

The learning process in the organization involves the gathering of information from the environment of the form and quantity necessary to make the appropriate inferences (Cyert and March 1963; Simon 1979). Within the organization it requires the information to be processed and presented in such a manner that judgments can be made about the significance of the information.

The information comes from participants in the organization who are interacting with the environment either in their official organizational roles or as individuals. This information is generally about rival firms' plans and market behavior. Salesmen and managers are an especially fruitful source of information of this kind. Their information comes from interactions with customers who have been in contact with salesmen of other firms and from direct interactions with rival salesmen. The information is most frequently about price or related selling conditions of the product such as credit terms. Any price changes, including attempts at secret price cuts will generally be picked up in this information net. This information will not be without bias, since salesmen, because of their payoff function, tend to press for changes in selling conditions that will increase sales. This bias in information is a factor that the organization must learn to evaluate and compensate for in the use of its information system (Cyert and March 1955).

It is obvious that the concept of learning in business organizations merits greater analysis than is relevant here (Crawford 1973; Grossman, Kihlstrom, and Mirman 1977; Nakagome 1982). Other approaches to information and uncertainty in Cournot and other duopolies and oligopolies are given by Novshek and Sonnenschein (1982), Palfrey (1982, 1985), and Green (1984). Duopoly behavior of public-good producers is discussed by McKinney (1984). Our purpose in the first part of this chapter has been to motivate some of the assumptions that will be made in the models presented in the next four sections.

An Additive Model

In this chapter we have given some illustrations of the way in which the expectations operator can be utilized in certain problems involving a single period with either simultaneous choice or alternating choice. Now we will show how the learning described in the preceding section can be incorporated into the models when the decisions are multiperiod and are made in different periods by the two firms.

The basic innovation in these models is the use of reaction functions that involve an unknown parameter and a random component. By using Bayesian analysis, the firm is able to adapt its decisions as it gains information about the unknown parameter from the rival's behavior.

As before, let q denote the quantity to be produced by firm 1, and let r denote the quantity to be produced by firm 2. We shall assume that the demand curve is of the form $p = a - bq - cr$, where a, b, and c are given positive constants. For any values of q and r chosen by the two firms, the resulting profit Q for firm 1, assuming no costs, is as follows:

$$Q = aq - bq^2 - cqr. \tag{7}$$

We shall make the following assumptions: (1) Firm 1 is the leader and makes its decision for q before firm 2 chooses the value for r. (2) After learning the value of q, firm 2 chooses r in accordance with the equation

$$r = q + \theta + \epsilon. \tag{8}$$

Here θ is a constant whose value is chosen and fixed by firm 2 before it learns the value of q, and ϵ is a random variable with mean 0 whose distribution is completely known to both firms. The exact value of θ that firm 2 is using is unknown to firm 1. This model will be referred to as an additive model because the parameter θ enters additively in equation (8).

The random variable ϵ represents the random part of firm 2's choice. It may reflect the effect of recent information about market conditions coming from a market survey, or it may result from firm 2's inability to control output in a completely accurate fashion. In short, the firm may decide on an output of $q + \theta$, but because of random disturbances it actually produces $q + \theta + \epsilon$. Firm 1 is fully aware of equation (8) and the distribution of ϵ but does not know the exact value of θ that firm 2 is using. However, firm 1 does have a prior distribution for θ.

By substituting the value of r given in (8) into (7), firm 1 can compute, for any value of q that it might choose, the expected profit as given by the following equation:

$$E(Q) = aq - (b + c)q^2 - cmq. \tag{9}$$

Here $m = E(\theta)$ is the mean of firm 1's prior distribution of θ. The value (9) is maximized when

$$q = \frac{a - cm}{2(b + c)}. \tag{10}$$

Thus, the value given in (10) represents the optimal choice of q for firm 1. The expected profit from this choice of q is

$$E(Q) = \frac{(a - cm)^2}{4(b + c)}. \tag{11}$$

A Multiplicative Model

Consider now the same problem as above, but suppose that firm 2's choice of r, instead of being given by (8), is now given by the following equation:

$$r = \theta q + \epsilon. \tag{12}$$

Again, θ is a positive constant chosen and fixed by firm 2 and ϵ represents the random element in firm 2's choice, with $E(\epsilon) = 0$. This model will be referred to as a multiplicative model because the parameter θ enters multiplicatively in equation (12).

When (12) is substituted into (7) we obtain

$$Q = (a - c\epsilon)q - (b + c\theta)q^2.$$

When expectations are taken the expected profit of firm 1 is found to be

$$E(Q) = aq - (b + cm)q^2. \tag{13}$$

Here again, $m = E(\theta)$ is computed under firm 1's prior distribution. From (13) we find that firm 1's optimal choice of q is

$$q = \frac{a}{2(b + cm)}, \tag{14}$$

and that the expected profit from this choice is

$$E(Q) = \frac{a^2}{4(b + cm)}.$$ (15)

In these two simple models, firm 2 is always restricted to a rather mechanical decision rule. In the additive model, firm 2 tries to produce a fixed amount θ more than firm 1 produces (or less than firm 1 produces if $\theta < 0$). In the multiplicative model, firm 2 always tries to produce a fixed fraction θ of the production of firm 1 (or a fixed multiple if $\theta > 1$). However, these two models will serve to illustrate the results that can be obtained and the difficulties that will be encountered in multiperiod problems in which learning is represented by a Bayesian analysis. As we shall show, the additive model can be handled relatively easily, but the multiplicative model has no optimal solution. A multiplicative model of this type has been introduced in a somewhat different multiperiod problem by Prescott (1972; see also Nguyen 1984).

A Multiperiod Problem with the Additive Model

Consider the additive model, and suppose now that the process continues through n periods. For $j = 1, \ldots, n$, let q_j denote the quantity to be produced by firm 1 in period j, let r_j denote the quantity to be produced by firm 2 in period j, and let Q_j denote the profit of firm 1 in period j. We assume, as before, that

$$Q_j = aq_j - bq_j^2 - cq_jr_j \quad (j = 1, \ldots, n).$$ (16)

We also assume that firm 2 chooses r_j in accordance with

$$r_j = q_j + \theta + \epsilon_j \quad (j = 1, \ldots, n).$$ (17)

Thus, firm 2 learns the value of q_j before choosing r_j. In equation (17), θ represents the systematic adjustment which firm 2 makes, and the value of θ remains fixed throughout the n periods; and ϵ_j represents the random component in the value of r_j that is ultimately chosen, and it is assumed that the random variables $\epsilon_1 \ldots \epsilon_n$ are independent and identically distributed. Specifically, we make the assumption that each ϵ_j is normally distributed with mean 0 and precision τ, where τ is a known number. As noted in chapter 2 the precision of a normal distribution is equal to the reciprocal of the variance of the distribution, that is, $\tau = 1/\sigma^2$. As we shall see, in many problems involving a Bayesian analysis based on normal distributions, it is simpler to represent these distributions by their mean and precision, rather than by their mean and variance.

It should be noted that by assuming that ϵ_j has a normal distribution and by allowing q_j, θ, and r_j to vary over all real numbers, we are not adhering to the physical restriction that the amount produced in any period must be nonnegative. This abstraction should not cause the reader any conceptual difficulties. Indeed, this restriction has been ignored throughout all of the earlier sections.

Bayes' theorem can be shown to be directly applicable to firm 1's information about θ. Suppose that, at a given period, firm 1's knowledge about θ can be represented by a normal distribution with mean m and precision h. By a standard application of Bayes' theorem (chapter 2, proposition 2), it can be shown that if we observe the value x of a random variable whose distribution for any given value of θ is normal with mean θ and precision τ, then the posterior distribution of θ will again be normal with mean m' and precision h' specified as follows:

$$m' = \frac{hm + \tau x}{h + \tau}, \quad h' = h + \tau. \tag{18}$$

Suppose now that when the prior distribution of θ is as specified above, firm 1 chooses the value q and observes that firm 2 chooses the value r in response. By equation (17), the distribution of $r - q$, for any given value of θ, is a normal distribution with mean θ and precision τ. Therefore, after firm 1 observes the value of r chosen by firm 2, the posterior distribution of θ will be normal with mean m' and precision h' specified as follows:

$$m' = \frac{hm + \tau(r - q)}{h + \tau}, \quad h' = h + \tau. \tag{19}$$

We assume that firm 1's objective is to maximize its expected total profit over the n periods; that is, firm 1 must find a sequential decision rule which maximizes

$$E(Q_1 + \ldots + Q_n). \tag{20}$$

We can now apply the method of backward induction (chapter 2) to find an optimal sequential rule of this type.

Suppose that the first $n - 1$ periods of the process are over and that firm 1 must now make its final choice q_n. Since all profits and losses in the first $n - 1$ periods have now been recorded and cannot be changed, firm 1 must choose q_n simply to maximize $E(Q_n)$, its expected profit in the final period. Further assume that at the beginning of the final period firm 1's distribution for θ is normal with mean m and precision h. It follows from the results (10) and (11) given earlier that firm 1 should choose

$$q_n = \frac{a - cm}{2(b + c)}, \tag{21}$$

and that the resulting expected profit $E(Q_n)$ on the final stage is

$$E(Q_n) = \frac{(a - cm)^2}{4(b + c)}.$$ (22)

We now move back one stage. Suppose that the first $n - 2$ periods are over and that firm 1 must now choose q_{n-1}. Suppose again that its distribution for θ at this time is normal with mean m and precision h. Firm 1 must now maximize the sum $E(Q_{n-1}) + E(Q_n)$. It follows from (19) and (22) that for any values of q_{n-1} and r_{n-1}, the optimal choice of q_n will yield

$$E(Q_n) = \frac{(a - cm')^2}{4(b + c)} = \frac{\left[a - c\, \dfrac{hm + \tau(r_{n-1} - q_{n-1})}{h + \tau}\right]^2}{4(b + c)}.$$ (23)

Furthermore, since r_{n-1} is given by (17), we can take the expectation over r_{n-1} in the final part of (23), for any given choice of q_{n-1}. In fact, when the distribution of θ is taken into account, it follows from (17) that the distribution of r_{n-1} is normal with mean $q_{n-1} + m$ and precision $h\tau/(h + \tau)$. It can thus be shown that for any given choice of q_{n-1},

$$E(Q_n) = (a - cm)^2 + \frac{\tau c^2}{h(\tau + h)}.$$ (24)

Since firm 1 must choose q_{n-1} to maximize the sum $E(Q_{n-1}) + E(Q_n)$, and since, by (24), the value of $E(Q_n)$ will not depend on the specific value of q_{n-1} which is chosen, firm 1 can choose q_{n-1} simply to maximize $E(Q_{n-1})$. In other words, the firm need not plan ahead. Again, from (10) and (11) or, equivalently, from (21) and (22), we find that the optimal choice is

$$q_{n-1} = \frac{a - cm}{2(b + c)},$$ (25)

which leads to the value

$$E(Q_{n-1}) = \frac{(a - cm)^2}{4(b + c)}.$$ (26)

Hence, by (26) and (24), it is seen that under the optimal procedure,

$$E(Q_{n-1}) + E(Q_n) = \left[1 + \frac{1}{4(b + c)}\right](a - cm)^2 + \frac{\tau c^2}{h(\tau + h)},$$ (27)

where m is the mean of firm 1's distribution for θ at the beginning of period $n - 1$ and h is the precision of this distribution. This argument can now be carried through successively earlier stages by induction.

Summarizing, we can say that when the additive model is appropriate, the optimal sequential decision procedure is the myopic procedure whereby firm 1 makes its choice in each period without regard to future periods. In other words, it makes choices as if each period were the final one, or as if it were in a one-period problem. It does, of course, update the posterior distribution of θ in each period based on the value of r which is observed in that period, as specified in equation (19).

A Multiperiod Problem with the Multiplicative Model

In this section we shall again consider a process with n periods, but we shall now assume that firm 2 chooses its output r in each period in accordance with the multiplicative model (12). We shall show that the optimal procedure for firm 1 in this problem will not be the myopic procedure whereby firm 1 chooses q in each period to maximize its expected profit in that period without regard to the effect of this choice on its expected profit in future periods. In fact, the optimal procedure cannot be determined, as will be made clear by attempting to apply the method of backward induction.

However, Bayes' theorem can still be applied easily to update firm 1's information about θ in each period. Again we shall suppose that, at a given time, firm 1's knowledge about θ can be represented by a normal distribution with mean m and precision h. It follows from equation (12) that for any given values of q and θ, the distribution of r/q will be normal with mean θ and precision τq^2. Therefore, by equation (18), if firm 1 chooses q and then observes that firm 2 chooses r, the posterior distribution of θ is again normal with mean m' and precision h' given as follows:

$$m' = \frac{hm + \tau rq}{h + \tau q^2}, \quad h' = h + \tau q^2. \tag{28}$$

These expressions can be compared with those given in (19). An indication that the optimal sequential procedure for the multiplicative model will be complicated is the appearance of q in the precision h' and, therefore, in the denominator of m'. This point raises the possibility of an obvious heuristic in approaching the problem. From (28) it can be seen that a large value of q leads to a large value of h', which means that firm 1 will have a very precise posterior distribution for θ. Hence, it might be worthwhile for firm 1 to sacrifice profits at the first stage by choosing a large value of q. It will then know the value of θ with high precision and will be able to exploit this knowledge to its advantage in later periods since it is assumed that θ remains constant. In other words, the interrelations among the periods are created by the appearance of the decision variable in the expression for the precision of the posterior distribution.

The optimal value of q for the final period is specified by (14), and the expected profit from this period is specified by (15). By making use of this result and (13), we find that firm 1 must choose q in period $n - 1$ to maximize the sum

$$E(Q_{n-1}) + E(Q_n) = aq - (b + cm)q^2 \tag{29}$$
$$+ \frac{a^2}{4} E\left[\left(b + c\frac{hm + \tau qr}{h + \tau q^2}\right)^{-1}\right],$$

where the random variable r in the final expectation has a normal distribution with mean mq and precision $h/(h + q^2)$. It follows that this expectation will be indeterminate, since the expectation of the reciprocal of a random variable with a normal distribution does not exist. Thus, it is impossible to determine an optimum value for q since the value of (29) is not well-defined.

It should not be inferred that either the concept of the multiplicative model or the method of backward induction is unreasonable. If the normal distribution assumed for r is replaced by a bounded distribution that is concentrated on positive values, then the difficulty of indeterminacy can be eliminated. Our major aim, to reiterate, has been to demonstrate the potential for adaptive models by introducing new tools and concepts.

5

Multiperiod Decision Models with Alternating Choice as a Solution to the Duopoly Problem

In the previous chapter we illustrated some of the ways that Bayesian analysis can be used in duopoly theory. Duopoly and oligopoly theory is characterized by the fact that an infinite number of models can be generated by assuming different values for the conjectural variations term (Cohen and Cyert 1975; Kamien and Schwartz 1983). No general solution exists and there is no basis, either empirical or theoretical, for preferring one of the models over the other.

In this chapter we develop a general solution to the duopoly problem as posed by Cournot. We mean by this a solution to the problem of two firms operating in a market with identical products in which the market demand function is known, in which each firm knows its own cost function (or an assumption of zero costs is made), and in which decisions are made in alternating periods rather than simultaneously. The further qualification is that the process is noncooperative; that is, there can be no explicit collusion. This qualification does not rule out a joint maximization solution brought about by some mechanism such as mutual restraint (Chamberlin 1946; Green and Porter 1984).

We shall first discuss the concept of a multiperiod process and sequential decisions, as opposed to single periods. Next, we shall consider models of simultaneous choice in a multiperiod process and discuss some of their shortcomings. We shall then study a multiperiod process with alternating choice and shall derive reaction functions for this process through the method of backward induction. We shall show the optimality of this rule for the duopoly problem and by this argument establish that the reaction functions derived by backward induction for multiperiod decision making provide a general solution to the duopoly problem posed by Cournot.

Single-Period versus Multiperiod Decision Making

Cournot recognized that it is necessary to derive a decision function as a solution to the duopoly problem. Although he viewed a single point, the equilibrium position, as the critical result, the utilization of a decision process in his model makes it dynamic. (See Smithies and Savage 1940, for an early version of a model that is explicitly dynamic.)

The argument as to why the problem should be viewed as a multiperiod problem instead of a one-period problem should be examined. As described in the last chapter, the basic reason for emphasizing longer horizons is that each period's decision affects the decisions in each of the subsequent periods. Unless the firm decides where it wants to be n periods later, it can be driven by the sequence of one-period reactions to a rival's behavior into a wide variety of positions and may not be maximizing as a result. The question of the nature of optimal behavior in a multiperiod problem, or really in any duopoly problem, is immediately raised by this discussion and needs to be examined before the multiperiod approach is described.

As in chapter 1, we assume a Cournot duopoly situation with a demand curve of the form $p = a - b(q + r)$. The reaction functions are then

$$q = \frac{a - br}{2b},$$

$$r = \frac{a - bq}{2b}, \tag{1}$$

and the equilibrium solution is

$$q = r = \frac{a}{3b}. \tag{2}$$

This equilibrium solution has the interesting property that if one firm insists on producing the equilibrium output $a/(3b)$, then there is *no* output that will enable the rival to do as well other than this same value.

If it is known that one firm will stick to the reaction function as given in (1) for n periods, then a rival can improve its own position by utilizing this information (Allen 1938). However, if one firm insists on using the equilibrium output (2), then the rival cannot use any output other than the equilibrium output to improve its position. Thus, wherever there is less than perfect collusion among the rivals—that is, wherever some mutual distrust exists—the equilibrium output is an optimum myopic strategy. The firm can produce this output without making any assumptions about the behavior of the rival and cannot in any sense be hurt by the rival without the rival being hurt at the same time. It follows that in a problem with n periods, the strategies of each firm choosing the output

$a/(3b)$ in every period are optimal against each other. They are in equilibrium, in the following sense: When one firm knows that the rival is following this strategy, its own profits are maximized over the n periods when it follows the same strategy.

If there is complete mutual trust, then the collusion output of $a/(4b)$ is clearly a better choice for each firm. Notice that in this case, however, in contrast to the equilibrium solution, the rival can do better by moving to an output of $3a/(8b)$ if one firm is producing the collusive output. Such an alternative does not exist for the rival when the equilibrium output $a/(3b)$ is being produced. Thus, without complete trust, the Cournot equilibrium point provides one solution of the duopoly problem. However, in a process with n periods this solution is still unsatisfactory because in the last few periods one of the firms can gain an advantage by moving away from the equilibrium output and thereby causing the rival to move away from this output also. Before presenting this discussion more formally, we shall first show that when the two firms must choose their outputs simultaneously in a multiperiod process, these equilibrium outputs characterize the only strategies for the two firms that will be optimal against each other.

Simultaneous Choice in a Multiperiod Process

Friedman (1968) has considered a duopoly process with n periods in which the two firms choose their outputs simultaneously in each period. This process may be summarized as follows:

For any value of i ($i = 1, 2, \ldots, n$), we shall let Q_i denote the profit function of firm 1 in period i and shall let R_i denote the profit function of firm 2 in period i. In other words, if the output of firm 1 in period i is q_i and the output of firm 2 is r_i, then $Q_i(q_i, r_i)$ is the profit of firm 1 in that period and $R_i(q_i, r_i)$ is the profit of firm 2. It should be noted that we are allowing the possibility that these profit functions may change from period to period. Hence, the model which will be described here is general enough to include a discounting factor, a demand function that changes from period to period, or a cost function for one or both firms that changes from period to period.

The total profit Q for firm 1 over the entire process will be

$$Q = \sum_{i=1}^{n} Q_i(q_i, r_i), \tag{3}$$

and the total profit R for firm 2 will be

$$R = \sum_{i=1}^{n} R_i(q_i, r_i). \tag{4}$$

It is assumed that in the ith period ($i = 1, \ldots, n$), firm 1 chooses its output q_i in accordance with a reaction function α_i which specifies q_i as a function of the output r_{i-1} of firm 2 in the preceding period. In other words, $q_i = \alpha_i(r_{i-1})$ for $i = 1, \ldots, n$. It is assumed that the initial value r_0 is given, so $q_1 = \alpha_1(r_0)$.

Similarly, it is assumed that the outputs $r_1, \ldots, r_n$ of firm 2 are chosen in accordance with a sequence of reaction functions $\beta_1, \ldots, \beta_n$ with the property that $r_i = \beta_i(q_{i-1})$ for $i = 1, \ldots, n$. Again, the initial value q_0 is assumed to be given.

For any given sequence of reaction functions $\beta_1, \ldots, \beta_n$ for firm 2, there will be a sequence of outputs $q_1, \ldots, q_n$ for firm 1 that will maximize its total profit Q. Similarly, for any given sequence of reaction functions $\alpha_1, \ldots, \alpha_n$ for firm 1, there will be a sequence of outputs $r_1, \ldots, r_n$ for firm 2 that will maximize its total profit R.

It is, therefore, natural to search for two sequences of reaction functions $\alpha_1, \ldots, \alpha_n$ and $\beta_1, \ldots, \beta_n$ with the following property: The sequence of outputs $q_1, \ldots, q_n$ for firm 1 that will be generated by these reaction functions will maximize Q against the functions $\beta_1, \ldots, \beta_n$ and, *simultaneously*, the sequence of outputs $r_1, \ldots, r_n$ for firm 2 that will be generated by these reaction functions will maximize R against the functions $\alpha_1, \ldots, \alpha_n$. Such reaction functions are said to be optimal against each other.

However, we shall now show that typically the only reaction functions that can possibly have this property are the trivial functions that specify that the outputs of the firms in each period must be equal to equilibrium values. The argument is simple and will be presented here for the special case considered earlier in which the demand function has the simple linear form $p = a - b(q + r)$ and costs are zero. In this case, the profit functions $Q_i(q_i, r_i)$ and $R_i(q_i, r_i)$ do not change from period to period. The profit functions for period i $(i = 1, \ldots, n)$ will be

$$Q_i(q_i, r_i) = aq_i - bq_i^2 - bq_ir_i, \tag{5}$$

and

$$R_i(q_i, r_i) = ar_i - br_i^2 - bq_ir_i. \tag{6}$$

If the reaction functions of the two firms are to be optimal against each other, then for any given values of the outputs $(q_1, r_1), \ldots, (q_{n-1}, r_{n-1})$ in the first $n - 1$ periods, the choices q_n^* and r_n^* in the final period must be optimal against each other. In other words, if the output of firm 2 in period n is going to be r_n^*, then the profit $Q_n(q_n, r_n^*)$ for firm 1 in that period must be maximized when $q_n = q_n^*$. Similarly, if the output of firm 1 in period n is going to be q_n^*, then the profit $R_n(q_n^*, r_n)$ for firm 2 must be maximized when $r_n = r_n^*$. Therefore, the values q_n^* and r_n^* must satisfy the relations

$$Q_n(q_n^*, r_n^*) = \max_{q_n} Q_n(q_n, r_n^*),\tag{7}$$

$$R_n(q_n^*, r_n^*) = \max_{r_n} R_n(q_n^*, r_n).\tag{8}$$

However, we have seen earlier in equations (1) and (2) that the only values of q_n^* and r_n^* that will satisfy these relations simultaneously are the equilibrium outputs $q_n^* = r_n^* = a/(3b)$.

By working backward from the final period, the same argument can be made in each of the n periods. Hence, the only sequences of reaction functions for the two firms that can possibly be optimal against each other are the functions that specify that the output of each firm in each period must be $a/(3b)$.

The trivial and static nature of these reaction functions is a result of the fact that the firms are selecting their outputs simultaneously in every period. In the models to be studied in the remainder of this chapter, the firms choose their outputs in alternate periods. For these models, there will exist more interesting and nontrivial sequences of reaction functions that are optimal against each other. In this way the dynamic nature of the duopoly process can be fully exhibited, and optimal strategies for the two firms that exploit these dynamic features can be constructed (Rao and Rutenberg 1979).

Alternating Choice in a Multiperiod Process

We shall now consider a process in which there are n periods, where n is a fixed positive integer ($n \geq 2$), and we shall suppose that the two firms choose their outputs in alternating periods as follows: In the first period, firm 1 chooses its output q_1. In the second period, firm 2 chooses its output r_2 while firm 1 must hold its output at the same level q_1 as in the preceding period. In the third period, firm 1 can choose a new output q_3, while firm 2 must hold its output at the same level r_2 as in the preceding period. In the fourth period, firm 2 chooses a new output r_4 while firm 1 again retains the same output q_3 as in the preceding period. In general, in each odd period $j\,(j = 3, 5, 7, \ldots)$, firm 1 chooses a new output q_j while firm 2 must produce the same output r_{j-1} as in period $j - 1$. In each even period $k\,(k = 2, 4, 6, \ldots)$, firm 2 chooses a new output r_k while firm 1 must produce the same output q_{k-1} as in period $k - 1$. To be specific, we shall assume that the total number of periods n is even. Hence, firm 2 will choose its output r_n in the final period of the process.

As before, for $i = 2, \ldots , n$ we shall let Q_i denote the profit function of firm 1 in period i and shall let R_i denote the profit function of firm 2 in period i. Since firm 1 chooses its initial output q_1 before firm 2 has chosen its first output, we shall assume for simplicity that neither firm realizes any profit in the first period. Hence, the total profit Q for firm 1 over the entire process will be

$$Q = Q_2(q_1, r_2) + Q_3(q_3, r_2) + Q_4(q_3, r_4) + \ldots + Q_n(q_{n-1}, r_n). \quad (9)$$

Similarly, the total profit R for firm 2 will be

$$R = R_2(q_1, r_2) + R_3(q_3, r_2) + R_4(q_3, r_4) + \ldots + R_n(q_{n-1}, r_n). \quad (10)$$

Before proceeding with the derivation of other solutions of the duopoly problem, we shall discuss the disadvantages of the Cournot equilibrium solution for this model. Suppose again that, for each period i, the profit functions Q_i and R_i are as specified by equations (5) and (6). It then follows as before that if firm 2 is going to choose the equilibrium value $a/(3b)$ for its output in every even period 2, 4, 6, $\ldots$, n, then the optimal strategy for firm 1 is to choose the same value $a/(3b)$ in every odd period. Also, if firm 1 is going to choose the output $a/(3b)$ in every odd period, then it is optimal for firm 2 to choose the output $a/(3b)$ in every even period. Thus, the constant choice of the equilibrium output by each firm, considered as n-period strategies, will be optimal for each firm against the other.

Nevertheless there is a strong incentive for the firms to depart from these outputs based on the following reasoning: If firm 1 chooses an output q_{n-1} in period $n - 1$ such that $q_{n-1} \neq a/(3b)$, then it would be foolish for firm 2 to choose $r_n = a/(3b)$ in period n, since its profit $R_n(q_{n-1}, r_n)$ in period n will be maximized by a different value of r_n. Therefore, firm 1 can presumably increase its total profit over the final two periods by deviating from the equilibrium output in period $n - 1$. However, if firm 2 anticipates this move by firm 1 in period $n - 1$, then firm 2 can protect itself to a certain extent by choosing its own output $r_{n-2} \neq a/(3b)$ in period $n - 2$. Thus, by this type of reasoning, the Cournot equilibrium is seen to be highly unstable in this model. The same reasoning makes it clear that the optimal sequences of reaction functions for the two firms can be derived by the method of backward induction, as we shall now describe.

Deriving Optimal Reaction Functions

We shall now assume that the total profits Q and R for the two firms are specified by equations (9) and (10) for arbitrary profit functions Q_j and R_j ($j = 1, \ldots, n$). We shall assume that each firm wishes to maximize its own profit and that each firm will choose its own sequence of outputs in order to accomplish this goal. This sequence will be determined by applying the method of backward induction as described in chapter 2. The aim of this section is to derive the optimal reaction functions in full generality for (9) and (10).

Suppose that all outputs $q_1, r_2, \ldots, q_{n-1}$ for the periods 1 to $n - 1$ have been chosen, and that firm 2 must now choose its final output r_n. Since firm 2 wishes to maximize the value of R, it follows from equation (10) that r_n should be chosen in order to maximize the value of $R_n(q_{n-1}, r_n)$. We shall suppose that this maximum value is finite and is attained by the choice

$$r_n^* = r_n^*(q_{n-1}). \tag{11}$$

Then the profit for firm 2 on period n will be

$$G_n(q_{n-1}) = R_n(q_{n-1}, r_n^*), \tag{12}$$

and the corresponding profit for firm 1 on period n will be

$$F_n(q_{n-1}) = Q_n(q_{n-1}, r_n^*). \tag{13}$$

We shall now move back one period. Suppose that the outputs $q_1, r_2, \ldots, r_{n-2}$ for periods 1 to $n - 2$ have been chosen, and that firm 1 must now choose its output q_{n-1} in period $n - 1$. Since firm 1 knows that firm 2 will respond in period n in accordance with equation (11), it follows from equation (9) that firm 1 should choose q_{n-1} to maximize the value of

$$Q_{n-1}(q_{n-1}, r_{n-2}) + F_n(q_{n-1}). \tag{14}$$

We shall suppose that this value is maximized by the choice

$$q_{n-1}^* = q_{n-1}^*(r_{n-2}). \tag{15}$$

Then the total profit for firm 1 from periods $n - 1$ and n will be

$$F_{n-1}(r_{n-2}) = Q_{n-1}(q_{n-1}^*, r_{n-2}) + F_n(q_{n-1}^*), \tag{16}$$

and the corresponding total profit for firm 2 from periods $n - 1$ and n will be

$$G_{n-1}(r_{n-2}) = R_{n-1}(q_{n-1}^*, r_{n-2}) + G_n(q_{n-1}^*). \tag{17}$$

Similarly, firm 2 should choose its output r_{n-2} in period $n - 2$ in order to maximize the value

$$R_{n-2}(q_{n-3}, r_{n-2}) + G_{n-1}(r_{n-2}). \tag{18}$$

The optimal choice r_{n-2}^* which maximizes (18) will be a function of the output q_{n-3} of firm 1.

By continuing backward induction, the entire sequence of optimal choices can be determined. It is, of course, assumed that in each period, the maximum value which is involved is finite and is actually attained at some finite value of the output which is being chosen in that period. In general, for any even period k ($k = 2, 4, \ldots, n$), let $G_k(q_{k-1})$ denote the total profit of firm 2 in periods k to n when the output of firm 1 in period $k - 1$ was q_{k-1} and the output r_k and all subsequent outputs are chosen according to the optimal rules which we have described. Also, let $F_k(q_{k-1})$ denote the total profit of firm 1 in periods k to n under these same conditions.

Similarly, for any odd period j ($j = 3, 5, \ldots, n - 1$), let $F_j(r_{j-1})$ denote the total profit of firm 1 in periods j to n when the output of firm 2 in period $j - 1$ was r_{j-1} and the output q_j and all subsequent outputs are chosen according to the optimal rules which we have described. Also, let $G_j(r_{j-1})$ denote the total profit of firm 2 in periods j to n under these same conditions.

For convenience, we shall define the functions F_{n+1} and G_{n+1} to be

$$F_{n+1}(r_n) = G_{n+1}(r_n) \equiv 0. \tag{19}$$

For any even value of k ($k = 2, 4, \ldots, n$) and any given values of the output q_{k-1} and all earlier outputs, the optimal choice of the output r_k can be derived from the following argument: For any possible choice of r_k, the profit for firm 2 in period k will be $R_k(q_{k-1}, r_k)$ and, assuming that all future outputs will be chosen optimally, its total profit from periods $k + 1$ to n will be $G_{k+1}(r_k)$. Hence, the total profit for firm 2 in periods k to n will be

$$R_k(q_{k-1}, r_k) + G_{k+1}(r_k), \tag{20}$$

and r_k should be chosen to maximize this sum.

Let $r_k^* = r_k^*(q_{k-1})$ denote such an optimal choice of r_k. Then it follows from the definition that the function G_k must satisfy the relation

$$\begin{aligned} G_k(q_{k-1}) &= \max_{r_k} \, [R_k(q_{k-1}, r_k) + G_{k+1}(r_k)] \\ &= R_k(q_{k-1}, r_k^*) + G_{k+1}(r_k^*). \end{aligned} \tag{21}$$

Furthermore, the total profit $F_k(q_{k-1})$ for firm 1 in periods k to n will be

$$F_k(q_{k-1}) = Q_k(q_{k-1}, r_k^*) + F_{k+1}(r_k^*). \tag{22}$$

Similarly, for any odd value of j ($j = 3, 5, \ldots, n - 1$) and any given values of the output r_{j-1} and all earlier outputs, the optimal choice of the output q_j can be derived as follows: For any choice of q_j, the total profit for firm 1 in periods j to n will be

$$Q_j(q_j, r_{j-1}) + F_{j+1}(q_j). \tag{23}$$

Hence, q_j should be chosen to maximize (23).

Let $q_j^* = q_j^*(r_{j-1})$ denote an optimal choice of q_j. Then it follows that

$$F_j(r_{j-1}) = \max_{q_j} [Q_j(q_j, r_{j-1}) + F_{j+1}(q_j)] \tag{24}$$

$$= Q_j(q_j^*, r_{j-1}) + F_{j+1}(q_j^*)$$

and that

$$G_j(r_{j-1}) = R_j(q_j^*, r_{j-1}) + G_{j+1}(q_j^*). \tag{25}$$

The sequence of functions G_n, F_n, G_{n-1}, F_{n-1}, ... , G_2, F_2 can be computed recursively from equations (21), (22), (24), and (25) and the boundary values (19). Furthermore the sequence of optimal outputs $r_n^*(q_{n-1})$, $q_{n-1}^*(r_{n-2})$, ... , $r_2^*(q_1)$ can also be obtained from these equations.

If, as we assumed earlier, firm 1 begins the process by making an initial choice of q_1, then it should choose a value $q_1 = q_1^*$ that maximizes $F_2(q_1)$. The entire sequence of outputs $q_1, r_2, q_3, \ldots, r_n$ by the two firms would then be specified by the values

$$q_1 = q_1^*, r_2 = r_2^*(q_1^*), q_3 = q_3^*(r_2^*), \ldots, r_n = r_n^*(q_{n-1}^*).$$

We summarize our results as follows:

The strategy that we have derived for firm 2 by the method of backward induction specified that in period k ($k = 2, 4, \ldots, n$), firm 2 should choose its output according to the reaction function $r_k = r_k^*(q_{k-1})$. Similarly, the strategy that has been derived for firm 1 specifies that in period j ($j = 3, 5, \ldots, n - 1$), firm 1 should choose its output according to the reaction function $q_j = q_j^*(r_{j-1})$. These strategies for the two firms are in equilibrium. That is, if firm 1 knows that firm 2 is going to choose its outputs according to the reaction functions $r_k = r_k^*(q_{k-1})$ for $k = 2$, $4, \ldots, n$, then it is optimal for firm 1 to choose its own outputs according to the reaction functions $q_j = q_j^*(r_{j-1})$. Furthermore, if firm 2 knows that firm 1 is going to choose its outputs according to the reaction functions $q_j = q_j^*(r_{j-1})$ for $j = 3, 5, \ldots, n - 1$, then it is optimal for firm 2 to choose its own outputs according to the reaction functions $r_k = r_k^*(q_{k-1})$ for $k = 2, 4, \ldots, n$.

For any given value of q_j ($j = 1, 3, \ldots, n - 1$), the total profit for firm 1 and firm 2 in periods $j + 1$ to n, when they follow the above strategies, will be $F_{j+1}(q_j)$ and $G_{j+1}(q_j)$. Similarly, for any given value of r_k ($k = 2, 4, \ldots, n - 2$) the total profit for firm 1 and firm 2 in period $k + 1$ to n will be $F_{k+1}(r_k)$ and $G_{k+1}(r_k)$. Hence, if firm 1 begins the process by choosing an optimal value q_1^*, the total profit for firm 1 over the entire process will be $F_2(q_1^*)$ and the total profit for firm 2 will be $G_2(q_1^*)$.

The limiting behavior of the reaction functions q_j^* and r_k^* as $n \to \infty$ is an open question. We conjecture that in most problems these reaction functions will converge to certain limiting functions. This convergence takes place for the quadratic profit functions that will be considered in the remainder of this chapter.

General Quadratic Profit Functions

We shall now consider some of the special properties that characterize the results obtained by the method of backward induction when the profit functions for the firms are assumed to be quadratic. Specifically, we shall assume that for each period i ($i = 2, 3, \ldots, n$), the functions Q_i and R_i are of the following form:

$$Q_i(q_i, r_i) = \alpha_{1i}q_i^2 + \beta_{1i}q_ir_i + \gamma_{1i}r_i^2 + \delta_{1i}q_i + \epsilon_{1i}r_i + \zeta_{1i} \qquad (26)$$

and

$$R_i(q_i, r_i) = \alpha_{2i}q_i^2 + \beta_{2i}q_ir_i + \gamma_{2i}r_i^2 + \delta_{2i}q_i + \epsilon_{2i}r_i + \zeta_{2i}. \qquad (27)$$

In equations (26) and (27), the coefficients α_{mi}, β_{mi}, γ_{mi}, δ_{mi}, ϵ_{mi}, and ζ_{mi} are known constants coming from the market demand curve and the cost functions of each firm for $m = 1, 2$ and $i = 2, 3, \ldots, n$. Thus, although Q_i and R_i are assumed to be quadratic functions, no restrictions have been placed on their coefficients and they are of the most general type. However, it must be assumed that the coefficients are such that each of the sums which must be maximized in carrying out the method of backward induction will actually have a finite maximum value.

When Q_i and R_i have the forms specified by (26) and (27) for each period i, the following results can be established by the method of backward induction:

For each value of k ($k = 2, 4, \ldots, n$) and any value of q_{k-1}, the optimal output r_k^* for firm 2 is specified by an equation of the form

$$r_k^* = t_k + u_kq_{k-1}. \qquad (28)$$

In other words, the optimal reaction function r_k^* will be a linear function of the output q_{k-1}. In equation (28), the coefficients t_k and u_k will be complicated, but specific, combinations of the coefficients that appear in (26) and (27).

Furthermore, for any given value of q_{k-1}, the total profits for the firms in periods k to n, when the optimal reaction functions are used by both firms in these periods, will be of the following form:

$$G_k(q_{k-1}) = A_{k-1} + B_{k-1}q_{k-1} + C_{k-1}q_{k-1}^2 \qquad (29)$$

and

$$F_k(q_{k-1}) = D_{k-1} + H_{k-1}q_{k-1} + L_{k-1}q_{k-1}^2. \qquad (30)$$

In other words, the total profits $G_k(q_{k-1})$ and $F_k(q_{k-1})$ in periods k to n will be quadratic functions of the output q_{k-1}. The coefficients A_{k-1}, B_{k-1}, C_{k-1}, D_{k-1}, H_{k-1}, and L_{k-1} that appear in (29) and (30) will again be complicated, but specific, combinations of the coefficients in (26) and (27).

Similarly, for each value of j ($j = 3, 5, \ldots, n - 1$) and any value of r_{j-1}, the optimal output q_j^* for firm 1 is specified by a linear equation of the form

$$q_j^* = t_j + u_j r_{j-1}. \tag{31}$$

Also, for any given value of r_{j-1}, the total profits for the firms in periods j to n will be quadratic functions of the following form:

$$F_j(r_{j-1}) = A_{j-1} + B_{j-1} r_{j-1} + C_{j-1} r_{j-1}^2 \tag{32}$$

and

$$G_j(r_{j-1}) = D_{j-1} + H_{j-1} r_{j-1} + L_{j-1} r_{j-1}^2. \tag{33}$$

Since firm 1 chooses a value for its output in each odd period j and firm 2 chooses a value in each even period k, we have attempted to reflect this alternation by denoting the coefficients for the function G_k in equation (29) and the coefficients for the function F_j in equation (32) by the same symbols. Similarly, we have denoted the coefficients for the function F_k in equation (30) and the coefficients for the function G_j in equation (33) by the same symbols.

It should be emphasized that there, as elsewhere in this chapter, we are using the symbol j to represent an odd integer, k to represent an even integer, and i to represent an arbitrary integer.

We shall not present the general formulas which are required for the computation of the coefficients in equations (28) and (33). Instead, we shall now consider a special class of problems in which the profit functions Q_i and R_i for each firm in each period are quadratic functions of a particularly simple but useful type.

Reduced Quadratic Profit Functions

Suppose that in any period i ($i = 2, \ldots, n$), if the output of firm 1 is q_i and the output of firm 2 is r_i, the demand function will be $p = \alpha - \beta q_i - \gamma r_i$. Here, α, β, and γ are given constants with the same fixed values in each period. If we assume no costs, it follows that the profits $Q_i(q_i, r_i)$ and $R_i(q_i, r_i)$ for firm 1 and firm 2 in period i will be specified by the equations:

$$Q_i(q_i, r_i) = q_i(\alpha - \beta q_i - \gamma r_i) = \alpha q_i - \beta q_i^2 - \gamma q_i r_i \tag{34}$$

and

$$R_i(q_i, r_i) = r_i(\alpha - \beta q_i - \gamma r_i) = \alpha r_i - \beta q_i r_i - \gamma r_i^2. \tag{35}$$

By suitably choosing the units in which the outputs q_i and r_i and the profits Q_i and R_i are measured, we can eliminate the parameters α, β, and γ from equations (34) and (35) and can reduce these equations to a simple canonical form. Specifically in (34) and (35), we shall replace q_i by $(\alpha/\beta)q_i$, replace r_i by $(\alpha/\beta)r_i$, replace Q_i by $(\alpha^2/\beta)Q_i$, and replace R_i by $(\alpha^2/\gamma)R_i$. Then (34) and (35) can be written in the simple form:

$$Q_i(q_i, r_i) = q_i - q_i^2 - q_i r_i \tag{36}$$

and

$$R_i(q_i, r_i) = r_i - q_i r_i - r_i^2. \tag{37}$$

The optimal reaction functions and the total profits for the two firms will have the forms specified in equations (28) and (33). The coefficients that appear in these equations can be determined recursively by the method of backward induction. We shall omit the derivation of these recursive relations and simply present the results. It can be shown that the coefficients must satisfy the following equations, for $i = 2, 3, \ldots, n$:

$$t_i = \frac{1 + H_i}{2(1 - L_i)}, \tag{38}$$

$$u_i = - \frac{1}{2(1 - L_i)}, \tag{39}$$

$$A_{i-1} = D_i - \frac{t_i^2}{2u_i}, \tag{40}$$

$$B_{i-1} = -t_i \tag{41}$$

$$C_{i-1} = - \frac{1}{2} u_i, \tag{42}$$

$$D_{i-1} = A_i + B_i t_i + C_i t_i^2, \tag{43}$$

$$H_{i-1} = 1 - t_i + B_i u_i + 2C_i t_i u_i, \tag{44}$$

$$L_{i-1} = C_i u_i^2 - u_i - 1. \tag{45}$$

The boundary values to be used with these equations are

$$A_n = B_n = C_n = D_n = H_n = L_n = 0. \tag{46}$$

All of the required values in equations (38) to (45) can now be computed,

Table 5.1   Coefficients for the Reaction Functions and the Loss Functions

i	t_i	u_i	A_{i-1}	B_{i-1}	C_{i-1}	D_{i-1}	H_{i-1}	L_{i-1}
n	0.5000	−0.5000	0.2500	−0.5000	0.2500	0	0.5000	−0.5000
$n-1$	0.5000	−0.3333	0.3750	−0.5000	0.1667	0.0625	0.5833	−0.6389
$n-2$	0.4831	−0.3051	0.4449	−0.4831	0.1525	0.1724	0.6204	−0.6794
$n-3$	0.4824	−0.2977	0.5632	−0.4824	0.1489	0.2474	0.6176	−0.6888
$n-4$	0.4789	−0.2961	0.6347	−0.4789	0.1480	0.3663	0.6217	−0.6909
$n-5$	0.4795	−0.2957	0.7552	−0.4795	0.1479	0.4391	0.6201	−0.6914
$n-6$	0.4789	−0.2956	0.8271	−0.4789	0.1478	0.5594	0.6210	−0.6915
$n-7$	0.4792	−0.2956	0.9477	−0.4792	0.1478	0.6315	0.6205	−0.6915
$n-8$	0.4790	−0.2956	1.0197	−0.4790	0.1478	0.7521	0.6208	−0.6915
$n-9$	0.4791	−0.2956	1.1404	−0.4791	0.1478	0.8241	0.6206	−0.6915
$n-10$	0.4791	−0.2956	1.2123	−0.4791	0.1478	0.9448	0.6207	−0.6915

first for $i = n$, next for $i = n - 1$, and then for each successively smaller value of i. The computed values are exhibited in table 5.1.

It is found, for example, from table 5.1 and equation (31) that at period $n - 3$, firm 1 should choose its output q_{n-3} according to the equation

$$q_{n-3} = 0.4824 - 0.2977r_{n-4}. \tag{47}$$

From table 5.1 and equation (32) the total gain for firm 1 from period $n - 3$ to period n is found to be

$$F_{n-3}(r_{n-4}) = 0.5632 - 0.4824r_{n-4} + 0.1489r_{n-4}^2. \tag{48}$$

From table 5.1 and equation (33) the total gain for firm 2 from period $n - 3$ to period n is found to be

$$G_{n-3}(r_{n-4}) = 0.2474 + 0.6176r_{n-4} - 0.6888r_{n-4}^2. \tag{49}$$

Asymptotic Results

It is evident from table 5.1 that as the index i moves back through successively smaller values, the values of t_i, u_i, B_{i-1}, C_{i-1}, H_{i-1}, and L_{i-1} converge to limiting values. Indeed, although these limiting values will not be attained precisely for any finite period, the values given in table 5.1 for period $n - 10$ are in fact equal to the limiting values calculated to four decimal places. The values of A_{i-1} and D_{i-1} will not converge to any finite limits, but will continue increasing as the index i moves back. This property reflects the fact that the total profit to each firm will continue increasing without bound as long as the number of periods being considered is increasing.

By utilizing the limiting stationary values presented in table 5.1, we may state that whenever at least 10 periods remain in the process, the optimal reaction function for firm 2 in any even period k is specified by the relation

$$r_k = 0.4791 - 0.2956q_{k-1}. \tag{50}$$

Similarly, the optimal reaction function for firm 1 in any odd period j is specified by the analogous relation

$$q_j = 0.4791 - 0.2956r_{j-1}. \tag{51}$$

In a process with a large number of periods, the firms will be choosing their outputs according to equations (50) and (51) over almost the entire process—more precisely, over all but the final ten periods of the process. It follows that when (50) and (51) are applied repeatedly for a long sequence of periods at the beginning of the process, the outputs q_j and r_k of each of the firms will converge to certain limiting values q^* and r^*. Furthermore, these limits q^* and r^* will be the same regardless of the initial output q_1 that is chosen by firm 1.

It can be shown that the limiting values r^* and q^* must be the unique pair of values of r and q that simultaneously satisfy both (50) and (51). Hence, it is found that

$$q^* = r^* = 0.3698. \tag{52}$$

Consider now the problem of how firm 1 will choose its initial output in a process with a large even number of periods n. It can be seen from table 5.1 and equation (30) that, for any value of q_1, the total profit $F_2(q_1)$ for firm 1 over the entire process will be of the form

$$F_2(q_1) = D_1 + 0.6207q_1 - 0.6915q_1^2. \tag{53}$$

Here, D_1 is a number whose value depends on the total number of periods n. Its exact value is not needed for our present purposes. Firm 1 should choose its output q_1 to maximize its total profit $F_2(q_1)$. Hence, the optimal value of q_1 will be

$$q_1 = 0.4488. \tag{54}$$

If firm 1 selects this value for its initial output q_1 in the first period of a long process, and if the firms then choose their successive outputs according to the stationary reaction functions given in (50) and (51), then the sequence of outputs $r_2, q_3, r_4, q_5, \ldots$ that will be generated is presented in table 5.2.

The values of q_j and r_k in this sequence will converge to the limiting value $q^* = r^*$ given by (52). Although these limiting values will not be attained precisely for any finite period, it is seen from table 5.2 that by

Table 5.2 Outputs from the Stationary Reaction Functions

i	q_i	r_i
1	0.4488	
2		0.3464
3	0.3767	
4		0.3677
5	0.3704	
6		0.3696
7	0.3698	
8		0.3698
9	0.3698	
10	•	0.3698
11	•	•
12	•	•

periods 7 and 8 the values of q^* and r^* have in fact been reached to within four decimal places.

Even if firm 1 selects a value for q_1 other than the optimal value given in (54), the convergence of the sequence of outputs, $r_2, q_3, r_4, q_5, \ldots$ to the limiting values r^* and q^* will still be fairly rapid. Indeed, it can be shown for any initial value between $q_1 = 0$ and $q_1 = 10^6$, that the limiting values q^* and r^* have been attained to within four decimal places by period 22.

Thus, in a process with a large but fixed number of periods, the behavior of the two firms according to the model we have presented here can be summarized as follows:

From the beginning of the process until about the final 10 periods, the firms will choose their outputs according to the reaction functions given in equations (50) and (51). After about the first 12 or 15 periods, their outputs will remain stationary at the values q^* and r^* specified by (52). These values will be used until about the final 10 periods. At that time, their outputs will be specified by the reaction functions (28) and (31) and the values given in table 5.1. Hence, except for the early periods and the late periods of the process, the outputs of the two firms will be q^* and r^*.

The Cost of Competition and the Benefits of Trust

We call the optimal strategies that have been derived here the *pure duopoly strategies,* and we shall now consider further the total profits for each firm when the pure duopoly strategies are followed. We shall show that when each firm is attempting to maximize its own total profits over the entire n-period process in accordance with these strategies, then the total profits are not as large for either firm as they otherwise might be through cooperative strategies.

Consider, for example, a process with four periods in which profits for each firm in periods 2 to 4 are given by (36) and (37). It can be found from (30) and table 5.1 that

$$F_2(q_1) = 0.1724 + 0.6204q_1 - 0.6794q_1^2. \tag{55}$$

The optimal output for firm 1 will be $q_1 = 0.4566$, and the subsequent outputs will be $r_2 = 0.3438$, $q_3 = 0.3854$, and $r_4 = 0.3073$. The total profits for the two firms resulting from this sequence of outputs will be

$$F_2(q_1) = 0.3140 \text{ and } G_2(q_1) = 0.2559. \tag{56}$$

There are cooperative strategies which lead to greater total profits for both firms, but require a certain degree of trust from each. It is well known that among all strategies for which the two firms will have the same total profit, the maximum for each is obtained from the outputs $q_1 = r_2 = q_3 = r_4 = 1/4$. We call these strategies the *pure cooperative strategies*. In each period, the profit for each firm will be 1/8. Hence, the total profit for each firm over the entire process will be $3/8 = 0.3750$.

The pure cooperative strategies are highly unstable. For example, if firm 2 knows that firm 1 will choose the outputs $q_1 = q_3 = 1/4$, then the optimal choices for firm 2 are $r_2 = r_4 = 3/8$. The resulting total profit for firm 2 will be 0.4219, whereas the total profit for firm 1 will be only 0.2813. Thus, the implementation of the pure cooperative strategies requires a high degree of trust on the part of each firm that the rival will not deviate from the strategy.

Other strategies will require an intermediate degree of trust from both firms and will yield profits that are intermediate between the profits from the pure cooperative strategies and the pure duopoly strategies. For example, the strategies whereby each firm chooses the Cournot equilibrium output at every stage are in equilibrium with each other but, as pointed out earlier, would require a certain degree of trust in an n-period problem with alternating choice. The profit for each firm in each period will be 1/9. Hence in a problem with $n = 4$, the total profits for each firm over periods 2, 3, and 4 will be 1/3. We will deal more formally with the concept of trust and its relationship to profits in the next chapter.

The greatest gain from the pure duopoly strategies will be to the consumer. When the pure cooperative strategies, the Cournot equilibrium strategies, and the pure duopoly strategies are compared, it is seen that the pure duopoly strategies result in the greatest total output in each period and the lowest price (M. Jones 1980).

The pure duopoly strategies that have just been derived represent the pure solution to the duopoly problem in the sense that no assumption of trust on the part of either firm need be made. These strategies specify the optimum decisions for each firm when nothing can be assumed about the rival other than that the rival desires to maximize its own profits over the *n* periods. Thus, we would argue that these strategies developed through backward induction represent the solution to the duopoly problem that has been sought by economists beginning with Cournot's model.

The firm should deviate from the pure duopoly strategy only when a pattern develops in the rival's strategy. If the rival deviates from the optimum path in a regular fashion, the firm can increase its profits by taking advantge of the pattern of decision making by the rival.

Other solutions in which one firm is viewed as operating less intelligently than the other or in which some other special behavioral assumptions are made are obviously possible (Laitner 1980)—many are already known and several have been and will be mentioned in this book. Such solutions which enable one firm to take advantage of the other may yield profits for one firm even exceeding those of the pure cooperative solution. Our solution has been in terms of the classical formulation of the problem and has been oriented toward situations in which the two firms are equal in size and in the ability to develop appropriate decision strategies. Within the limits of these constraints we argue that the theoretical duopoly problem as originally conceived is solved.

6

Cooperation and Learning
in a Duopoly Context

In the multiperiod models that we have thus far discussed, certain assumptions about the behavior of the two firms have been made, and optimal strategies have been developed for the firms. In the model discussed in chapter 5, an equilibrium position for the two firms was ultimately established. The particular equilibrium that will be attained can be deduced in advance from the fixed behavioral assumptions that were built into the model. A model is needed that enables the firms to change their behavioral assumptions and their strategies during the multiperiod process in order to change the equilibrium position.

In this chapter we develop such a model. The firms move in a rational fashion from a path leading to a noncooperative equilibrium to paths leading to equilibria defined by various degrees of cooperation and ultimately to the cooperative (collusive) solution. In the process of constructing this model we will introduce the concept of a coefficient of cooperation, and will derive mutually optimal reaction functions for various coefficients of cooperation.

Coefficient of Cooperation

Consider a duopoly problem in which the demand function in any given period i is $p_i = f(q_i, r_i)$, where again q_i is the output of firm 1 in period i and r_i is the output of firm 2. If $c_1(q_i)$ denotes the cost of firm 1 in period i and $c_2(r_i)$ denotes the cost of firm 2, then the profits Q_i and R_i of the firms in period i will be

$$Q_i(q_i, r_i) = q_i f(q_i, r_i) - c_1(q_i),$$

$$R_i(q_i, r_i) = r_i f(q_i, r_i) - c_2(r_i).$$

Thus, in a process with n periods, the total profits Q and R of the two firms over the n periods will be given by equations (3) and (4) of chapter 5. The basic goal of each firm is to maximize its total profit, and this total profit will be higher for both firms when they cooperate with each other than it will be when each firm attempts to maximize its own profit without regard to its rival. Cooperation requires trust and, as we indicated in chapter 5, we propose to deal with this concept in a formal manner. We will do that by introducing a utility function for each firm that will encompass the degree of cooperation that each firm is prepared to demonstrate toward its rival.

We shall assume that there exists a constant γ $(0 \leq \gamma \leq 1)$ such that firm 1 desires to maximize the sum

$$V_1 = \sum_{i=1}^{n} [Q_i(q_i, r_i) + \gamma R_i(q_i, r_i)], \qquad (1)$$

and, therefore, we will refer to V_1 as the utility function for firm 1. The number γ will be called the coefficient of cooperation of firm 1. If $\gamma = 0$, then firm 1 is not cooperating with firm 2 and the sum in (1) is simply the total profit of firm 1 over the n periods. If $0 < \gamma < 1$, firm 1 is interested in some degree of cooperation with firm 2 and desires to maximize its own total profit plus a fraction of the profit of firm 2. If $\gamma = 1$, firm 1 is interested in complete cooperation with firm 2 and desires to maximize the total profit of the two firms. Values of $\gamma > 1$ do not seem to be of practical interest. Values of $\gamma < 0$ indicate that firm 1 derives positive utility from reductions of firm 2's profits and therefore imply some form of intense antagonism between the two firms. However, we will not explore that range of values in this book.

We shall also assume that there exists a constant δ $(0 \leq \delta \leq 1)$ such that firm 2 desires to maximize a utility function V_2 of the following form:

$$V_2 = \sum_{i=1}^{n} [R_i(q_i, r_i) + \delta Q_i(q_i, r_i)]. \qquad (2)$$

Thus, δ is the coefficient of cooperation of firm 2.

It should be emphasized that, in the theory to be presented here, there is a reason why each firm attempts to maximize a linear combination such as V_1 or V_2 rather than simply trying to maximize its own profit. The firms recognize that for certain pairs of positive values of γ and δ, their profits will actually be larger when they try to maximize V_1 and V_2 than when each firm tries to maximize its own profit directly. We have called V_1 and V_2 the utility functions of the firms because they choose their outputs in order to maximize these functions. This terminology is slightly inappropriate, however, since the firms ultimately evaluate the usefulness of given coefficients γ and δ, not in terms of how large the values of V_1

and V_2 are, but in terms of how large their individual profits are.

It is interesting to note that our development of the concept of a coefficient of cooperation was anticipated more than 100 years ago by Edgeworth (1881, page 53). In a footnote describing the contract curve for economic agents X and Y with utility functions P and Π respectively, Edgeworth introduces the *coefficient of effective sympathy*:

> Where the *contract-curve* is $(dP/dx)(d\Pi/dy) - (d\Pi/dx)(dP/dy) = 0$, the *utilitarian point* has co-ordinates determined by the equations
>
> $$\left(\frac{d}{dx}\right)[P + \Pi] = 0, \left(\frac{d}{dy}\right)[P + \Pi] = 0;$$
>
> the roots of which evidently satisfy the contract-equation. The theorem is quite general.
>
> Here may be the place to observe that if we suppose our contractors to be in a sensible degree *not* 'economic' agents, but actuated in effective moments by a sympathy with each other's interests (as even now in *domestic*, and one day perhaps in political, contracts), we might suppose that the object which X (whose own utility is P) tends—in a calm, effective moment—to maximize, is not P, but $P + \lambda\Pi$; where λ is a *coefficient of effective sympathy*. And similarly Y—not of course while rushing to self-gratification, but in those regnant moments which characterize an ethical 'method'—may propose to himself as end $\Pi + \mu P$. What, then, will be the contract-curve of these modified contractors? *The old contract curve between narrower limits* . . . As the coefficients of sympathy increase, utilitarianism becomes more *pure*, ... the *contract-curve narrows down to the utilitarian point.*

We are indebted to Martin Shubik for calling our attention to this historical precedent.

Mutually Optimal Reaction Functions

Ignoring the values of the coefficients of cooperation for the moment, we define two reaction functions to be mutually optimal if the intersection point of the two reaction functions is also the point of maximum profit for each firm relative to the reaction function of the rival. This concept can be made clearer by again looking at the traditional Cournot model, where the reaction functions are not mutually optimal because, as explained in chapter 5, if firm 1 knows that firm 2 is using the Cournot assumption, then firm 1 can use this information to develop a new reaction function that will intersect the reaction function of firm 2 at a point that is more profitable for firm 1. On the other hand, two reaction functions, one vertical and one horizontal that intersect at the Cournot equilibrium point are mutually optimal. With this preface we undertake a more complete definition and analysis.

Consider now a duopoly problem in which the number of periods n is

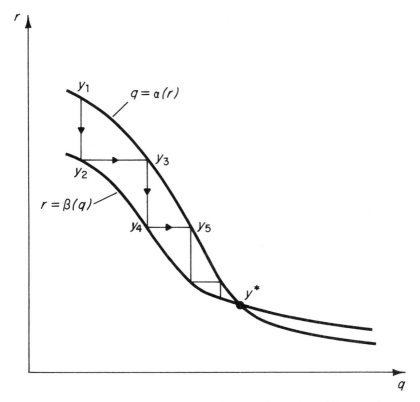

Figure 6.1. Convergence of the outputs to the point of intersection.

large. We shall continue to assume that the two firms choose their outputs in alternating periods. Furthermore, we shall suppose that firm 1 chooses its output q according to a reaction function $q = \alpha(r)$, and that firm 2 chooses its output r according to a reaction function $r = \beta(q)$. In other words, if firm 2 has just chosen its output in a given period i to be r_i, then firm 1 will choose its output in the *next* period to be $q_{i+1} = \alpha(r_i)$ while firm 2 holds its output at r_i. In the following period, firm 2 will then choose its output to be $r_{i+2} = \beta(q_{i+1})$ while firm 1 holds its output at q_{i+1}. The choices continue to be made in this alternating fashion through successive periods.

If the curves $q = \alpha(r)$ and $r = \beta(q)$ intersect at the point $y^* = (q^*, r^*)$, then, as indicated in figure 6.1, the sequence of successive points $y_1 = (q_1, r_0)$, $y_2 = (q_1, r_2)$, $y_3 = (q_3, r_2)$, $y_4 = (q_3, r_4)$, ... will typically converge to the point y^*. This convergence to the point of intersection y^* (see figure 6.1) will take place for any reaction functions α and β satisfying the following three properties:

1. Both the curves $q = \alpha(r)$ and $r = \beta(q)$ are decreasing (or nonincreasing).
2. The curve $q = \alpha(r)$ lies above the curve $r = \beta(q)$ for all points (q, r) such that $q < q^*$.
3. The curve $q = \alpha(r)$ lies below the curve $r = \beta(q)$ for all points (q, r) such that $q > q^*$.

Thus, under these conditions, if the two firms repeatedly use the reaction functions $q = \alpha(r)$ and $r = \beta(q)$, their outputs will converge to q^* and r^*, regardless of the initial outputs at which the process starts.

Suppose now that the coefficients of cooperation of firms 1 and 2 are γ and δ, respectively, and that each firm knows the rival's cost and reaction functions. In any given period i, firm 1 knows that corresponding to any value that it chooses for its output q_i, firm 2 will react in the next period by choosing the value $r_{i+1} = \beta(q_i)$. The profits of firms 1 and 2 in period $i + 1$ will then be

$$Q_{i+1}[q_i, \beta(q_i)] = q_i f[q_i, \beta(q_i)] - c_1(q_i)$$

and

$$R_{i+1}[q_i, \beta(q_i)] = \beta(q_i) f[q_i, \beta(q_i)] - c_2[\beta(q_i)].$$

Since the coefficient of cooperation of firm 1 is γ, firm 1 is interested in maximizing the value of the utility.

$$v_1 = Q_{i+1}[q_i, \beta(q_i)] + \gamma R_{i+1}[q_i, \beta(q_i)]. \tag{3}$$

Suppose that this utility is maximized at the value $q_i = q_M$. Because of the convergence which we have described, we know that in the long run, the output of firm 1 will be close to q^* in every period. It follows, therefore, that from the point of view of firm 1, the most desirable value of q^* is q_M.

For this reason, we shall say that the reaction function $q = \alpha(r)$ of firm 1 *is optimal against* the reaction function $r = \beta(q)$ of firm 2 if $q^* = q_M$. In other words, the reaction function $q = \alpha(r)$ of firm 1 is optimal against the reaction function $r = \beta(q)$ of firm 2 if the point of intersection (q^*, r^*) of the two reaction functions, toward which the outputs of the two firms converge, is also the point on the curve $r = \beta(q)$ at which the utility (3) of firm 1 is a maximum.

Similarly, for any choice of output r_j by firm 2 in some period j, the reaction of firm 1 will be $q_{j+1} = \alpha(r_j)$ and the profits of the two firms will be $Q_{j+1}[\alpha(r_j), r_j]$ and $R_{j+1}[\alpha(r_j), r_j]$.

The utility function of firm 2 is

$$v_2 = R_{j+1}[\alpha(r_j), r_j] + \delta Q_{j+1}[\alpha(r_j), r_j] \tag{4}$$

and we shall let r_M denote the value of r_j for which (4) is maximized. Then we say that the reaction function $r = \beta(q)$ of firm 2 is optimal against the reaction function $q = \alpha(r)$ of firm 1 if $r^* = r_M$.

Finally, we say that the two reaction functions are mutually optimal if both $q_M = q^*$ and $r_M = r^*$. In other words, the two reaction functions are mutually optimal if the preferred position of firm 1 along the curve $r = \beta(q)$ is at the point (q^*, r^*) and the preferred position of firm 2 along the curve $q = \alpha(r)$ is also at the point (q^*, r^*). It should be emphasized that the coefficients of cooperation γ and δ are assumed to have given values in this definition and that two reactions are considered to be mutually optimal *relative to the given values of γ and δ*. When the two reaction functions are mutually optimal, neither firm will desire to change the point of intersection toward which the outputs are converging by changing its own reaction function *as long as the rival firm does not change*.

Linear Reaction Functions

We shall now apply these concepts to the special but important case in which the demand function is linear and the cost functions of both firms are 0. As described in chapter 5, we can assume without loss of generality that the demand function is of the form $p = 1 - q - r$, so that the profit functions for the firms are [see (36) and (37) of chapter 5]

$$Q_i(q_i, r_i) = q_i - q_i^2 - q_i r_i, \tag{5}$$

$$R_i(q_i, r_i) = r_i - q_i r_i - r_i^2.$$

Suppose also that both the reaction function $q = \alpha(r)$ of firm 1 and the reaction function $r = \beta(q)$ of firm 2 are linear functions specified as follows:

$$\alpha(r) = T_1 + U_1 r,$$

$$\beta(q) = T_2 + U_2 q, \tag{6}$$

where $|U_i| < 1$ for $i = 1, 2$. Finally, assume that the coefficient of cooperation of firm 1 is γ and that of firm 2 is δ.

For $0 \leq \gamma \leq 1$, the value q_M that maximizes (3) can now be found by elementary differentiation to be

$$q_M = \frac{1 - T_2 + \gamma(U_2 - T_2 - 2T_2 U_2)}{2(1 + \gamma U_2)(1 + U_2)}. \tag{7}$$

Similarly, for $0 \leq \delta \leq 1$, the value r_M that maximizes (4) will be

$$r_M = \frac{1 - T_1 + \delta(U_1 - T_1 - 2T_1U_1)}{2(1 + \delta U_1)(1 + U_1)}. \tag{8}$$

Furthermore, the coordinates of the point of intersection of the reaction functions specified by (6) are

$$q^* = \frac{T_1 + T_2U_1}{1 - U_1U_2} \tag{9}$$

and

$$r^* = \frac{T_2 + T_1U_2}{1 - U_1U_2}. \tag{10}$$

The reaction functions specified by (6) will be mutually optimal if and only if $q_M = q^*$ and $r_M = r^*$.

For any given values of γ and δ, there will be an infinite number of pairs of reaction functions that are mutually optimal. In fact, a pair of reaction functions specified by (6) will be mutually optimal if and only if the four numbers T_1, U_1, T_2 and U_2 satisfy the two constraints $q_M = q^*$ and $r_M = r^*$.

For example, consider the pure duopoly case in which $\gamma = \delta = 0$ and each firm attempts to maximize only its own profits. In this case it follows from (7) to (10) that the reaction functions given in (6) will be mutually optimal if and only if

$$\frac{1 - T_2}{2(1 + U_2)} = \frac{T_1 + T_2U_1}{1 - U_1U_2} \tag{11}$$

and

$$\frac{1 - T_1}{2(1 + U_1)} = \frac{T_2 + T_1U_2}{1 - U_1U_2}. \tag{12}$$

After simplification, (11) and (12) can be rewritten as

$$T_1 = T_2 = \frac{1 - U_1U_2}{(2 + U_1)(2 + U_2) - 1}. \tag{13}$$

It can be seen from (13) that for any choice of the slopes U_1 and U_2 such that $|U_i| < 1$ ($i = 1, 2$), there is a pair of mutually optimal reaction functions having those slopes. Furthermore, it is seen from (13) that the intercepts T_1 and T_2 must be equal in every pair of mutually optimal reaction functions.

The profits of the two firms will, of course, be different for different pairs of mutually optimal reaction functions. In particular, for a pair such that $U_1 = U_2 = U$, the point of intersection will be $q^* = r^* = 1/(3 + U)$ and the profit for each firm at this point will be

$$Q_i = R_i = \frac{1 + U}{(3 + U)^2}. \tag{14}$$

It follows from (14) that as U increases from -1 to $+1$, the profit for each firm increases from 0 to $1/8$, which is the profit that each can obtain by dividing the monopoly profits between them equally.

When $U = 0$, the mutually optimal reaction functions specify that both firms will repeatedly choose their outputs at the Cournot equilibrium point $q = r = 1/3$. As previously noted, the usual Cournot reaction functions $q = (1/2)(1 - r)$ and $r = (1/2)(1 - q)$ are not mutually optimal even though their point of intersection is also $q = r = 1/3$.

Optimal Strategies in Multiperiod Decision Problems with Alternating Choice

We shall now consider again a process with n periods and shall continue to assume that the two firms choose their outputs in alternating periods. In chapter 5 we developed pure duopoly strategies for the two firms by using the method of backward induction based on the assumption that each firm desired to maximize its total profit over the n periods. Here we shall generalize this development to a problem in which the coefficients of cooperation γ and δ of the two firms are fixed, firm 1 desires to maximize the utility V_1 given by (1), and firm 2 desires to maximize the utility V_2 given by (2).

For each different pair of values of γ and δ, the method of backward induction specifies a different sequence of outputs for the two firms which, in turn, yields a different sequence of profits for the firms over the n periods. Thus, the choice of γ and δ by the firms fixes their profit stream over the n periods. Suppose, for example, that $\gamma = \delta$, so the firms are using the same coefficient of cooperation, and suppose that c_1 and c_2 are numbers such that $0 \leq c_1 < c_2 \leq 1$. Then, in general, the profits of both firms will be higher when $\gamma = \delta = c_2$ than they will be when $\gamma = \delta = c_1$. In other words, it will be mutually profitable for the firms to use a common coefficient of cooperation that is as large as possible. The development given in chapter 5 corresponds to the problem in which $\gamma = \delta = 0$, and the development to be sketched here for arbitrary values of γ and δ is completely analogous to the development given there.

We shall assume for convenience that the total number of periods n is even and that firm 2 must choose its output r_n in the final period n. After the output q_{n-1} of firm 1 in period $n - 1$ is known, firm 2 will choose

r_n to maximize its utility $R_n(q_{n-1}, r_n) + \delta Q_n(q_{n-1}, r_n)$. Thus, when firm 1 chooses its output q_{n-1} in period $n - 1$, it knows the output r_{n-2} of firm 2 in period $n - 2$ as well as the reaction function that firm 2 will use in period n. Hence, subject to these conditions, it can choose q_{n-1} to maximize its utility over the final two periods

$$[Q_{n-1}(q_{n-1}, r_{n-2}) + \gamma R_{n-1}(q_{n-1}, r_{n-2})] + [Q_n(q_{n-1}, r_n) + \gamma R_n(q_{n-1}, r_n)].$$

By moving backward through the process in this way, it is seen that at any given period, the firm which must choose its output in that period will know the reaction functions that will be used by the rival firm and by itself in all later periods. Hence, for any given output of the rival in the preceding period, it can choose its own output to maximize the sum of its utilities over all the remaining periods. The sequences of reaction functions for the two firms constructed in this way are called the *pure duopoly strategies relative to the given coefficients of cooperation* γ *and* δ.

If this process of backward induction is continued indefinitely and the reaction functions for the firms are derived for earlier and earlier periods, then these reaction functions will typically converge to certain limiting reaction functions. These limiting reaction functions are presented in the appendix to this chapter for the problem in which the demand function is linear and the profit functions of the two firms are given by (5). In this problem, the reaction functions used in each period and the limiting reaction functions of both firms are linear functions.

It is shown in the appendix that when the profit functions of the two firms are given by (5) and the coefficients of cooperation γ and δ are fixed, the limiting reaction functions are mutually optimal. Since quadratic profit functions can be reduced to the form (5) by an appropriate choice of the units of measurement, it follows that in any problem in which the demand function is linear and the costs of the two firms are assumed to be zero, the limiting reaction functions will be mutually optimal.

Because of the nature of the process by which the pure duopoly strategies are derived, we believe that for a wide class of profit functions other than quadratic ones, it will remain true that the limiting reaction functions are mutually optimal. However, this property has been established only for the quadratic functions described here.

Changing Coefficients of Cooperation

Up to this point we have derived the following results:

1. For each fixed pair of coefficients of cooperation γ and δ, there

exists an equilibrium point obtained from mutually optimal limiting reaction functions.

2. There exists a unique pair of paths leading to each such equilibrium point established by a process of backward induction in which each firm wants to be in the optimal position vis à vis its competitor at the final period.

3. When $\gamma = \delta = 0$, the equilibrium point is the pure duopoly solution. When $\gamma = \delta$ and their common value increases toward the value 1, the equilibrium points yield increasing profits for both firms.

These conclusions mean that each firm can be viewed as facing a decision set consisting of an infinite number of pairs of multiperiod decision paths. Each of these pairs of paths leads to an equilibrium point established from mutually optimal reaction functions. Each pair is identified by the values of the coefficients of cooperation held by the firms. Each path is based on a model of alternating decisions. In each period the firm making the decision makes the optimum decision, given the rival's decision in the previous period, for maximizing its utility over the infinite horizon. This entire process is based on the assumption that neither demand nor cost conditions are changing and that the firm knows its rival's coefficient of cooperation.

It is not, however, necessary to assume that the coefficients of cooperation are fixed throughout the entire process. Each firm can change its coefficient of cooperation at any time. Hence, no firm need stay on a fixed path.

In order to illustrate the model's potential, let us start with a situation in which both firms are on the paths consistent with the values $\gamma = \delta = 0$. Assume that through the process of learning, one of the firms develops a probability distribution on the rival's likelihood of cooperating with a larger value for the coefficient of cooperation. As an example, suppose that firm 1 is uncertain about the maximum coefficient of cooperation δ^* to which firm 2 is willing to move. We assume that firm 1 regards each value of δ^* in the interval $0 < \delta^* < d,$ to be equally likely and, therefore, assigns a uniform prior distribution over this interval. The value d is the upper bound of the maximum level of the coefficient of cooperation to which firm 1 believes firm 2 will implicitly consent. Let us further assume that if δ^* is less than the value of γ to which firm 1 moves in a given period, then firm 2 will keep δ at the value 0 in the next period. On the other hand, if δ^* is greater than or equal to the new value of γ, then firm 2 will choose a new δ that will match the γ to which firm 1 has moved, so the two coefficients of cooperation will again be equal.

If we assume a two-period analysis, then it is possible to determine an optimal value for γ, the value that firm 1 should set. Let $W_1(\gamma|0,d)$ stand for the expected utility of firm 1 over the two periods for a given value of γ $(0 \leq \gamma < d)$. The expression for W_1 must take into account the fact that decisions are made in alternating periods. We assume a process in which each firm is proceeding along the optimum paths for $\gamma = \delta = 0$. In the period appropriate for firm 1 to make its output decision, it does so on the basis of the previous output r_0 of firm 2, but with a new choice of γ. By choosing an output q^* that is consistent with r_0 and a new value of $\gamma > 0$, firm 1 indicates to firm 2 that it is prepared to operate at a higher level of cooperation than previously. Firm 2 then has the opportunity to respond positively, that is, to choose r_1^* based on q^* and $\delta = \gamma > 0$, or to continue to hold $\delta = 0$ and choose r_2^* based on $\delta = 0$ and q^*. In this model, firm 1 must choose γ to maximize the following expected utility:

$$W_1(\gamma|0,d) = [Q_1(q^*, r_0) + \gamma R_1(q^*, r_0)]$$
$$+ \frac{d - \gamma}{d} [Q_2(q^*, r_1^*) + \gamma R_2(q^*, r_1^*)]$$
$$+ \frac{\gamma}{d} [Q_2(q^*, r_2^*) + \gamma R_2(q^*, r_2^*)].$$

Since q^*, r_1^*, *and* r_2^* are also functions of γ, the maximization process becomes messy although straightforward. The question is whether there is a value of $\gamma > 0$ such that $W_1(\gamma|0,d) > W_1(0|0,d)$. Some economic insight can be gained by regrouping the terms in $W_1(\gamma|0,d)$ and examining the resulting expression. We have

$$W_1(\gamma|0,d) = [Q_1(q^*, r_0) + Q_2(q^*, r_1^*)] + \gamma[R_1(q^*, r_0)$$
$$+ R_2(q^*, r_1^*)] + \frac{\gamma}{d} [Q_2(q^*, r_2^*) - Q_2(q^*, r_1^*)]$$
$$+ \frac{\gamma^2}{d} [R_2(q^*, r_2^*) - R_2(q^*, r_1^*)].$$

It is reasonable to assume that the first two bracketed expressions are positive. The third one should be negative since we would expect firm 1 to make more profit when firm 2 cooperated by matching so that $\delta = \gamma$. The fourth term should be positive since we would expect firm 2 to make more profit by being uncooperative (while firm 1 is being cooperative) than by being cooperative. Thus, the impact of firm 2's noncooperative action on firm 1 becomes decisive in determining whether the expected utility is increasing and, therefore, in determining whether γ should be increased.

Though this analysis is for the two-period case, it illustrates the process by which the firms can move from one track to another, each leading to an equilibrium determined by the intersection of two mutually optimal reaction functions. It is possible in this way for the firm to move from the pure duopoly track, $\gamma = \delta = 0$, to the higher profits corresponding to $\gamma = \delta = 1$. Once learning takes place and the optimal value of γ becomes $\gamma^* > 0$, firm 1 can rationally attempt to move to the new track, namely the one for which both $\gamma = \delta = \gamma^*$. Firm 2 then has two alternatives. On the one hand, it can refuse to follow and make larger profits than it did previously. However, it can expect firm 1 to come back eventually to the track represented by $\gamma = \delta = 0$. Under such a situation firm 2 is back to its original profit position. On the other hand, firm 2 can move to the new track by making $\delta = \gamma^*$. If it does so, its profits will be greater than they were for $\delta = \gamma = 0$. With the usual assumptions about demand and cost curves, it is reasonable to assume that profits and hence utility become greater as $\gamma = \delta \to 1$.

The process just described continues to occur over time. If firm 1's efforts succeed and firm 2 increases its δ to make it equal to γ, then both firms are on a track leading toward a new equilibrium point. Both firms are making more profits than they were when each was on the uncooperative track. Both firms continue to learn and form priors about the new values toward which the other firm will raise its coefficient of cooperation. At some point when the decision rule being used shows that the expected gain in utility is worth the risk of increasing the coefficient of cooperation, one of the firms will make the move and eventually the firms will move to another pair of tracks where the profit is higher. In this model either firm may initiate the movement.

Even if the first move should fail to stimulate the rival to match the new coefficient of cooperation, eventually the process will succeed. The temporary gains from not matching will be lost as soon as the firm initiating the upward movement reduces its coefficient of cooperation back to the old. Punishment is as effective a stimulus for learning by firms in the real world as it is for subjects in an experiment in a laboratory (Axelrod 1984).

We argue, therefore, that this model demonstrates the kind of behavior that many economists have speculated does occur in duopoly and oligopoly. We have shown how firms progress from a noncooperative solution to situations of increasing profit and ultimately to the tracks characterized by $\gamma = \delta = 1$.

The dynamicization of the duopoly model has been accomplished by the introduction of the concept of firm learning, by the formalization of this learning through Bayesian analysis, and by utilizing the concept of mutually optimal reaction functions and their associated equilibria, all within the format of multiperiod analysis. This pattern of concepts will be used to extend and improve other duopoly and oligopoly models in chapter 7.

Discounting

Up to this point no mention has been made of the discounting process. We have made our analysis with the discount rate equal to zero. Such an assumption is, of course, unrealistic.

We shall continue to consider an n-period problem in which the coefficients of cooperation of the two firms are γ and δ. We shall assume now, however, that instead of desiring to maximize the sum (1), firm 1 desires to maximize the following discounted sum

$$V_1 = \sum_{i=1}^{n} \rho^{i-1}[Q_i(q_i,r_i) + \gamma R_i(q_i,r_i)], \tag{15}$$

where ρ is the discount factor. Thus $\rho \to 1$ implies no discounting and $\rho \to 0$ implies complete discounting so that only the first period matters. Similarly, it is assumed that firm 2 desires to maximize the discounted sum

$$V_2 = \sum_{i=1}^{n} \rho^{i-1}[R_i(q_i,r_i) + \delta Q_i(q_i,r_i)]. \tag{16}$$

When the firms choose their outputs in alternating periods, the optimal sequence of reaction functions can again be found by backward induction. As before, if the process of backward induction is continued indefinitely and the reaction functions are derived for earlier and earlier periods, these reaction functions will typically converge to certain limiting functions.

These limits are presented in table 6.1 for various values of γ and δ (with $\gamma = \delta$) and various values of ρ, for the simple model for which the profit functions Q_i and R_i of the two firms are given by (5). The relations governing the backward induction process in this model are presented in the appendix to this chapter.

It follows from the relations given in the appendix, and it can be seen in table 6.1, that for a discount factor of 0, the solution for both coefficients of cooperation equal to 0 is the Cournot solution. However, as the discount factor increases so that the future is weighted more heavily, these coefficients of cooperation do not lead to the Cournot solution. In fact, for higher discount factors the Cournot output and profit (but not the Cournot reaction functions) can be found at higher coefficients of cooperation. This fact reemphasizes the point made in chapter 5 that the Cournot solution requires a certain amount of trust. Thus, for the true noncooperative solution ($\gamma = \delta = 0$) the profit continues to fall as the

Table 6.1 Limiting Values for Various Discount Factors when γ = δ

ρ	γ = δ	$T_1 = T_2$	$U_1 = U_2$	$q^* = r^*$	$Q_i = R_i$
.95	0	.4805	− .3031	.3687	.0968
	.2	.4953	− .3931	.3556	.1027
	.5	.5346	− .5719	.3401	.1088
	.9	.6133	− .9185	.3197	.1153
	1.0	.5000	−1.0000	.2500	.1250
.8	0	.4848	− .3275	.3652	.0984
	.2	.4994	− .4238	.3508	.1047
	.5	.5350	− .6122	.3318	.1116
	.9	.5601	− .9381	.2890	.1220
	1.0	.5000	−1.0000	.2500	.1250
.5	0	.4931	− .3844	.3562	.1025
	.2	.5047	− .4901	.3387	.1093
	.5	.5256	− .6787	.3131	.1170
	.9	.5198	− .9459	.2671	.1244
	1.0	.5000	−1.0000	.2500	.1250
.2	0	.4988	− .4513	.3437	.1075
	.2	.5038	− .5571	.3236	.1142
	.5	.5100	− .7253	.2956	.1208
	.9	.5053	− .9486	.2595	.1248
	1.0	.5000	−1.0000	.2500	.1250
0	0	.5000	− .5000	.3333	.1111
	.2	.5000	− .6000	.3125	.1172
	.5	.5000	− .7500	.2857	.1224
	.9	.5000	− .9500	.2564	.1249
	1.0	.5000	−1.0000	.2500	.1250

discount factor increases. For any discount factor $ρ < 1$ it can be seen that the firms move toward the monopoly solution as the coefficients of cooperation increase, and they attain it when $γ = δ = 1$.

Discussion of Results

Table 6.2 shows the limiting reaction functions for different values of γ and δ when $ρ = 1$, that is, there is no discounting. It is proved in the appendix that the limiting reaction functions are mutually optimal when $ρ = 1$ and $γ = δ$. An analytic proof that the limiting reaction functions are mutually optimal when $ρ = 1$ and $γ ≠ δ$ has not been obtained. However, these limiting reaction functions have been computed numerically by carrying out the backward induction process for a wide range of values of γ and δ and it has been verified that in every case the limiting

Bayesian Analysis and Uncertainty in Economic Theory

Table 6.2 Limiting Values for Various Coefficients of Cooperation when There Is No Discounting

γ	δ	T_1	U_1	T_2	U_2	q^*	r^*	Q_i	R_i
0	0	.4791	−.2956	.4791	−.2956	.3698	.3698	.0963	.0963
0	.1	.5001	−.3023	.4641	−.3295	.3996	.3325	.1071	.0891
0	.2	.5244	−.3096	.4472	−.3646	.4350	.2886	.1202	.0798
0	.3	.5527	−.3178	.4277	−.4009	.4777	.2362	.1367	.0676
0	.4	.5866	−.3269	.4049	−.4389	.5303	.1721	.1578	.0512
0	.5	.6279	−.3372	.3776	−.4786	.5969	.0919	.1857	.0286
0	.6	.6799	−.3491	.3440	−.5205	.6841	−.0121	.2244	−.0040
0	.7	.7482	−.3632	.3010	−.5652	.8039	−.1534	.2810	−.0536
0	.8	.8435	−.3802	.2425	−.6135	.9799	−.3587	.3712	−.1359
0	.9	.9903	−.4020	.1552	−.6668	1.2677	−.6901	.5355	−.2915
.2	.2	.4938	−.3834	.4938	−.3834	.3570	.3570	.1021	.1021
.2	.3	.5229	−.3942	.4750	−.4226	.4027	.3048	.1178	.0891
.2	.4	.5574	−.4062	.4529	−.4636	.4601	.2395	.1382	.0719
.2	.5	.5996	−.4196	.4262	−.5069	.5344	.1553	.1658	.0482
.2	.6	.6529	−.4350	.3929	−.5527	.6345	.0422	.2051	.0136
.2	.7	.7237	−.4531	.3496	−.6020	.7773	−.1183	.2651	−.0403
.2	.8	.8251	−.4752	.2891	−.6556	.9989	−.3658	.3665	−.1342
.2	.9	.9901	−.5038	.1940	−.7159	1.3957	−.8051	.5714	−.3296
.5	.5	.5337	−.5580	.5337	−.5580	.3425	.3425	.1079	.1079
.5	.6	.5872	−.5787	.5003	−.6094	.4598	.2201	.1472	.0705
.5	.7	.6585	−.6022	.4561	−.6645	.6399	.0309	.2107	.0102
.5	.8	.7630	−.6303	.3926	−.7246	.9490	−.2951	.3284	−.1021
.5	.9	.9465	−.6664	.2856	−.7924	1.6022	−.9840	.6117	−.3757
.8	.8	.6038	−.8042	.6038	−.8042	.3346	.3346	.1107	.1107
.8	.9	.7760	−.8382	.4790	−.8710	1.3872	−.7293	.4745	−.2494
.9	.9	.6341	−.9005	.6341	−.9005	.3337	.3337	.1110	.1110

reaction functions are indeed mutually optimal. Several such pairs are shown in table 6.2.

For $\rho < 1$ the limiting reaction functions are not mutually optimal. Thus the pairs of functions shown in table 6.1 are not mutually optimal as we have defined that term [equations (7)–(10)]. For example when $\rho = 0$ and $\gamma = \delta = 0$, the limiting reaction functions are the Cournot reaction functions [equation (1) of chapter 5], but as we have shown these functions are not mutually optimal. Nevertheless, the Cournot equilibrium is a stable equilibrium for a one-period problem, which is the meaning of $\rho = 0$. More generally, these limiting functions determine a stable equilibrium position even though they are not mutually optimal. We believe that our definition of mutual optimality is deficient in that it does not take account of the discount factor. In fact the limiting reaction functions defined in the appendix [(A11)–(A13)] should be mutually optimal in that they result from a process in which each firm maximizes its cumulative discounted utility over γ periods. For a related problem, see Shapiro (1980, p. 76).

When $\gamma = \delta$ and $\rho = 1$, the profits of both firms at the equilibrium point increase as the common value of γ and δ increases. As this common value of γ and δ approaches the value 1, the equilibrium point converges to the Cournot equilibrium point and the profits converge to the Cournot equilibrium profits. However, the reaction functions do not converge to the Cournot reaction functions. They converge to a mutually optimal pair of reaction functions intersecting at the Cournot equilibrium point.

At the actual value $\gamma = \delta = 1$, the reaction functions of the two firms coincide. The common reaction function is $q + r = 1/2$. Thus the total of the two firms will be the monopoly output. The firms will remain at the same point on this single reaction function throughout the multiperiod process. The exact point selected will depend upon the arbitrary initial decision on output.

If $\gamma < \delta$, then the profits of firm 1 at the equilibrium point will be greater than the profits of firm 2. As firm 1 increases γ up to the level of δ, the profits of firm 1 may continue to increase until γ gets close to δ. For example, for $\delta = 0.9$, the profit of firm 1 increases as γ increases from $\gamma = 0$ to $\gamma = 0.2$. Interestingly, in this example, as firm 1 becomes more cooperative by increasing γ, firm 2's profit decreases.

This chapter in a real sense represents the culmination of the work that Cournot began in 1839. We have analyzed a multiperiod process and have introduced the concept of the coefficient of cooperation. We have shown that by varying the discount factor ρ and the values of the coefficients of cooperation γ and δ, an infinite number of equilibrium positions are possible. Only one combination, $\rho = 0$ and $\gamma = \delta = 0$, gives the classical Cournot solution; although the Cournot equilibrium values are shown to exist for $\gamma = \delta > 0$ and $\rho < 1$. In fact, for any value of ρ there is a value of γ and δ that will give the Cournot solution.

Cournot had to restrict his firms to a single assumption about their rival's behavior. By the introduction of the concept of learning and by making the management of each of the firms Bayesians, we have removed this restriction. We have also freed the analysis from the traditional criticism against Cournot that the management of each firm is stupid and does not learn even though the rival firm repeatedly behaves contrary to assumption (Stigler 1940; Simon, Puig, and Aschoff 1973). In our model the firm can learn about the strategy of its rival, and this learning affects the value of the coefficient of cooperation set by the firm. In the model developed in this chapter either firm may function as the leader in trying to move the two firms to a higher profit track represented by increased values of the coefficients of cooperation. The decision is made (or not made) to move to a higher track by one of the firms on the basis of a probability distribution on higher values of the rival's coefficient of cooperation. The process of learning enables the firms to move to the monopoly solution.

APPENDIX:
Derivation of the Pure Duopoly Strategies Given γ and δ

We shall derive here the optimal strategies for each firm when the profit functions in each period are given by (5), the coefficients of cooperation are γ and δ, and the firms desire to maximize the discounted sums V_1 and V_2 given by (15) and (16). When $\rho = 1$, (15) and (16) reduce to (1) and (2), so the discussion which follows includes as a special case the problem in which there is no discounting ($\rho = 1$).

As far as possible, we shall follow the notation of chapter 5. It is assumed that the total number of periods n is even, that firm 1 must choose its output q_j in each odd period j, and that firm 2 must choose its output r_k in each even period k.

By backward induction the optimal choice of firm 1 can be shown to be a linear function of the output r_{j-1} of firm 2 in period $j - 1$. We shall denote this optimal choice by

$$q_j^* = t_j + u_j r_{j-1}. \tag{A1}$$

When firm 1 chooses the output q_j^* and all subsequent choices by the two firms in periods $j + 1$ to n are also made optimally, it can be shown by backward induction that the sum of the utilities for both firm 1 and firm 2 in periods j to n will be quadratic functions of r_{j-1}. If $F_j(r_{j-1})$ denotes the sum of these utilities for firm 1 and $G_j(r_{j-1})$ denotes the sum for firm 2, then these sums are of the form:

$$F_j(r_{j-1}) = A_{j-1} + B_{j-1} r_{j-1} + C_{j-1} r_{j-1}^2, \tag{A2}$$

$$G_j(r_{j-1}) = D_{j-1} + H_{j-1} r_{j-1} + L_{j-1} r_{j-1}^2. \tag{A3}$$

Similarly, firm 2 must choose the output r_k in each even period k. The optimal value of r_k will be a linear function of q_{k-1} which we shall denote

$$r_k^* = t_k + u_k q_{k-1}. \tag{A4}$$

With this choice of r_k and optimal choices of outputs by the two firms in all subsequent periods from $k + 1$ to n, the sum of the utilities for firm 2 in periods k to n, as a function of q_{k-1}, will be denoted

$$G_k(q_{k-1}) = A_{k-1} + B_{k-1} q_{k-1} + C_{k-1} q_{k-1}^2. \tag{A5}$$

The sum of the utilities for firm 1 will be denoted

$$F_k(q_{k-1}) = D_{k-1} + H_{k-1}q_{k-1} + L_{k-1}q_{k-1}^2. \tag{A6}$$

All the coefficients in (A1) to (A6) can be found by backward induction beginning with the final period n. For any even integer k and any given value of q_{k-1}, we have

$$G_k(q_{-1}) = \sup_r [R_k(q_{k-1},r) + \delta Q_k(q_{k-1},r) + \rho G_{k+1}(r)]. \tag{A7}$$

The value of r that yields the supremum on the right side of (A7) is r_k^*. The value of $F_k(q_{k-1})$ can then be determined by the relation

$$F_k(q_{k-1}) = Q_k(q_{k-1},r_k^*) + \gamma R_k(q_{k-1},r_k^*) + \rho F_{k+1}(r_k^*). \tag{A8}$$

For any odd integer j, similar relations exist for determining the values of $F_j(r_{j-1})$, q_j^*, and $G_j(r_{j-1})$.

Since the values of $G_{n+1}(r_n)$ and $F_{n+1}(r_n)$ must be 0, the backward induction begins with the boundary values

$$A_n = B_n = C_n = D_n = H_n = L_n = 0. \tag{A9}$$

For any even integer k, the following relations can be derived from (A4) to (A8):

$$t_k = \frac{1 + \rho H_k}{2(1 - \rho L_k)},$$

$$u_k = -\frac{1 + \delta}{2(1 - \rho L_k)},$$

$$A_{k-1} = \rho D_k - \frac{(1 + \delta)t_k^2}{2u_k},$$

$$E_{k-1} = \delta - (1 + \delta)t_k, \tag{A10}$$

$$C_{k-1} = -\left[\delta + \frac{(1 + \delta)u_k}{2}\right],$$

$$D_{k-1} = \rho A_k + (\gamma + \rho B_k)t_k + (\rho C_k - \gamma)t_k^2,$$

$$H_{k-1} = 1 - (1 + \gamma)t_k + (\rho B_k + \gamma)u_k + 2(\rho C_k - \gamma)t_k u_k,$$

$$L_{k-1} = (\rho C_k - \gamma)u_k^2 - (1 + \gamma)u_k - 1.$$

Similarly, for any odd integer j, an analogous set of eight equations can be derived by replacing k by j everywhere in (A10) and interchanging γ and δ wherever they occur in (A10).

If the backward induction process is continued indefinitely and the values of t_k and u_k are calculated for successively smaller even integers k, it is found that these values converge to certain limiting values, which we shall denote by T_2 and U_2. Similarly, the values of t_j and u_j for odd integers j will converge to certain limiting values T_1 and U_1. In other words, the reaction functions (A1) and (A4) converge to certain limiting reaction functions of the form

$$q_j^* = T_1 + U_1 r_{j-1}, \tag{A11}$$

$$r_k^* = T_2 + U_2 q_{k-1}. \tag{A12}$$

By replacing t_k, u_k, B_{k-1}, B_k, C_{k-1}, C_k, H_{k-1}, and L_{k-1} by their limiting values in (A10), and replacing t_j, u_j, B_{j-1}, B_j, C_{j-1}, C_j, H_{j-1}, and L_{j-1} by their limiting values in the analogous equations for odd integers j, it is found that the limiting values T_1, U_1, T_2 and U_2 must satisfy

$$\delta = \frac{(1 + \rho)(1 + \rho T_1 - 2T_2) - \rho(2 + \rho + \rho U_1 U_2)(T_1 + T_2 U_1)}{\rho[2 + \rho + 2(1 + \rho)U_1 + \rho U_1 U_2](T_1 + T_2 U_1) - \rho(1 + \rho)(T_1 + U_1)},$$

$$\delta = -\frac{(1 + \rho U_1 U_2)^2 + 2(1 + \rho)U_2}{(1 + \rho U_1 U_2)^2 + 2\rho(1 + \rho)U_1^2 U_2},$$

$$\gamma = \frac{(1 + \rho)(1 + \rho T_2 - 2T_1) - \rho(2 + \rho + \rho U_1 U_2)(T_2 + T_1 U_2)}{\rho[2 + \rho + 2(1 + \rho)U_2 + \rho U_1 U_2](T_2 + T_1 U_2) - \rho(1 + \rho)(T_2 + U_2)},$$

$$\gamma = -\frac{(1 + \rho U_1 U_2)^2 + 2(1 + \rho)U_1}{(1 + \rho U_1 U_2)^2 + 2\rho(1 + \rho)U_1 U_2^2}.$$

(A13)

If $\gamma = \delta$, then $T_1 = T_2$ and $U_1 = U_2$, and it can be found from (A13) that the common value of T and common value of U must satisfy the relations:

$$\rho^2(1 + \delta)U^4 + 2\rho(1 + \rho)\delta U^3$$
$$+ 2\rho(1 + \rho)U^2 + 2(1 + \rho)U + 1 + \delta = 0, \tag{A14}$$

$$T = -\frac{(1 + \rho)(1 + \rho\delta U)U}{1 + \delta - \rho(1 + \delta)U - (\rho^2 + 3\rho^2\delta + 2\rho\delta)U^2 - \rho^2(1 + \delta)U^3}.$$

Now suppose that $\rho = 1$, so that there is no discounting. When $\gamma = \delta$ it follows from equations (7) to (10) in this chapter that the limiting reaction functions given by (A11) and (A12) will be mutually optimal if and only if

$$T = \frac{(1 - U)(1 + \delta U)}{3 + \delta + (1 + 3\delta)U}. \tag{A15}$$

It can now be verified that if T and U satisfy the relations (A14), then they also satisfy (A15). Hence, the limiting reaction functions (A11) and (A12) are mutually optimal.

7

Interfirm Learning and the Kinked Demand Curve

The last three chapters have been concerned primarily with duopoly models. In this chapter we apply Bayesian analysis to an oligopoly model known as the kinked demand curve. The kinked demand curve represents a theoretical dilemma that is not uncommon in the social sciences (Stigler 1978). The dilemma concerns the inclusion or the exclusion of the model from the mixed bag represented by the classification "oligopoly theory." The model has been in the literature for a number of years and is still in an ambiguous position. Sweezy (1939) proposed the model as an explanation of rigid oligopoly prices, which were taken as an empirical observation (see also Hall and Hitch 1939). The basic assumption underlying the kinked demand curve is that rivals will not follow an attempted increase in price by one of the firms but will follow a decrease. The result is that for each firm the portion of the demand curve above the current price is elastic and the portion below the curve is inelastic. Hence, in the firm's view, the demand curve appears kinked at the current price and the firm has no incentive to modify its price. Because of the paucity of good alternatives, the model was quickly accepted as the theory of oligopoly by many textbook writers. The theory did not explain how oligopoly prices reached a particular level, but it did offer an explanation of their stability.

Stigler (1947) challenged the basic assumption of the kink by producing a number of empirical examples that contradicted the predictions of the model. Stigler's work cast doubt on the validity of the kink theory, but it certainly did not prove it wrong—nor did Stigler claim that it did. As a result, the kink continues to live on in the literature though in an ambiguous state. One reason for its continued existence is that even casual empiricism enables one to produce examples of the kind of behavior predicted by the model (even in Stigler's data there was one).

One such example is the price behavior of the aluminum industry in the summer of 1969. The *Wall Street Journal,* of August 8, 1969, reported on page 5 that

> Two more aluminum producers indicated they don't plan to raise the selling price of basic aluminum ingot. The statements, following a similar declaration late Wednesday by Aluminum Co. of America, raised the possibility that price increases announced earlier this week by Reynolds Metals Co. of Richmond, Va., Kaiser Aluminum and Chemical Corp. of Oakland, Calif. and Revere Copper & Brass, Inc. of New York would be rescinded.

Three days later, on page 10 of the same newspaper, it was reported that

> Aluminum Co. of America has won the latest aluminum price battle. Kaiser Aluminum & Chemical Corp., Oakland, Calif., and Reynolds Metals Co., Richmond, Va., were balked by the opposition of their giant competitor and backed down Friday on a Kaiser-led attempt to raise the price of primary aluminum ingot one cent a pound to 28 cents. Kaiser, the country's third largest producer, said in a brief announcement that it is rescinding the price increase on ingot, the basic form of the metal, that it announced last Wednesday. The increase would have been effective with orders today. Reynolds announced its callback a few hours before Kaiser. The second largest producer said: "We feel an increase was justified at this time. However, we intend to be competitive."

A second reason for the continued existence of the model is that the implications of the theory for behavior during a period when the demand curve is falling or rising are not well specified. Thus any attempts such as Stigler's can be criticized by "believers" who will not accept the data as a true test (Efroymson 1955).

We will not attempt to prove the kink valid or invalid. Rather, we will try to embed the kink in a broader model that incorporates the concepts of learning and search behavior that we have discussed in chapters 4, 5, and 6. This model will reveal conditions under which firm behavior will be consistent with the kink and conditions under which it will be inconsistent. In other words, we accept the fact that both kinds of behavior have been observed, and we attempt to develop a theory which will explain these phenomena.

The Kink Reviewed

A review of the conventional analysis of the kink is unnecessary since it is contained in most textbooks. It will be useful, however, to look at the kink in terms of reaction functions. As given in figure 7.1, *OAC* is the reaction curve of firm 1 and *OAB* is the reaction curve of firm 2. Each of these is the reaction function as expected by the rival. Here we have reduced the kink to a duopoly situation to simplify the analysis that will

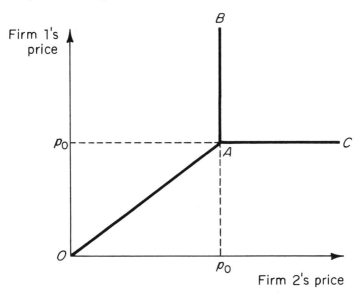

Figure 7.1. Kink assumptions as conjectural variations

follow. In terms of conjectural variations the model can be described as follows:

$$\frac{dp_1}{dp_2} = \begin{cases} 1 & \text{for } p_2 < p_0, \\ 0 & \text{for } p_2 > p_0, \end{cases} \tag{1}$$

$$\frac{dp_2}{dp_1} = \begin{cases} 1 & \text{for } p_1 < p_0, \\ 0 & \text{for } p_1 > p_0. \end{cases}$$

It is of interest to compare these values with those in the Cournot model. There, as pointed out in chapter 1, the derivatives for the two firms are always zero. The possible falseness of the assumptions in (1) is not exposed as dramatically as in the Cournot model because in the kinked model the firms are locked into one position by the assumptions and hence never move. Thus, it is not as obvious as in the Cournot model that the firms never learn, since there is no dynamic process in the kinked-demand-curve model.

The point of this analysis of the kink and the comparison with the Cournot model is to emphasize the static relationship that is assumed between the rivals. The equilibrium price, which is the kink, continues to exist because each firm continues to assume that its rival will always react to any change in price by behavior that will inflict the maximum damage on the firm. Because of this assumption the firm will never be in a position to learn anything about its rival that will lead it to change its price behavior. In Bayesian terms the prior probability is one that the rival will match any decrease in price and that it will not change price in response to an increase.

Interfirm Learning

The model as stated in its simple form cannot be validated empirically. One reason is that the model allows for no learning, but learning about the rival's behavior does take place in the environment of real firms. If we allow that firms learn, then, as we shall show in this chapter, it is possible to get behavior that is sometimes consistent with the kink and sometimes inconsistent, as seems to be true in the data observed. The value of the model will then depend upon finding the conditions under which each type of behavior should be expected. Specifically, starting from given prior probabilities for the behavior of the rival, we will use the concept of firm learning as a mechanism for changing these probabilities. As new posterior probabilities are formed on the basis of new knowledge, the reaction functions will change. At some point the expected gain from experimentation with price will be greater than the expected loss. At this point a firm will make an attempt to change price and through this behavior to find a new equilibrium position.

As mentioned in chapter 4, there is ample evidence to suggest that a multitude of legal ways exist in which firms can learn about the strategies and plans of rivals. There are a wide variety of conference and trade meetings where managers in corresponding organizational roles within rival organizations can meet. We are not implying that collusive agreements are made at such meetings. Antitrust lawyers abound in oligopolistic firms and have educated managers on the kind of behavior that is legal and, in particular, on the kinds of information that can be legally exchanged. In particular, this means that some operating problems can be discussed and possibly some projected plans. At the same time such occasions give opportunities for evaluating the character of rival managers and forming judgments about the goals of rival firms. Individuals within the firm interact with participants of other organizations and thereby both give and receive information about their own and rival organizations.

Another source of learning develops as an industry matures. Trade journals further the spread of knowledge about industry trends in demand and costs, as well as providing information about the price plans and expectations of individual firms. For some industries similar information is published in the daily newspapers.

The role of learning in our theory is to enable the firm to develop a prior probability distribution that is a change from the implicit one assumed in the original theory and portrayed in figure 7.1. The process by which information inputs gathered from the kinds of sources described are transformed into a probability distribution will not be formalized in the model. Once the new prior probability distribution has been developed, the model will explicitly specify whether or not a new equilibrium will be established and, if so, the process by which it will be reached. Thus, instead of the kinked demand curve determining a long-run equilibrium situation, it represents only a starting position when we introduce the concept of learning by firms.

A Learning Approach to the Kinked Demand Curve

Once learning is admitted into the model, although the learning takes place outside the market assumed by the model, the consequences of either a price increase or a price decrease by the firm are no longer as definite as portrayed in figure 7.1. The firm is led by the learning that occurs to a prior probability distribution that encourages it to attempt to forsake the kink by trying to increase price. More specifically, we will assume that we are dealing with a duopoly and that firm 1 is the firm that is learning. Further, we assume that firm 1 has learned that firm 2 has a maximum price θ to which it will match the price increases of firm 1. However, firm 1 does not know the value of θ with certainty, but instead has a prior probability density function $h(\theta)$. This approach is similar to the one used in chapter 6 for an unknown maximum coefficient of cooperation.

We can then, with the aid of figure 7.2, analyze the possible cases. First, let us suppose that firm 1 raises its price from p_0, the current kink price, to p_2. Firm 1 makes this move because its prior $h(\theta)$ leads the firm to conclude that the probability of firm 2's matching is high enough to warrant the risk of loss if firm 2 does not match. The increase of price is a first step on the part of firm 1 in the search for the value of θ. If firm 2 matches the price increase to p_2 then both firms move up the DD' curve to p_2, and the new kinked demand curve is $p_2'p_2D'$. Firm 1 will then continue to increase price as long as expected profits are positive, and firm 2 will continue to match the price increase until reaching θ or coming as close as possible to it. Each experience results in the prior density for θ being transformed into a posterior density and the latter becoming the new prior.

A second case arises when firm 1 increases price, say, to p_2, and firm 2 does not follow. We assume then that firm 1 moves to the upward branch of the kink $p_0'p_0$ and produces where the price p_2 intersects the kink which is at an output of q_1. In the next period, the firm moves back to p_0 and the original equilibrium is reestablished, with no further attempts to increase price above the kink until a new prior is found.

A third case develops when the response by firm 2 is only a partial

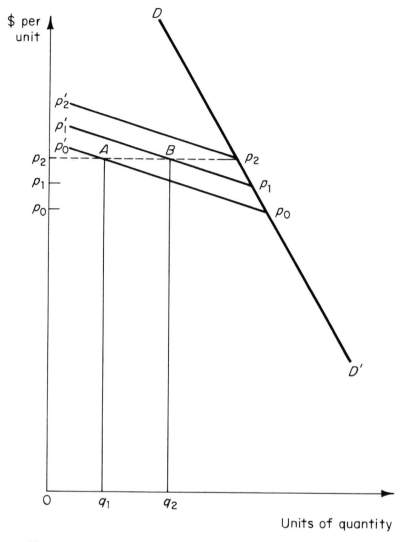

Figure 7.2. Kinked demand curve with various price changes

increase. For example, in figure 7.2 suppose that firm 1 increases price to p_2 and firm 2 increases only to p_1. The immediate effect is for firm 1 to operate at the point where price is equal to p_2 and output is q_2. In the next period, firm 1 moves down to p_1. Since the increase by firm 2 was less than the increase by firm 1, the latter can infer that p_1 is equal to θ and that any further increases are not feasible until a new prior may develop out of the learning process discussed earlier.

Thus, in each period firm 1 must decide between keeping its price at the current level or raising its price to a new value p. If it raises its price to a value $p \leq \theta$, then the rival will match this new price and firm 1 will attain increased profits. If it raises its price to a value $p > \theta$, then the rival will not match this new price and firm 1 will suffer reduced profits. A decision problem arises because firm 1 does not know the value of θ with certainty, but will learn about θ as the process evolves and it observes the response of the rival to different prices of firm 1. To be more specific, assume that firm 1's prior distribution for θ at the beginning of the process is represented by some density function $h(\theta)$ on the interval $l < \theta \leq u$, where l and u are given numbers ($l \geq 0$). The lower limit l is the price level at the beginning of the process, and the upper limit u can be regarded as the monopoly price for the market.

In the first period, firm 1 must choose a price p in the interval $l \leq p \leq u$. If the rival matches this price, then it is known that $p \leq \theta$ and the posterior distribution of θ will be represented by a new density function $h'(\theta)$ defined in the interval $p \leq \theta \leq u$. The new density function is obtained by truncating $h(\theta)$ at $\theta = p$, eliminating that portion of the distribution where $\theta < p$, and renormalizing $h(\theta)$ on the interval $p \leq \theta \leq u$ so that the total probability of this interval is one. Thus $h'(\theta)$ is a proper density function. If firm 2 does not increase price at all or increases only partially, then the second or third case described prevails and price changes cease until a new prior is developed.

In this general discussion, no special assumptions have been made about the form of the demand or cost functions, nor about the prior density function. The discussion has been focused on a general formulation of the problem. In this regard it may be well to amplify the concept of the maximum matching price θ. We are treating firm 1 as the more aggressive firm in the market and firm 2 as the responder. This is a special behavioral assumption that is necessary because of the analytic difficulties that arise if both firms initiate price changes. The concept behind a maximum matching price is merely the notion that firm 2 has a view as to how high, in absolute terms, the price should be in this market. It holds this view independently of the action that firm 1 takes. It should be noted that u is the monopoly price and, therefore, matched price increases less than or equal to u will result in increased profit for both firms.

A Specific Model

In the rest of this chapter we shall consider in detail a specific model in which the profit function of firm 1 has a particularly simple form and in which the only response that firm 2 is allowed to make to any increase in price by firm 1 is either to match the increase or to keep its own price

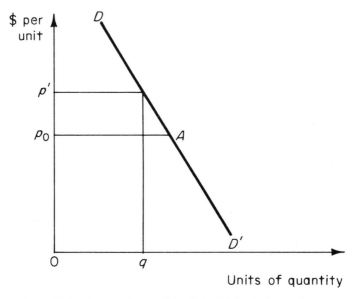

Figure 7.3. A specific model of the kinked demand curve

at the current level. This model is a slight modification of the kink model which has just been discussed. We assume that the demand curve facing the two firms when prices are equal is DD', as given in figure 7.3. The kinked demand curve is $p_0 AD'$. In other words, if firm 1 increases its price above p_0 and firm 2 does not follow, then firm 1's demand goes to zero. If firm 2 matches the increase, then the total demand is determined by DD'. At price p' the total demand is q and this demand is divided equally between the firms.

The profit function for firm 1 that will be used in this model retains many of the important features of more realistic profit functions and has the advantage that certain aspects of the optimal policy for firm 1 can be determined explicitly in terms of simple functions. Specifically, we shall assume that if in some period firm 1 chooses a value p and if the rival does not match this value (because $p > \theta$), then the profit as well as the demand of firm 1 in that period is 0. In other words, we assume that the firm has no fixed costs.

Furthermore, we shall assume that if the rival does match the value p that is chosen by firm 1 in some period (because $p \leq \theta$), then the profit of firm 1 in that period will be simply p. Explicit forms of the demand function and the cost function for firm 1 could be developed which, for all values of p in a certain bounded interval, would result in a profit that was precisely equal to p, as we are assuming. More importantly, however, if the actual profit function in some problem is an increasing function of p over some short interval of values of p, then it will typically be possible to approximate this profit function over the given interval by a linear function of p. By an appropriate choice of units, we can assume without loss of generality that this approximate profit function over the given interval is simply equal to p itself.

However, the main consideration that has led us to choose the function p in this model is the simplicity of the resulting mathematical development. This model is taken purely to simplify the exposition and is not a restriction dictated by our approach. For similar reasons we assume that there are discrete periods and that the prices can be changed only once during the period.

Uniform Prior Distribution

Again to simplify the exposition, we shall assume that firm 1's prior distribution for θ at the beginning of the process is a uniform distribution on the interval $l \leq \theta \leq u$, where l is the price level at the beginning of the process. In the first period, firm 1 must choose a price p in the interval $l \leq p \leq u$. If the rival matches this price, then it is known that $p \leq \theta$ and the posterior distribution of θ will be a uniform distribution on the interval $p \leq \theta \leq u$. If the rival does not match the price p, then it is known that $\theta < p$ and the posterior distribution of θ will be a uniform distribution on the interval $l \leq \theta \leq p$. In either case, the prior distribution of θ at the beginning of the second period will again be a uniform distribution.

A similar argument can be applied at any stage of the process and it follows that the distribution of θ at any stage will always be a uniform distribution.

Single-Period Analysis

In a process with just a single period, the optimal value of p can be determined as follows: For any value of p in the interval $l \leq p \leq u$, let $W_1(p|l,u)$ denote the expected profit from this choice of p. Since θ has a uniform distribution on the interval $l \leq \theta \leq u$, then

$$W_1(p|l,u) = p \Pr(\theta \geq p) + 0 \Pr(\theta < p)$$

$$= p \frac{u - p}{u - l}$$

As indicated in figure 7.4, the maximizing value of p will depend on the relative magnitudes of l and u. The function $W_1(p|l,u)$ is sketched in figure 7.4 for all values of p. However, because of the kink at l, the

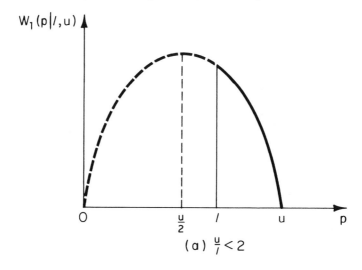

(a) $\frac{u}{l} < 2$

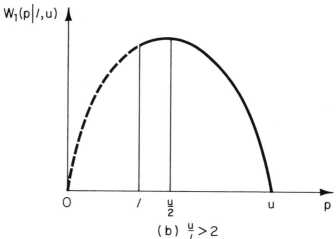

(b) $\frac{u}{l} > 2$

Figure 7.4. Expected profit curve

portion of the curve to the left of l will not represent expected profit for prices below l. Among all values of p in the interval $l \le p \le u$, the expected profit $W_1(p|l,u)$ will be maximized when $p = p_1$, where

$$
p_1 = \begin{cases} l & \text{if } \dfrac{u}{l} \le 2, \\[2ex] \dfrac{u}{2} & \text{if } \dfrac{u}{l} > 2. \end{cases}
$$

If we let $V_1(l,u)$ denote the expected profit that results from this optimum choice of p, then

$$V_1(l,u) = \begin{cases} l & \text{if } \dfrac{u}{l} \le 2, \\[3mm] \dfrac{u^2}{4(u - l)} & \text{if } \dfrac{u}{l} > 2. \end{cases}$$

This result has a simple interpretation. If the maximum possible value u of θ is not more than twice the current price l, then the risk of suffering zero profit is so great for any possible price increase that firm 1 should simply retain the price l. On the other hand, if $(u/l) > 2$, then the probability of increased profit is sufficiently large for firm 1 to risk at least a slight price increase. The size of this particular threshold is a direct result of making the elasticity of the upper branch of the kinked demand curve infinite. As the elasticity is reduced, the size of the threshold will also be reduced.

Multiperiod Analysis

We shall now consider the problem of finding an optimum sequence of prices for firm 1 in a multiperiod process. We shall assume that the goal of firm 1 is to maximize its total discounted expected profit over a fixed number n of stages. In other words, we shall assume that there is a given discount factor α $(0 < \alpha \le 1)$ such that, if Q_i is the profit of firm 1 in the ith period, then firm 1 must choose its prices sequentially over the n stages to maximize the expectation of $Q_1 + \alpha Q_2 + \dots + \alpha^{n-1} Q_n$.

For any numbers $0 < x < y$ and any positive integer j, let $V_j(x,y)$ denote the maximum total expected discounted profit that can be obtained in a problem with j periods in which the prior distribution of θ is a uniform distribution over the interval $x \le \theta \le y$. Consider now a problem with $j + 1$ periods in which the prior distribution of θ is uniform on the interval $l \le \theta \le u$. Suppose that firm 1 chooses the price p $(l \le p \le u)$ in the first period. Then, as previously calculated, its expected profit in the first period is $p(u - p)/(u - l)$.

Furthermore, if $\theta < p$, then the posterior distribution of θ will be uniform on the interval $l \le \theta \le p$. In this case, if firm 1 chooses an optimal sequence of prices over the final j periods of the process, then the discounted expected profit over those j periods will be $\alpha V_j(l,p)$.

On the other hand, if $\theta \ge p$, then the posterior distribution of θ will be uniform on the interval $p \le \theta \le u$. In this case, if firm 1 chooses an optimal sequence of prices over the final j periods, then the discounted expected profit over those j periods will be $\alpha V_j(p,u)$.

Since $\Pr(\theta < p) = (p - l)/(u - l)$ and $\Pr(\theta \geq p) = (u - p)/(u - l)$,   the discounted expected profit over the final j stages, when the price p is chosen on the first stage, will be

$$\alpha \left[\frac{p - l}{u - l} V_j(l,p) + \frac{u - p}{u - l} V_j(p,u) \right].$$

By adding the expected profit in the first period to the above value, we obtain the following value $W_{j+1}(p|l, u)$ for the total discounted expected profit over all $j + 1$ periods, when a price p (not necessarily optimal) is chosen in the first period and optimal prices are chosen in the remaining j periods:

$$W_{j+1}(p|l,u) = \frac{p(u - p)}{u - l} +$$

$$\frac{\alpha}{u - l} [(p - l) V_j(l,p) + (u - p) V_j(p,u)]. \qquad (2)$$

An optimal choice of p in the first period will be a value of p for which $W_{j+1}(p|l,u)$ is maximized.

It will be convenient for the later exposition to denote this value of p by $p_{j+1}(l,u)$. The subscript should be understood to mean the number of periods remaining in the process. Thus in an n-period problem, p_1 denotes the optimal choice in the final period and p_2 denotes the optimal choice in period $n - 1$. With this optimal choice $p_{j+1}(l,u)$ in the first period and optimal choices in the j remaining periods, $W_{j+1}(p_{j+1}|l,u)$ becomes $V_{j+1}(l,u)$, the maximum discounted expected profit that can be obtained over all $j + 1$ periods. Thus we have obtained the following basic relations among V_j, and V_{j+1} and W_{j+1}: For $j = 1, 2, \ldots$ and for $0 \leq l < u$,

$$V_{j+1}(l,u) = \max_{l \leq p \leq u} \left\{ \frac{p(u - p)}{u - l} + \right.$$

$$\left. \frac{\alpha}{u - l} [(p - l) V_j(l,p) + (u - p) V_j(p,u)] \right\} \qquad (3)$$

$$= \max_{l \leq p \leq u} W_{j+1}(p|l,u) = W_{j+1}(p_{j+1}|l,u).$$

The values of p_1 and V_1 were determined for the single-period case earlier in this paper. From these values it is now possible, at least in principle, to use the basic relation (3) to determine, in succession, the values of p_j and V_j for $j = 2, 3, \ldots$. Algebraic expressions for p_2 and V_2 can be derived by a tedious but straightforward analysis of (3). Since the tediousness is a rapidly increasing funciton of j and the additional values will not be needed in the remainder of this chapter, we will not present any further values of p_j and V_j here. However, it is important, as we indicated earlier, to obtain the conditions under which the optimal decision for firm 1 is to retain the current price l, that is, $p_j(l,u) = l$. This shall be done in the next section.

Analysis of the Threshold

We shall now establish the conditions for maintaining the kink. It will be convenient to introduce the following notation: For $0 < \alpha < 1$ and $j = 1, 2, \ldots$, we shall define

$$\pi_j(\alpha) = \frac{\alpha + \alpha^2 + \cdots + \alpha^j}{1 + \alpha + \alpha^2 + \cdots + \alpha^j} = \frac{\alpha(1 - \alpha^j)}{1 - \alpha^{j+1}}. \tag{4}$$

For $j = 0$, we shall define $\pi_0(\alpha) = 0$. Finally, for $\alpha = 1$ and $j = 0, 1, 2, \ldots$, we shall define $\pi_j(\alpha) = j/(1 + j)$.

Theorem: For any positive integer j, $p_j(l,u) = l$ and

$$V_j(l,u) = l \sum_{i=0}^{j-1} \alpha^i$$

if and only if $(u/l) \leq 2 - \pi_{j-1}(\alpha)$.

This theorem is proved in the appendix to this chapter. It is clear from the nature of the problem being considered, as well as from the condition stated in the theorem, that if it is optimal for firm 1 to choose the price $p = l$ at some stage of the process, then it is optimal for firm 1 to continue to choose the price $p = l$ in all the remaining periods of the process.

The theorem applies to any multiperiod process in which there are j periods remaining in the process. It should be noted that the l and u referred to in the theorem are the end points of the current posterior distribution. They can be different from the end points of the original prior distribution. In the process of searching for θ, both l and u could have been modified several times.

It follows from the theorem that when there are j periods remaining, firm 1 should make no attempt to increase the price level and should simply choose the price $p = l$ on all j periods if and only if $u/l \leq 2 - \pi_{j-1}(\alpha)$. This strategy is, of course, posited on the assumption that no additional learning takes place in the remaining periods so that the current distribution remains stationary. In other words, this condition represents precisely the implications underlying the kinked demand curve theory. As long as the current distribution fulfills the condition specified in the theorem and there is no change in the distribution, the kink is a valid description of the world.

The value $2 - \pi_{j-1}(\alpha)$ serves as an experimental threshold, in the sense that u/l must be larger than this value for experimentation to proceed. As α grows larger, the profits in future periods are discounted less and, therefore, contribute more to the cumulative profit function over the remaining j periods. It follows that the experimental threshold should be reduced to encourage experimentation, since future profits become more valuable relative to current profits. This feature is exhibited in our model as indicated by the fact that the experimental threshold $2 - \pi_{j-1}(\alpha)$ given in the theorem is a decreasing function of α for any fixed value of j. There will always be a threshold for any j-period problem as can be seen from the value of $\pi_{j-1}(\alpha)$ when $\alpha = 1$. For this value of α it can be verified that the threshold becomes $(j + 1)/j$. Furthermore, for any fixed α the threshold will decrease as the value of j increases. This can be seen from the expression for $\pi_j(\alpha)$ given earlier.

Infinite-Period Case

When $0 < \alpha < 1$, the general approach we have taken can be extended to an infinite number of periods. Under such conditions, firm 1 should continue to try a new price in each period until the posterior uniform distribution of θ becomes restricted to an interval $l \leq \theta \leq u$ such that $u/l \leq 2 - \alpha$. The latter is the condition for the kink to prevail. That is, firm 1 should simply choose the price $p = l$ for each period. Obviously, the propositions about the effects of changes in the size of α on the threshold hold also for the infinite-period case.

Even in the infinite-period case, experimentation will eventually terminate if prices are restricted to integer multiples of some fixed unit. A period will be reached at which $u/l \leq 2 - \alpha$ because each experiment reduces the value of u/l by at least some minimum positive amount. Once the interval becomes small enough, firm 1 will find that further experimentation will not be profitable and will accept a given amount of uncertainty as to the precise value of θ. Given that $\theta < u$ and that the terminal price $p^* = l$, it follows that $1 \leq \theta/p^* \leq 2 - \alpha$.

Summary and Conclusions

Our objective in this chapter has been to develop a theoretical model around the kinked demand curve that is consistent with empirical observations. We have accomplished this objective by introducing an interfirm learning mechanism. We have postulated that this learning results in the development of a prior uniform distribution by firm 1's management on the upper limit θ of a price increase that will be matched by the rival. When the prior meets the condition for the firm to attempt a price increase, the firm learns more about the precise location of θ. This information about θ is incorporated into the prior to form a posterior distribution and, in the usual manner, the latter becomes the new prior.

In developing our analytic model, we made a number of simplifying assumptions that enabled us to make specific calculations (for extensions see Holthaus 1979). This simplified model has been in some sense justified by the fact that it has led to propositions about the effects on the threshold of changes in the discount rate and the number of periods that are consistent with the results that would be expected from basic theory. For both the multiperiod and the infinite-period case, we have developed the conditions that make the kink a valid description, on the one hand, and the conditions that will lead to a deviation from the kink, on the other.

Both of these conditions are essentially limiting conditions that follow from something like "one-shot" learning. That is, learning takes place in some institutional or extra-model sense to the extent that a prior distribution can be specified on the limiting price that would be matched by the rival. After that, further learning takes place only through actual price experimentation. In the real world, the extra-model learning continues to occur and can have effects on the current probability distribution. Thus, one can see how it would be possible at one instant of time to have the kink prevail and at another instant of time have it fail to prevail. Automobiles, steel, aluminum, potash, and cigarettes all provide instances where each type of situation has been observed when a long-time series of prices is considered (Cyert 1955).

This chapter has provided insight into the kind of empirical research that is necssary to develop predictive models about firm behavior. Specifically, our work points in the direction of isolating the sources of learning in the industry and finding methods for describing the effects of this learning on the probability distributions that are used in the decision process.

APPENDIX:
Proof of Theorem

The purpose of this appendix is to prove the following theorem: For any positive integer j, $p_j(l,u) = l$ and $V_j(l,u) = l \sum_{i=0}^{j-1} \alpha^i$ if and only if $u/l \leq 2 - \pi_{j-1}(\alpha)$, where $\pi_{j-1}(\alpha)$ is defined by (4). We shall prove this theorem by an induction argument on the value of j. It can be verified from the expressions for p_1 and V_1 derived earlier that the statement is true for $j = 1$. Suppose now that the statement is true for an arbitrary positive integer j. We shall show that it must also be true for $j + 1$.

Consider any values of l and u such that $u/l \leq 2 - \pi_j(\alpha)$. Since

$\pi_j(\alpha) > \pi_{j-1}(\alpha)$ it follows that $u/l \leq 2 - \pi_{j-1}(\alpha)$. Furthermore, for any value of p in the interval $l \leq p \leq u$, it will also be true that $p/l \leq 2 - \pi_{j-1}(\alpha)$. Therefore, by the induction hypothesis,

$$V_j(l,p) = l \sum_{i=0}^{j-1} \alpha^i$$

and

$$V_j(p,u) = p \sum_{i=0}^{j-1} \alpha^i.$$

By equation (2), it now follows after some simplification that

$$W_{j+1}(p|l,u) = \frac{1 + \alpha + \cdots + \alpha^j}{u - l} [p(u - p) + \pi_j(\alpha) l(p - l)].$$

The maximum value of $W_{j+1}(p|l,u)$ over all values of p in the interval $l \leq p \leq u$ will occur at $p = l$ if and only if $u/l \leq 2 - \pi_j(\alpha)$. Therefore, if $u/l \leq 2 - \pi_j(\alpha)$, then $p_{j+1}(l,u) = l$ and $V_{j+1}(l,u)$ has the desired value. On the other hand, if

$$2 - \pi_j(\alpha) < \frac{u}{l} \leq 2 - \pi_{j-1}(\alpha),$$

then $W_{j+1}(p|l,u)$ will still be of the form that has just been derived, but its maximum value will not occur at $p = l$. Therefore, $p_{j+1}(l,u) \neq l$.

To complete the proof, we note that if $p_{j+1}(l, u) > l$ for some value of the ratio u/l, then it must also be true that $p_{j+1}(l,u) > l$ for all larger values of the ratio u/l. Hence, if $u/l > 2 - \pi_j(\alpha)$, then $p_{j+1}(l,u) > l$. The desired result has now been established.

8

Sequential Strategies in Dual Control Problems

In this chapter* we show how some of the concepts we have developed in our work on duopoly can be applied to other types of decision problems. In particular, we will apply our methodology to some problems in control theory. As indicated in chapter 3, we believe that control theory is appropriate for building mathematical models of the firm. We will develop an extension of the usual linear-quadratic, stochastic control problems in discrete time (Simon 1956; DeGroot 1970, sec. 14.10; Chow 1975; Whittle 1982) to problems in which there are two decision-makers or players, both of whom are trying to control the same stochastic system in order to maximize their own individual payoffs or, equivalently, to minimize their own individual losses. The control problems we shall be considering can be regarded as a special class of non-zero-sum, two-person games (for other applications see Grossman 1975a; Fogelman-Soulie, Munier, and Shakun 1983).

We shall confine ourselves to the simplest type of stochastic control model. We assume a sequence of real-valued random variables X_0, X_1, ... , X_n, where X_i represents the state of a certain stochastic system in period i ($i = 0, 1, \ldots , n$) and the system evolves in accordance with the relation

$$X_i = \alpha_i X_{i-1} + \beta_i + u_i + \epsilon_i \ (i = 1, \ldots , n). \tag{1}$$

Here, α_i and β_i are given constants, u_i is a control variable whose value is to be chosen by the decision maker after observing the value of X_{i-1}, and ϵ_1, ... , ϵ_n are independent random error terms with $E(\epsilon_i) = 0$ and $\mathrm{Var}(\epsilon_i) = \sigma_i^2$, for $i = 1, \ldots , n$.

---

*The reader may omit this chapter without any break in continuity.

In this simple, traditional model it is assumed that there is a given sequence of real numbers $s_1, \ldots, s_n$ which serve as the targets or goals of the decision-maker. It is also assumed that the loss in period i is of the form*

$$q_{1i}(X_i - s_i)^2 + q_{2i}u_i^2, \tag{2}$$

where q_{1i} and q_{2i} are nonnegative constants. The first term in (2) is the loss due to the state X_i being away from the target s_i and the second term is the cost of using the control u_i in period i. The total loss over the entire n periods is, therefore,

$$\sum_{i=1}^{n} [q_{1i}(X_i - s_i)^2 + q_{2i}u_i^2]. \tag{3}$$

For any given initial state X_0, it is assumed that the decision-maker must choose the controls $u_1, \ldots, u_n$ sequentially in order to minimize the expected value of the total loss (3).

Now we shall consider a similar process with two decision-makers or players: player 1 and player 2. The system equation (1) is now replaced by a relation of the form

$$X_i = \alpha_i X_{i-1} + \beta_i + u_i + v_i + \epsilon_i \ (i = 1, \ldots, n). \tag{4}$$

Here, u_i represents the control which is to be chosen by player 1 after observing the value of X_{i-1}, and v_i represents the control which is to be chosen by player 2. It is assumed that the loss function of player 1 is given by (3) and that the loss function of player 2 is of the form

$$\sum_{i=1}^{n} [r_{1i}(X_i - t_i)^2 + r_{2i}v_i^2], \tag{5}$$

where $t_1, \ldots, t_n$ represent the targets of player 2 and r_{1i} and r_{2i} are non-negative numbers. Finally, it is assumed that the players wish to minimize the expected value of their own loss function.

The targets of the two players may be either the same or different. If the targets $s_1, \ldots, s_n$ of player 1 are different from the targets $t_1, \ldots, t_n$ of player 2, then in general, the players will try to control the system to keep it near their own targets. If the targets $s_1, \ldots, s_n$ are the same as or similar to the targets $t_1, \ldots, t_n$, then, in general, each player will try to get the other player to pay the control costs of moving the system near

---

*In this chapter, the symbols q and r have a different meaning from that in the previous chapters but conform to standard usage in control theory.

their common targets and of keeping it there. We shall call problems of this type, problems of *dual control*.

Alternating Choice and Backward Induction

When both player 1 and player 2 can choose values for their control variables simultaneously in each period, there is no clear-cut solution to the dual control problem being considered here. Indeed, it is not clear what is meant by a solution in this context, and various concepts of a solution in a non-zero sum, two-person game have been proposed (see Luce and Raiffa 1957; A. J. Jones 1980). The difficulty is that since the players must make their choices simultaneously in each period, each player will make a choice based (1) on the choice he or she thinks the other player will make, (2) on the choice he or she thinks the other player thinks that he or she will make, and so on.

Some methods of avoiding the infinite regress to which this type of reasoning leads were described in chapter 4. As in chapters 5 and 6, we shall avoid this difficulty by assuming that the players make their choices in alternating periods. Specifically we shall assume that in period 1, player 1 can choose any value for the control variable u_1 but player 2 must choose the value $v_1 = 0$. In period 2, player 2 can choose any value for the control variable v_2 but player 1 must choose the value $u_2 = 0$. In period 3, it is again the turn of player 1 to choose a value for u_3 while $v_3 = 0$. The process continues in this way with player 1 choosing a value for the control variable u_j in each odd period j while $v_j = 0$, and player 2 choosing a value for the control variable v_k in each even period k while $u_k = 0$. Processes similar to this one have been introduced in the theory of differential games to obtain approximations and bounds for the strategies and expected losses in the continuous-time processes considered in that theory (see Friedman 1971).

With this alternating-choice model, all guesswork is removed for the two players and there is a well-defined sequence of optimal controls that can be determined by the method of backward induction. We shall assume, for convenience, that the number of periods n is even, so that player 2 must choose the value of v_n to minimize the expected loss in period n, which is

$$E_{n-1}[r_{1n}(X_n - t_n)^2] + r_{2n}v_n^2. \qquad (6)$$

The symbol E_{n-1} in (6) indicates that the expectation is to be calculated conditionally on the history of the process over the first $n - 1$ periods being given. It is easily found in this way that the optimal value of v_n, that is, the value of v_n that minimizes (6), will be a certain linear function of the state X_{n-1}.

Next, the method of backward induction specifies moving back to period $n - 1$. After the value of X_{n-2} has been observed, player 1 must choose the value of u_{n-1}. Since player 1 knows that player 2 will use the strategy that we have just developed for choosing v_n on period n, player 1 can, for any given value of X_{n-2}, choose u_{n-1} in order to minimize the expected total loss over periods $n - 1$ and n.

By continuing to move backward toward the first period in this way, we can develop the entire sequence of optimal controls for both players. It can be shown that in any given period i, the optimal value of the control for the player who must choose in that period will be a linear function of the previous state X_{i-1}. The coefficient of X_{i-1} and the constant term in this linear function will depend on the future targets s_j and t_j and on the values of the constants q_{1j}, q_{2j}, r_{1j}, and r_{2j} for $j = i, i + 1, \ldots, n$, but they will not depend on the variances $\sigma_i^2, \ldots, \sigma_n^2$ of the random error terms and, hence, these variances need not actually be known to the players. In fact, if all the variances are 0, the process is actually deterministic and not random. It follows from this discussion that the players can make their optimal choices as if the process were deterministic, even though it is actually random.

Limiting Strategies

In order to move the discussion forward conveniently, we shall now simplify the model further by assuming that $\alpha_i = 1$ and $\beta_i = 0$ for $i = 1, \ldots, n$ in equation (4). Furthermore, we shall assume that in (3) and (5), we have $q_{1i} = q > 0$, $q_{2i} = 1$, $r_{1i} = r > 0$, and $r_{2i} = 1$ for $i = 1, \ldots, n$. Finally, we shall assume that all the targets $s_1, \ldots, s_n$ of player 1 have the same value s and all the targets $t_1, \ldots, t_n$ of player 2 have the same value t. Without loss of generality we shall assume that $s = 0$ and $t > 0$.

In summary, we are now considering a dual control problem in which the system evolves in accordance with the relation

$$X_i = X_{i-1} + u_i + v_i + \epsilon_i \ (i = 1, \ldots, n), \tag{7}$$

and in which the loss functions of the two players are as follows:

Player 1: $\quad \displaystyle\sum_{i=1}^{n} (q\,X_i^2 + u_i^2),$

$$\tag{8}$$

Player 2: $\quad \displaystyle\sum_{i=1}^{n} [r(X_i - t)^2 + v_i^2].$

As previously mentioned, in each odd period j, the optimal value of u_j will be a linear function of the form

Table 8.1   Optimal Strategies for $q=1$, $r=1$, $t=1$

i	μ_i	v_i	ϕ_i	ψ_i
n			0.000	0.500
$n-1$	0.111	0.556		
$n-2$			0.194	0.565
$n-3$	0.245	0.564		
$n-4$			0.277	0.565
$n-5$	0.296	0.565		
$n-6$			0.308	0.565
$n-7$	0.315	0.565		
$n-8$			0.319	0.565
$n-9$	0.322	0.565		
$n-10$			0.323	0.565
$n-11$	0.324	0.565		
$n-12$			0.325	0.565
$n-13$	0.325	0.565		
$n-14$			0.326	0.565
$n-15$	0.326	0.565		
$n-16$			0.326	0.565
$n-17$	0.326	0.565		

$$u_j = -\mu_j - v_j X_{j-1}, \tag{9}$$

and in each even period k, the optimal value of v_k will be a linear function of the form

$$v_k = -\phi_k + \psi_k(t - X_{k-1}). \tag{10}$$

The values of μ_j, v_j, ϕ_k, and ψ_k can be determined by backward induction. The sequence of optimal values is presented in table 8.1 for the problem in which $q = r = t = 1$, and in table 8.2 for the problem in which $q = 1$, $r = 2$, and $t = 10$.

It can be seen from tables 8.1 and 8.2—and it is true for any given positive values of q, r, and t—that as we move backward from the final period, the values of μ_j, v_j, ϕ_k, ψ_k converge to certain limiting values which we shall denote by μ^*, v^*, ϕ^*, and ψ^*. For example, it can be seen from table 8.2 that $\mu^* = 2.387$, $v^* = 0.528$, $\phi^* = 3.144$, and $\psi^* = 0.723$. These limiting values are given in table 8.3 for a few sets of values of q and r and for $t = 1$. For any other value of t, the tabulated values of μ^* and ϕ^* must be multiplied by t, but the tabulated values of v^* and ψ^* remain unchanged. Whenever $q = r$, it will be true that $\mu^* = \phi^*$ and $v^* = \psi^*$.

It follows from this discussion that as we move backward from the final period, the optimal strategies u_j and v_k given in equations (9) and

Table 8.2 Optimal Strategies for $q=1$, $r=2$, $t=10$

i	μ_i	v_i	ϕ_i	ψ_i
n			0.000	0.667
$n-1$	1.053	0.526		
$n-2$			2.217	0.722
$n-3$	2.028	0.528		
$n-4$			2.894	0.723
$n-5$	2.290	0.528		
$n-6$			3.076	0.723
$n-7$	2.361	0.528		
$n-8$			3.126	0.723
$n-9$	2.380	0.528		
$n-10$			3.139	0.723
$n-11$	2.385	0.528		
$n-12$			3.142	0.723
$n-13$	2.386	0.528		
$n-14$			3.143	0.723
$n-15$	2.387	0.528		
$n-16$			3.144	0.723
$n-17$	2.387	0.528		
$n-18$			3.144	0.723

(10) will converge to certain limiting strategies of the form

$$u_j = -\mu^* - v^* X_{j-1} \tag{11}$$

and

$$v_k = \phi^* + \psi^*(t - X_{k-1}). \tag{12}$$

By analogy with chapters 5 and 6, we shall call these strategies the *limiting pure duopoly strategies*. Thus, in a process with many periods, the players will be using strategies for u_j and v_k that are essentially given by (11) and (12) over most of the periods of the process, up until the final

Table 8.3 The Limiting Strategies

q	r	t	μ^*	v^*	ϕ^*	ψ^*
1	1	1	0.326	0.565	0.326	0.565
1	2	1	0.239	0.528	0.314	0.723
2	2	1	0.270	0.693	0.270	0.693
0.5	1	1	0.255	0.387	0.319	0.617
0.5	2	1	0.161	0.355	0.262	0.759

few periods. During these final few periods, the players will move away from the limiting strategies given in (11) and (12) and will begin to change their strategies in each period, as indicated in tables 8.1 and 8.2, in preparation for the termination of the process.

Equilibrium

We shall now assume that the random error term ϵ_i in (7) has a normal distribution with mean 0 and the same variance σ^2 in every period of the process. It then follows that since the players choose their controls in each of the earlier periods of the process in accordance with the limiting strategies (11) and (12), the process will be brought into an equilibrium that is similar to the pure duopoly equilibrium defined in chapter 6 and will remain in equilibrium until the final few periods. In the rest of this chapter we shall concentrate on this equilibrium, which will be maintained over the vast middle part of a process with many periods.

When the process is in equilibrium the state will have one stationary distribution in the odd periods and a different stationary distribution in the even periods. This result follows from the fact that the state of the system is a random variable because of the random error terms, and the behavior of the system in odd periods differs from its behavior in even periods due to the alternating choices. Furthermore, since the random error terms in equation (7) are now assumed to be normally distributed, and since the controls are being chosen in each period in accordance with (11) and (12), it follows that for any given initial state X_0, the state X_i of the system in any period i will itself have a normal distribution. We shall now determine the stationary normal distribution for both the odd periods and the even periods.

Suppose that in equilibrium, the stationary distribution of the state X_j in any odd period j is a normal distribution with mean m_1 and variance σ_1^2, and the stationary distribution of X_k in any even period k is a normal distribution with mean m_2 and variance σ_2^2. For any odd period j, we have $v_j = 0$ and $E(\epsilon_j) = 0$. It follows, therefore, by taking expectations of both sides of (7) and using (11) that

$$m_1 = E(X_j) = E(X_{j-1}) + E(u_j)$$

$$= m_2 - \mu^* - v^*m_2 \tag{13}$$

$$= -\mu^* + (1 - v^*)m_2.$$

Similarly, it follows from considering (7) for an even period k and using (12) that

$$m_2 = m_1 + \phi^* + \psi^*(t - m_1)$$
$$= \phi^* + \psi^*t + (1 - \psi^*)m_1. \tag{14}$$

Together, (13) and (14) imply that

$$m_1 = \frac{-\mu^* + (1 - v^*)(\phi^* + \psi^*t)}{1 - (1 - v^*)(1 - \psi^*)} \tag{15}$$

and

$$m_2 = \frac{-(1 - \psi^*)\mu^* + \phi^* + \psi^*t}{1 - (1 - v^*)(1 - \psi^*)}. \tag{16}$$

Next, by considering the variance of each side of equation (7) for an odd period j, and using (11) and the fact that Var $(\epsilon_j) = \sigma^2$, we obtain the relation

$$\sigma_1^2 = \text{Var}(X_j) = \text{Var}(X_{j-1} - \mu^* - v^*X_{j-1}) + \sigma^2$$
$$= (1 - v^*)^2\sigma_2^2 + \sigma^2. \tag{17}$$

Similarly, we can also obtain the relation

$$\sigma_2^2 = \text{Var}(X_k) = (1 - \psi^*)^2\sigma_1^2 + \sigma^2. \tag{18}$$

It follows from (17) and (18) that

$$\sigma_1^2 = \frac{[1 + (1 - v^*)^2]\sigma^2}{1 - (1 - v^*)^2(1 - \psi^*)^2} \tag{19}$$

and

$$\sigma_2^2 = \frac{[1 + (1 - \psi^*)^2]\sigma^2}{1 - (1 - v^*)^2(1 - \psi^*)^2}. \tag{20}$$

Thus, the stationary distributions of X_j in odd periods and of X_k in even periods are now completely specified by equations (15), (16), (19), and (20). We have not shown here that these stationary distributions are actually the limiting distributions that will become established in equilibrium when the players use the strategies (11) and (12) repeatedly, but that result could be demonstrated as well.

The values of m_1, σ_1^2, m_2, and σ_2^2 for a few sets of values of q and r and for $t = 1$ are given in table 8.4. These values have been calculated from the values given in table 8.3 and equations (15), (16), (19), and (20). For any other value of t, the tabulated values of m_1 and m_2 must be multiplied by t, but the tabulated values of σ_1^2 and σ_2^2 remain unchanged. For the cases included in table 8.4, the target of player 1 in each period is 0 and the target of player 2 in each period is 1. When

Table 8.4   Means and Variances in Equilibrium

q	r	t	m_1	σ_1^2	m_2	σ_2^2
1	1	1	0.076	$1.234\sigma^2$	0.924	$1.234\sigma^2$
1	2	1	0.289	$1.244\sigma^2$	1.117	$1.096\sigma^2$
2	2	1	0.028	$1.104\sigma^2$	0.972	$1.104\sigma^2$
0.5	1	1	0.417	$1.457\sigma^2$	1.095	$1.214\sigma^2$
0.5	2	1	0.590	$1.451\sigma^2$	1.163	$1.084\sigma^2$

$q = r = 1$, the values $m_1 = 0.076$ and $m_2 = 0.924$ indicate that in odd periods player 1 will tend to use the control u_j to move the state of the process down to 0.076, and in even periods player 2 will tend to use the control v_k to move the state of the process back up to 0.924. Indeed, when $\sigma^2 = 0$ and the process is deterministic, this is *exactly* what will happen.

However, for $q = 0.5$ and $r = 2$, the values $m_1 = 0.590$ and $m_2 = 1.163$ presented in table 8.4 reveal an interesting phenomenon. In this case, player 1 allocates less weight to the losses due to missing the target than is allocated to the losses due to control costs, whereas player 2 allocates more weight to losses due to missing the target than is allocated to control costs. The result of these considerations is that in odd periods, player 1 will tend to use the control u_j to move the state of the process down to 0.590 and in even periods, player 2 will tend to use the control v_k to move the state of the process *beyond* his target to the value 1.163. Offhand, this strategy would not appear to be optimal because player 2 could attain the same loss due to being away from the target and a smaller loss due to control costs in each even period by using the control v_k to move the state of the process just to the value $1 - 0.163 = 0.837$ rather than to the value 1.163. Should this procedure be followed, however, player 1 would find it optimal to use the control u_j in each odd period to pull the state of the process down to a value lower than 0.590, and the result to player 2 would be a total loss larger than that incurred by the strategy summarized in tables 8.3 and 8.4.

Losses

The expected total loss to player 1 in any two successive periods will be

$$L_1 = E(qX_j^2 + u_j^2) + E(qX_{j+1}^2), \tag{21}$$

where j is an odd integer and $j + 1$ is, therefore, an even integer. Since in equilibrium the random variable X_j has mean m_1 and variance σ_1^2, the random variable X_{j+1} has mean m_2 and variance σ_2^2, and u_j is given by (11), it follows from (21) that

$$L_1 = q(\sigma_1^2 + m_1^2) + v^{*2}\sigma_2^2 + (\mu^* + v^*m_2)^2 + q(\sigma_2^2 + m_2^2). \tag{22}$$

In turn, it follows from (19) and (20) that

$$L_1 = q(m_1^2 + m_2^2) + (\mu^* + v^*m_2)^2 \tag{23}$$
$$+ \frac{q[1 + (1 - v^*)^2] + (q + v^{*2})[1 + (1 - \psi^*)^2]}{1 - (1 - v^*)^2(1 - \psi^*)^2} \sigma^2$$

Similarly, the expected total loss to player 2 in any two successive periods will be

$$L_2 = E[r(X_k - t)^2 + v_k^2] + E[r(X_{k-1} - t)^2], \tag{24}$$

where k is even and $k + 1$ is odd. It can be shown that in equilibrium

$$L_2 = r[(m_2 - t)^2 + (m_1 - t)^2] + [\phi^* + \psi^*(t - m_1)]^2 \tag{25}$$
$$+ \frac{r[1 + (1 - \psi^*)^2] + (r + \psi^{*2})[1 + (1 - v^*)^2]}{1 - (1 - v^*)^2(1 - \psi^*)^2} \sigma^2.$$

The values of L_1 and L_2, as determined from (23) and (25) are presented in table 8.5 for a few sets of values of q and r and for $t = 1$. For any other value of t, the coefficients of σ^2 in both L_1 and L_2 will remain unchanged, but the constant term in both L_1 and L_2 must be multiplied by t^2.

Table 8.5 exhibits another unusual phenomenon. When $q = 0.5$ and $r = 2$, the loss incurred by player 2 when missing the target t by any given amount is four times as large as the loss incurred by player 1 when missing the target 0 by the same amount. Furthermore, the costs of control are the same for both players. However, it can be seen from table 8.5 that when $\sigma^2 = 0$, the expected loss of player 1 will be $L_1 = 1.179$ and the expected loss of player 2 will be $L_2 = 0.718$. Thus, although the loss function of player 2 is larger than that of player 1, the equilibrium becomes established in such a way that the actual loss per period of player 1 will be greater than that of player 2. Part of the explanation of this unusual feature lies in the values of m_1 and m_2 which were given in table 8.4.

It can also be seen from table 8.5 that if σ^2 is large, then the value of L_2 will be much larger than the value of L_1. In fact, $L_2 > L_1$ if $\sigma^2 > 0.102$.

Finally, it can be seen from table 8.5 that a similar phenomenon occurs when $q = 1$ and $r = 2$, and also when $q = 0.5$ and $r = 1$.

Table 8.5 **Expected Total Loss for Each Player in Two Successive Periods from Limiting Pure Competitive Strategies**

q	r	t	L_1	L_2
1	1	1	$1.577 + 2.861\sigma^2$	$1.577 + 2.861\sigma^2$
1	2	1	$2.018 + 2.645\sigma^2$	$1.725 + 5.330\sigma^2$
2	2	1	$2.781 + 4.947\sigma^2$	$2.781 + 4.947\sigma^2$
0.5	1	1	$1.147 + 1.517\sigma^2$	$0.810 + 3.225\sigma^2$
0.5	2	1	$1.179 + 1.404\sigma^2$	$0.718 + 5.908\sigma^2$

Mutually Optimal Strategies

It can be shown that if player 1 chooses the control u_j in every odd period j in accordance with a function of the form (11), for some fixed values of μ^* and ν^*; if player 2 chooses the control v_k in every even period k in accordance with a function of the form (12), for some fixed values of ϕ^* and ψ^*; and if $0 < \nu^* < 1$ and $0 < \psi^* < 1$, then the process will converge to an equilibrium. In this equilibrium, the distribution of the state X_j in any odd period j will have mean m_1 and variance σ_1^2, as given by (15) and (19), and the state X_k in any even period k will have mean m_2 and variance σ_2^2, as given by (16) and (20). Furthermore, in equilibrium, the expected total loss L_1 of player 1 in any two successive periods will be given by (23) and the expected total loss L_2 of player 2 will be given by (25).

For any given values of μ^* and ν^* to be used by player 1 in (11)—not necessarily the optimal values as given in table 8.3—it would be of interest to player 2 to find values of ϕ^* and ψ^* to be used in (12) which would minimize the value of the expected loss L_2. Similarly, for any given values of ϕ^* and ψ^* to be used by player 2, it would be of interest to player 1 to find values of μ^* and ν^* which would minimize the value of L_1. If four values μ^*, ν^*, ϕ^*, and ψ^* have the property that for these given values of μ^* and ν^*, L_2 is minimized by the given values of ϕ^* and ψ^*, and for these given values of ϕ^* and ψ^*, L_1 is minimized by the given values of μ^* and ν^*, then it is said that the strategies u_j and v_k defined by (11) and (12) are *mutually optimal*. Although (11) and (12) are not viewed as reaction functions in control theory, they are similar. The term "mutually optimal" is used here in the same sense as in chapters 5 and 6. If the strategies u_j and v_k are mutually optimal, then in equilibrium, as long as player 1 continues to choose the control u_j in every odd period in accordance with (11), it will be optimal for player 2 to continue to choose the control v_k in every even period in accordance with (12), and vice versa.

For any given values of q, r, t, and σ^2, the limiting pure duopoly strategies are mutually optimal. It appears to be difficult to establish this property analytically, but it has been verified numerically for a wide class of values of q, r, t, and σ^2. These numerical computations, together with the method by which the limiting pure competitive strategies were derived as limits of sequences of choices which minimize the expected total loss of each player relative to the strategies being used by the other player, leave no doubt that the limiting pure competitive strategies are mutually optimal in all cases.

Myopic Strategies

Suppose now that instead of planning an optimal sequence of choices during the process, each player in turn chooses the control to minimize the expected loss in that particular period without regard for the future. In any odd period j, the expected loss to player 1 for any given values of the state X_{j-1} and the control u_j is

$$E(qX_j^2) + u_j^2 = E[q(X_{j-1} + u_j + \epsilon_j)^2] + u_j^2. \tag{26}$$

It can be shown that the value of u_j which minimizes (26) is

$$u_j = \frac{-q}{1+q} X_{j-1}. \tag{27}$$

Similarly, in any even period k, for any given value of X_{k-1}, the value of v_k which minimizes the expected loss to player 2 in period k is

$$v_k = \frac{r}{1+r}(t - X_{k-1}). \tag{28}$$

The strategies u_j and v_k given by (27) and (28) are called the *myopic strategies* of the players.

By comparing (27) and (28) with (11) and (12), we see that the myopic strategies have the form given in (11) and (12) with $\mu^* = \phi^* = 0$, $v^* = q/(1+q)$ and $\psi^* = r/(1+r)$. Hence, if the players repeatedly use their myopic strategies, an equilibrium will be established in which the expected loss L_1 to player 1 in any two successive periods can be determined from (23), and the expected loss L_2 to player 2 in any two successive periods can be determined from (25). The calculated values of L_1 and L_2 are given in table 8.6.

By comparing the values given in table 8.6 with those given in table 8.5, it can be seen that if $\sigma^2 = 0$, then in every case included in these tables, the losses for both players are smaller when they use their myopic strategies than when they use the limiting pure competitive strategies.

Table 8.6 Expected Total Loss for Each Player in Two Successive Periods from Myopic Strategies

q	r	t	L_1	L_2
1	1	1	$0.667 + 3\sigma^2$	$0.667 + 3\sigma^2$
1	2	1	$0.960 + 2.714\sigma^2$	$0.960 + 5.428\sigma^2$
2	2	1	$1.5 + 5\sigma^2$	$1.5 + 5\sigma^2$
0.5	1	1	$0.469 + 1.672\sigma^2$	$0.375 + 3.437\sigma^2$
0.5	2	1	$0.612 + 1.474\sigma^2$	$0.490 + 6.052\sigma^2$

Thus, if σ^2 is sufficiently small, when each player chooses the controls in an optimal way, with due regard for the fact that the future choices of the other player will be made in accordance with the pure duopoly strategies, the total loss to each player is larger than it would be if both players chose their controls myopically.

If we keep in mind that when $t = 10$, the constant terms in both L_1 and L_2 are 100 times as large as their values when $t = 1$, and the coefficients of σ^2 remain the same as when $t = 1$, then it can be seen from table 8.6 that when $q = 1$, $r = 2$, and $t = 10$, the myopic strategies yield the losses $L_1 = 96 + 2.714\sigma^2$ and $L_2 = 96 + 5.428\sigma^2$. The losses in this case from the limiting pure competitive strategies are found from table 8.5 to be $L_1 = 201.8 + 2.645\sigma^2$ and $L_2 = 172.5 + 5.330\sigma^2$. Hence, for these values, in equilibrium the myopic strategies will yield a smaller loss to player 1 as long as $\sigma^2 < 1533$, and they will yield a smaller loss to player 2 as long as $\sigma^2 < 780$.

These calculations reveal that the players can do better when they both behave in a somewhat stupid fashion and make their choices myopically, than they can when they try to minimize their losses competitively. Of course, both players can do better when they cooperate, and we shall now consider this possibility.

Pure Cooperative Strategies

Suppose now that both players are actually employed by the same organization and have the common objective of minimizing the sum of their expected losses. In other words, the players choose their controls in order to minimize the expected total loss to both players over the n periods. This total loss will be

$$\sum_{i=1}^{n} [qX_i^2 + r(X_i - t)^2 + c_i^2], \tag{29}$$

where $c_j = u_j$ in any odd period j and $c_k = v_k$ in any even period k. This situation is analogous to the maximization of V_1 and V_2, as given by equations (1) and (2) in chapter 6, when $\gamma = \delta = 1$. In that case $V_1 = V_2$ and each firm attempts to maximize the total profit of both itself and its rival.

The total loss (29) can be written as

$$\sum_{i=1}^{n} \left[(q + r) \left(X_i - \frac{rt}{q + r} \right)^2 + c_i^2 \right] + \frac{nqrt^2}{q + r}. \tag{30}$$

It follows from (30) that the control c_i should be chosen in each period by either player 1 or player 2, depending on whose turn it is, as if there were only one player in a standard, stochastic control problem in which the target in each period is $rt/(q + r)$ and the coefficient q in the loss function is replaced by $q + r$.

The optimal sequence of values of c_i can be determined by backward induction. Furthermore, it can be shown (DeGroot 1970, p. 440) that as we move backward from the final period, the optimal strategy for the control c_i will converge to a limiting strategy of the form

$$c_i = \alpha^* \left(\frac{rt}{q + r} - X_{i-1} \right) \tag{31}$$

where

$$\alpha^* = \frac{1}{2} \left[\sqrt{(q + r)^2 + 4(q + r)} - (q + r) \right]. \tag{32}$$

We call the strategies for the players defined by (31) and (32) the *limiting pure cooperative strategies*.

Since $X_i = X_{i-1} + c_i + \epsilon_i$, it can be shown that if the strategy c_i is used repeatedly by each player, then the process will converge to an equilibrium in which the stationary distribution of X_i will be a normal distribution with

$$E(X_i) = \frac{rt}{q + r} \tag{33}$$

and

$$\text{Var}(X_i) = \frac{\sigma^2}{1 - (1 - \alpha^*)^2}. \tag{34}$$

Furthermore, the expected total loss L to the two players in any given period in equilibrium will be

$$L = E[qX_i^2 + r(X_i - t)^2 + c_i^2]. \tag{35}$$

Table 8.7 **Expected Total Loss to the Two Players in a Given Period from Limiting Pure Cooperative Strategies**

q	r	t	L
1	1	1	$0.5 + 2.732\sigma^2$
1	2	1	$0.667 + 3.791\sigma^2$
2	2	1	$1 + 4.824\sigma^2$
0.5	1	1	$0.333 + 2.186\sigma^2$
0.5	2	1	$0.4 + 3.266\sigma^2$

Since c_i is given by (31) and (32), and the mean and variance of both X_i and X_{i-1} are given by (33) and (34), it can be shown that

$$L = \frac{qrt^2}{q+r} + \frac{q+r+\alpha^{*2}}{1-(1-\alpha^*)^2}\sigma^2. \tag{36}$$

The values of L are given in table 8.7. Since the value of L is the expected total loss to both players in a single period, it follows that if the players share their total losses equally, then this value of L will also be the expected loss for each of the players in any two successive periods in equilibrium. Because of the way in which the limiting pure cooperative strategies were derived, it follows that the sum of the expected total losses to the two players over two successive periods, which will be equal to $2L$, will be smaller than the corresponding sum $L_1 + L_2$ when the players use either the limiting pure competitive strategies or their myopic strategies. It can be verified that the values given in tables 8.5 to 8.7 are in agreement with this fact.

One difficulty with applying the limiting pure cooperative strategies is that if $q \neq r$, there is no reason why the two players should incur equal losses and there is no other natural method for allocating the total loss L between the two players in a more reasonable manner. Furthermore, these strategies require the complete cooperation of the two players and provide no other alternatives to players who may wish to avoid the pure competitive or myopic strategies, but who do not necessarily wish to commit themselves to the pure cooperative strategies, either because they think they can reduce their losses with other strategies or because each player is unsure whether the other player is willing to cooperate. We shall now introduce a class of strategies that permits all degrees of cooperation by utilizing the concept of coefficients of cooperation γ and δ, as in chapter 6.

Coefficients of Cooperation

Suppose now that player 1 tries to cooperate with player 2 by minimizing a function of the form

$$\Lambda_1 = \sum_{i=1}^{n} [qX_i^2 + \gamma r(X_i - t)^2 + u_i^2].$$ (37)

In other words, we shall suppose that player 1 chooses controls over the n periods in order to minimize the expected value of Λ_1, a function that takes into account not only how far the state X_i of the system is from the target 0 of player 1 and the control costs of player 1, but also how far the state X_i is from the target t of player 2. As in chapter 6, player 1 attempts to minimize (37) by cooperating with player 2 in order to reduce the loss function (8) below the values obtained from competitive strategies. Similarly, player 2 chooses controls to minimize

$$\Lambda_2 = \sum_{i=1}^{n} [r(X_i - t)^2 + \delta qX_i^2 + v_i^2].$$ (38)

We continue to assume that the players choose their controls in alternating periods. It can again be shown that as we move backward from the final period, the optimal strategies for the two players will converge to certain limiting strategies of the form given in (11) and (12). Furthermore, it can again be shown that when the players use these limiting strategies repeatedly, a stochastic equilibrium will be established, and the expected losses of the players in equilibrium can be calculated.

As before, we shall let L_1 denote the expected total loss to player 1 in two successive periods in equilibrium, and shall let L_2 denote the corresponding expected total loss to player 2. It should be emphasized that L_1 and L_2 are calculated from the original loss functions given in (8), even though the players are choosing their controls on the basis of the cooperative functions Λ_1, and Λ_2. The values of L_1 and L_2 for various coefficients of cooperation γ and δ are given in table 8.8 for the problem in which $q = 1$, $r = 1$, and $t = 1$, and in table 8.9 for the problem in which $q = 1$, $r = 2$ and $t = 1$.

The gain from cooperation is exhibited in these tables. When $q = 1$ and $r = 1$, it can be seen from table 8.8 that the losses of both players are reduced as γ and δ increase together from 0 to 1. The same phenomenon can be observed in table 8.9, provided that $\sigma^2 = 0$, or $\sigma^2 > 0$ but very small. Another interesting feature can be noted in both tables 8.8 and 8.9 when player 2 is using a large coefficient of cooperation, such as $\delta = 0.9$. As player 1 increases γ from 0 to 0.9, the loss of player 2 decreases monotonically, as seems natural, but the loss of player 1 does not necessarily increase monotonically. These results are similar to those

Table 8.8 **Expected Total Loss for Each Player in Two Successive Periods from Cooperative Strategies when $q=1$, $r=1$, and $t=1$**

γ	δ	L_1	L_2
0	0	$1.577 + 2.861\sigma^2$	$1.577 + 2.861\sigma^2$
0.1	0.1	$1.250 + 2.834\sigma^2$	$1.250 + 2.834\sigma^2$
0.2	0.2	$1.014 + 2.812\sigma^2$	$1.014 + 2.812\sigma^2$
0.3	0.3	$0.845 + 2.794\sigma^2$	$0.845 + 2.794\sigma^2$
0.4	0.4	$0.724 + 2.780\sigma^2$	$0.724 + 2.780\sigma^2$
0.5	0.5	$0.638 + 2.768\sigma^2$	$0.638 + 2.768\sigma^2$
0.6	0.6	$0.579 + 2.759\sigma^2$	$0.579 + 2.759\sigma^2$
0.7	0.7	$0.540 + 2.752\sigma^2$	$0.540 + 2.752\sigma^2$
0.8	0.8	$0.516 + 2.746\sigma^2$	$0.516 + 2.746\sigma^2$
0.9	0.9	$0.504 + 2.742\sigma^2$	$0.504 + 2.742\sigma^2$
1.0	1.0	$0.500 + 2.738\sigma^2$	$0.500 + 2.738\sigma^2$
0	0.5	$0.839 + 2.717\sigma^2$	$1.154 + 2.927\sigma^2$
0.1	0.5	$0.759 + 2.725\sigma^2$	$1.013 + 2.885\sigma^2$
0.2	0.5	$0.704 + 2.735\sigma^2$	$0.895 + 2.849\sigma^2$
0.3	0.5	$0.668 + 2.746\sigma^2$	$0.795 + 2.818\sigma^2$
0.4	0.5	$0.648 + 2.757\sigma^2$	$0.710 + 2.792\sigma^2$
0.5	0.5	$0.638 + 2.768\sigma^2$	$0.638 + 2.768\sigma^2$
0	0.9	$0.554 + 2.656\sigma^2$	$1.097 + 2.978\sigma^2$
0.1	0.9	$0.498 + 2.663\sigma^2$	$0.980 + 2.935\sigma^2$
0.2	0.9	$0.462 + 2.671\sigma^2$	$0.881 + 2.898\sigma^2$
0.3	0.9	$0.443 + 2.680\sigma^2$	$0.798 + 2.866\sigma^2$
0.4	0.9	$0.437 + 2.690\sigma^2$	$0.728 + 2.838\sigma^2$
0.5	0.9	$0.439 + 2.700\sigma^2$	$0.668 + 2.814\sigma^2$
0.6	0.9	$0.449 + 2.711\sigma^2$	$0.617 + 2.792\sigma^2$
0.7	0.9	$0.464 + 2.721\sigma^2$	$0.573 + 2.773\sigma^2$
0.8	0.9	$0.482 + 2.732\sigma^2$	$0.536 + 2.757\sigma^2$
0.9	0.9	$0.504 + 2.742\sigma^2$	$0.504 + 2.742\sigma^2$

found in table 6.2. In general, it should be possible for each player to explore the willingness of the other player to cooperate by trying different values for the coefficient of cooperation, and it should be possible for both players to reduce their losses by increasing their coefficients of cooperation along paths that are mutually beneficial.

Table 8.9   Expected Total Loss for Each Player in Two Successive Periods from Cooperative Strategies when $q=1$, $r=2$, and $t=1$

γ	δ	L_1	L_2
0	0	$2.018 + 2.645\sigma^2$	$1.725 + 5.330\sigma^2$
0.1	0.1	$1.642 + 2.649\sigma^2$	$1.337 + 5.212\sigma^2$
0.2	0.2	$1.385 + 2.657\sigma^2$	$1.055 + 5.125\sigma^2$
0.3	0.3	$1.209 + 2.667\sigma^2$	$0.853 + 5.058\sigma^2$
0.4	0.4	$1.090 + 2.677\sigma^2$	$0.708 + 5.007\sigma^2$
0.5	0.5	$1.009 + 2.688\sigma^2$	$0.607 + 4.967\sigma^2$
0.6	0.6	$0.956 + 2.699\sigma^2$	$0.537 + 4.934\sigma^2$
0.7	0.7	$0.922 + 2.709\sigma^2$	$0.491 + 4.908\sigma^2$
0.8	0.8	$0.902 + 2.718\sigma^2$	$0.463 + 4.887\sigma^2$
0.9	0.9	$0.892 + 2.727\sigma^2$	$0.449 + 4.870\sigma^2$
1.0	1.0	$0.889 + 2.736\sigma^2$	$0.444 + 4.855\sigma^2$
0	0.5	$1.331 + 2.604\sigma^2$	$1.476 + 5.359\sigma^2$
0.1	0.5	$1.179 + 2.616\sigma^2$	$1.206 + 5.234\sigma^2$
0.2	0.5	$1.088 + 2.632\sigma^2$	$0.997 + 5.140\sigma^2$
0.3	0.5	$1.038 + 2.650\sigma^2$	$0.835 + 5.068\sigma^2$
0.4	0.5	$1.015 + 2.669\sigma^2$	$0.707 + 5.012\sigma^2$
0.5	0.5	$1.009 + 2.688\sigma^2$	$0.607 + 4.967\sigma^2$
0	0.9	$1.003 + 2.583\sigma^2$	$1.468 + 5.382\sigma^2$
0.1	0.9	$0.883 + 2.593\sigma^2$	$1.218 + 5.256\sigma^2$
0.2	0.9	$0.819 + 2.608\sigma^2$	$1.026 + 5.161\sigma^2$
0.3	0.9	$0.791 + 2.625\sigma^2$	$0.877 + 5.088\sigma^2$
0.4	0.9	$0.786 + 2.644\sigma^2$	$0.761 + 5.031\sigma^2$
0.5	0.9	$0.795 + 2.662\sigma^2$	$0.669 + 4.985\sigma^2$
0.6	0.9	$0.814 + 2.679\sigma^2$	$0.596 + 4.948\sigma^2$
0.7	0.9	$0.837 + 2.696\sigma^2$	$0.537 + 4.917\sigma^2$
0.8	0.9	$0.864 + 2.712\sigma^2$	$0.488 + 4.891\sigma^2$
0.9	0.9	$0.892 + 2.727\sigma^2$	$0.449 + 4.870\sigma^2$
0.5	0	$1.459 + 2.738\sigma^2$	$0.695 + 4.947\sigma^2$
0.5	0.1	$1.346 + 2.726\sigma^2$	$0.654 + 4.950\sigma^2$
0.5	0.2	$1.246 + 2.715\sigma^2$	$0.626 + 4.954\sigma^2$
0.5	0.3	$1.158 + 2.705\sigma^2$	$0.611 + 4.958\sigma^2$
0.5	0.4	$1.079 + 2.696\sigma^2$	$0.605 + 4.962\sigma^2$
0.5	0.5	$1.009 + 2.688\sigma^2$	$0.607 + 4.967\sigma^2$
0.9	0	$1.429 + 2.809\sigma^2$	$0.400 + 4.838\sigma^2$
0.9	0.1	$1.337 + 2.796\sigma^2$	$0.372 + 4.841\sigma^2$
0.9	0.2	$1.256 + 2.785\sigma^2$	$0.358 + 4.843\sigma^2$
0.9	0.3	$1.184 + 2.774\sigma^2$	$0.353 + 4.847\sigma^2$
0.9	0.4	$1.121 + 2.765\sigma^2$	$0.356 + 4.850\sigma^2$
0.9	0.5	$1.064 + 2.756\sigma^2$	$0.365 + 4.854\sigma^2$
0.9	0.6	$1.014 + 2.748\sigma^2$	$0.380 + 4.857\sigma^2$
0.9	0.7	$0.969 + 2.740\sigma^2$	$0.400 + 4.861\sigma^2$
0.9	0.8	$0.928 + 2.734\sigma^2$	$0.423 + 4.865\sigma^2$
0.9	0.9	$0.892 + 2.727\sigma^2$	$0.449 + 4.870\sigma^2$

9

Adaptive Utility

In chapter 2, we discussed the concept of decision making and noted that the two central components of a decision problem under uncertainty are the decision maker's subjective probabilities, which characterize knowledge and beliefs, and subjective utilities, which characterize preferences and tastes. In the usual development of decision theory and descriptions of decision making, provision is made for the decision maker to change probabilities in the light of new information, but no provision is made for changing utilities in the light of such information. As a result, examples such as the "Allais paradox" have been constructed which show that a decision maker may make a sequence of choices which are inconsistent with any fixed utility function (Allais 1953; DeGroot 1970; Allais and Hagen 1979). Attempts to allow for such inconsistencies in the choices of a decision maker have led to the development of stochastic models of choice behavior and the notion of a stochastic utility function (Luce and Suppes 1965; Manski and McFadden 1981).

It is our belief that the concept of learning can be applied to utilities as well as to probabilities. For example, when utility is a weighted average of several variables, we will argue that the particular weights used in the utility function are subject to change as a result of learning through experiencing particular values of the variables. The common use of utility functions assumes that an individual can calculate accurately the utility that will be received from any specified values of the variables (Stigler and Becker 1977). We are proposing instead the concept of an adaptive utility function in which the utility that will be received by the individual from specified values of the variables is to some extent uncertain, and the expected utility from these values will change as a result of learning through experience. The notion of utility being known only through experience is consistent with casual empiricism. We have reference to the fads in style, food, automobiles, soaps, and other products in the economy. Only a small number of the new products can lay claim to legitimate technical improvements over older products. In the marketing literature such shifts have been institutionalized in the concept of a product life cycle (see any of a number of texts on marketing). In other words, it is expected that products will have a limited life, partly because of preference changes.

We postulate a process in which the individual envisions the consequences of an event and derives conceptually the expected utility that will be realized from those consequences. A decision may be made on the basis of this expected utility but actually experiencing the consequences may result in the realization of a significantly different level of utility. Simon (1955) has put this well: "The consequences that the organism experiences may change the pay-off function—it doesn't know how well it likes cheese until it has eaten cheese." As a result of the experience, the expected utility of similar consequences will be changed and another decision under the same circumstances may be quite different. Once it is recognized that utilities are uncertain and that expected utilities can change by virtue of experience, it becomes important to incorporate these concepts in the theory of decision making (Peston 1967; Krelle 1973; Witsenhausen 1974; Marschak 1978; Pessemier 1978; Pollak 1978; Cohen and Axelrod 1984; White 1984). Related ideas of adaptive demand theory are contained in Long and Manning (1976) and Manning (1978).

The concept of an adaptive utility function is fundamental in a world in which uncertainty exists for the individual. In the theory of perfect competition, it is assumed that individuals have complete knowledge of any variables that might affect their actions, and there is no need for a concept of learning. The basic assumption underlying adaptive utility functions is that individuals are always dealing with an uncertain but fairly stable world about which they can learn. In particular, they are uncertain about their own preferences for goods, and combinations of goods and money, that they have never experienced.

In this chapter we shall attempt to present a full description of the impact of adaptive utility functions on the theory of decision making and to present some formal models for incorporating adaptive utility into standard demand theory.

Expected and Realized Utility

In classical utility theory, a utility function is assumed to exist for any individual decision maker. It is also assumed that this function is fully known to the individual so that it is even possible for the person to make hypothetical choices. Thus, the demand curve for a product can be determined by having each consumer indicate the quantity that would be purchased at different prices. After a decision is made, it is assumed that the utility realized by the decision maker is the amount indicated by the utility function. Thus, it is implicitly assumed that the utility that the individual expects from a particular decision is the utility realized when the decision is made. There are no surprises with respect to the amount of utility received. There is no gap between the expectation and the utility realized for each possible set of values of the variables in the utility function. There is only one utility function. It is known by the decision maker and it accurately reflects the utility that will be realized from the consequences of a particular event. The mathematical statement of these properties of utility has been presented in chapter 2.

In the approach that we are taking it is assumed that there are two types of utility functions. The first one is represented by the concept of expected utility. Here the individual may have a complete utility function for consequences that have not been experienced previously, but for which the individual estimates expected utility. This utility function is somewhat analogous to the prior probability distribution that is used in Bayesian analysis. We assume that the individual is capable of deriving expected utility for any consequences that may be relevant. One way that this expected utility might be derived for any particular consequence of specified values of the variables in the utility function would be for the individual to utilize mathematical expectation. The individual constructs a probability distribution for the different amounts of utility that might be realized from the specified values of the variables and then calculates the mathematical expectation of this distribution. This value would become a point of the expected utility function which is composed of all such points. We do not believe that each individual actually goes through such calculations in determining the expected utility function. Rather we believe that the expected utility function is a heuristic used by the decision maker and is not typically derived in full from the kind of detailed calculation just described. In whatever manner it is derived, the expected utility function becomes the basis for the individual's decision-making behavior.

Once a decision is made, and the individual experiences the consequences, the actual utility experienced is compared with the expected utility. There will usually be a gap between these utilities. For example, in trying out a new food or in buying a new product, the prior expectation will usually not be realized exactly. In a different type of problem, an individual may have an expected utility for the net revenue that will be received from selling a product, such as a house, at a particular price. However, the actual experience of having the price offered to the individual may result in a new expected utility that is different from the previous expected utility, and as a result, a price that the individual had previously expected to accept may be rejected.

The result of the difference between the experienced and expected utility is that the individual modifies the expected utility function when it is relevant for future decisions. In order to treat the problem formally, which we do in subsequent sections, we will assume that the expected utility function has been derived from the calculation of mathematical expectations as described earlier, and that this function is modified by the standard Bayesian analysis. This updating of the expected utility function could be based on a variety of models, depending on the type of information extracted by the individual from the realized utility. For example, the individual might be able to perceive only that the actual utility was above or below the expected value and must apply Bayes' theorem to these limited observations to determine a new set of probabilities that will in turn determine a new expected utility function.

We do not explore the trivial case of modification in which the actual and expected functions can be brought into conformity on the basis of a few observations. This would be the case if the actual utility function depended on a small number of parameters which could be determined exactly from a small number of observations. Rather, we shall consider utility functions in which there is some element of randomness that prevents the parameters from ever being determined exactly.

The approach that we are postulating concentrates on the interactions between these two functions—the expected utility function and the actual function. It should be emphasized that we assume that the individual is capable of comparing the actual realized utility with the expected utility of the consequences of an event.

Maximizing Expected Utility

If the individual does not know the utility function and gains information through experience, what kind of process is followed to gain the maximum utility? Our assumption is that the individual has the objective of maximizing expected utility. Suppose, as in chapter 2, that an individual must choose a decision δ from some available class Δ of possible decisions, and that each decision $\delta \in \Delta$ induces a probability distribution $P(\delta)$ on a given space R of possible consequences r. In the classical theory, it is assumed that there exists a real-valued utility function V defined on the space R such that one decision δ_1 is preferred to another decision δ_2 if and only if $E[V \mid P(\delta_1)] > E[V \mid P(\delta_2)]$, where $E[V \mid P(\delta_i)]$ denotes the expectation of V with respect to the distribution $P(\delta_i)$. If a decision δ must be chosen from a specified subset Δ_0 of the set Δ, then one will be chosen for which $E[V \mid P(\delta)]$ is a maximum, assuming that such a decision exists.

In accordance with this theory, if an individual could simply choose a consequence r from a given available subset of R, one would be chosen for which $V(r)$ was a maximum. The theory indicates that this choice would be straightforward and could be made without difficulty because there are no elements of uncertainty in the decision. Uncertainty enters the classical theory only if the individual is uncertain about the consequence that will result from at least one of the available decisions. Thus, this theory assumes that an individual's preferences among sure things are fixed, and then determines the preferences among probability distributions involving the same consequences.

In our approach, however, there are no sure things. A person who can choose a consequence, or reward, from among an available set of rewards may have difficulty making a choice because of uncertainty about the utility of each of the rewards. Thus, regardless of whether the reward is a meal at a new restaurant, a new household appliance, a stock certificate, or twenty dollars, the utility of the reward will be uncertain. Therefore, the utility that the person does assign to a reward should itself be regarded as an expected utility. Here, the expectation is taken, formally or heuristically, over the possible values that the utility of the reward might have, and is taken with respect to the person's subjective distribution for these possible values. Thus, from our point of view, an individual will typically be uncertain about the actual utility of any particular consequence, no matter how well specified that consequence might be.

Nevertheless, in a single-period decision problem in which the individual must choose a decision δ from some specified subset Δ_0 of Δ, it is irrelevant whether $V(r)$ is the actual utility that will be realized from the consequence r or merely the expected utility that will be realized from r. In either case, $E[V \mid P(\delta)]$ will be the overall expected utility from choosing the decision δ, and the individual will try to choose a decision that maximizes $E[V \mid P(\delta)]$.

However, in a multiperiod decision problem in which the individual must choose decisions from Δ_0 repeatedly, the definition and underlying structure of the function V can be important. In a multiperiod problem of this type, the individual will try to maximize the expectation of some function, such as the sum, of the utilities that are realized in each period. This maximization must, in general, now be a sequential process. The individual will typically be able to increase the total utility realized over the entire process by explicitly taking into account the fact that the utility $V(r)$ assigned to a particular consequence r at the beginning of the process is merely an expectation and may be higher or lower than the actual utility that would be realized from r in any given period. By exploring the actual utilities of various consequences in the early stages of the process, one can learn about one's own utility function. This learning will result in the elimination of some or all of the uncertainty that is present in a utility function and an individual can thereby make decisions in later periods that will have a high probability of yielding conformance between actual utility and expected utility.

To formalize our description, consider a process with n periods, and suppose that in each period a decision maker must choose a decision $\delta \in \Delta$ after observing the consequences of the preceding periods. Let u_i denote the utility function for period i ($i = 1, \ldots, n$). The function u_i is defined on the space R of possible consequences. It is assumed that the decision maker is uncertain about the exact values of the function u_i and that this uncertainty is represented by the presence in the function u_i of a parameter θ whose value is unknown. Thus, if the consequence r occurs in period i, the realized utility will be $u_i(r \mid \theta)$. The parameter θ will in general be a vector taking values in some parameter space Ω.

For $i = 1, \ldots, n$, we shall let r_i denote the consequence that occurs in period i, and we shall assume that the total utility U over the entire process is simply the sum of the utilities realized in each of the n periods.

Thus, we assume that $U = \sum_{i=1}^{n} u_i(r_i \mid \theta)$.

As is typical in statistical decision problems, we shall also assume that the probability distribution on the space R induced by each decision $\delta \in \Delta$ is not completely known and depends on a vector parameter ϕ. We shall let $P(r \mid \phi, \delta)$ denote that distribution. The parameter ϕ will, in general, also be a vector taking values in a parameter space Φ. In some problems, some of the components of ϕ may be related to, or even identical with, some of the components of θ. In other problems, the parameters θ and ϕ may be completely unrelated. For example, the parameter θ which determines how much utility or enjoyment an individual will derive from ordering a steak dinner at a particular restaurant will be closely related to the parameter ϕ which determines whether or not the restaurant prepares good steak dinners. As another example, the parameter θ which determines how much utility an individual will realize from owning a stock that yields a particular gain is only slightly related to the parameter ϕ representing external conditions which determine whether or not the stock will yield that gain. At the beginning of the process, the available information about the values of θ and ϕ can be represented by specifying a joint prior distribution $\xi(\theta, \phi)$ for these parameters.

In the first period, there are two types of information that become available to the decision maker. First, after a decision δ_1 has been chosen in period 1, the consequence r_1 that actually occurs is observed. Second, the decision maker gains some information about the utility $u_1(r_1 \mid \theta)$ actually received from r_1 in period 1. In general, the exact numerical value of $u_1(r_1 \mid \theta)$ can be learned only with error. For example, the decision maker might learn only whether this value is greater than or less than his or her prior expected value $\int_\Omega u_1(r_1 \mid \theta) d\xi_1(\theta)$, where $\xi_1(\theta)$ denotes the marginal prior distribution of θ.

Together, these two types of information lead to a posterior joint distribution of θ and ϕ that serves as the relevant prior distribution when a decision $\delta_2 \epsilon \Delta$ is chosen in the second period. The decision maker must choose a sequence of decisions $\delta_1, \ldots, \delta_n$ that will maximize the expected total utility $E(U)$.

In general, the optimal decision δ_1 in the first period of this multiperiod problem will be different from the decision specified by the myopic rule which considers only the first period and ignores future periods. It will, in general, also be different from the decision specified by the rule which ignores possible changes in utility and assumes that the same expected utility function which pertains to the first period will also pertain to all future periods. Indeed, even in a two-period problem in which the parameters θ and ϕ are independent, and the information obtained about θ in the first period does not depend on which decision δ_1 is chosen or which consequence r_1 occurs, the decision maker must take possible changes in utility into account when choosing δ_1.

For example, suppose that θ and ϕ are independent under their joint prior distribution, and that information about θ is obtained at the end of the first period by observing the value x of a random variable X whose distribution $F(x \mid \theta)$ depends on θ but does not depend on which decision δ_1 was chosen or on which consequence r_1 occurred. The random variable X will in general be a function of the actual utility received from the realized consequence. As mentioned earlier, X may be an indicator of whether the actual utility is greater or smaller than the expected utility for that consequence. The assumption in this example that $F(x \mid \theta)$ does not depend on which consequence occurs is special and need not be retained in the general theory. Under these conditions, the information obtained about θ is independent of the information obtained about ϕ, and it follows that θ and ϕ will again be independent under their joint posterior distribution. We shall let $\xi_1'(\theta)$ and $\xi_2'(\phi)$ denote the posterior distributions of θ and ϕ, given δ_1, r_1, and x. If a particular decision δ_2 is then chosen on the second (and final) period, the expected utility resulting from this decision will be

$$\int_\Phi \int_\Omega \int_R u_2(r \mid \theta) \, dP(r \mid \phi, \delta_2) \, d\xi_1'(\theta) \, d\xi_2'(\phi)$$

$$= \int_\Phi \int_R v_2(r \mid x) \, dP(r \mid \phi, \delta_2) \, d\xi_2'(\phi). \tag{1}$$

Here $v_2(r \mid x)$ is the expected utility function for the second period, as determined by the relation

$$v_2(r \mid x) = \int_\Omega u_2(r \mid \theta) \, d\xi_1'(\theta) \, .$$

Since the posterior distribution $\xi_1'(\theta)$ depends on x, so also will the expected utility function $v_2(r \mid x)$, and we have explicitly exhibited this dependence in the notation we are using. Next, for any possible decision δ_2, we can use the conditional distribution $P(r \mid \phi, \delta_2)$ of r_2 given ϕ, together with the marginal distribution $\xi_2'(\phi)$ of ϕ, to determine the marginal (or predictive) distribution $P(r \mid \delta_2)$ of r_2. Since the posterior distribution $\xi_2'(\phi)$ depends on the decision δ_1 that was chosen in the first period and on the observed consequence r_1, this marginal distribution should more properly be written as $P(r \mid \delta_2, \delta_1, r_1)$. The expected utility (1) can now be expressed as

$$\int_R v_2(r \mid x) \, dP(r \mid \delta_2, \delta_1, r_1) \, . \tag{2}$$

At the beginning of the second period, a decision δ_2 should be chosen for which the integral (2) is a maximum. We shall let

$$U_2(\delta_1, r_1, x) = \sup_{\delta_2 \in \Delta} \int_R v_2(r \mid x) dP(r \mid \delta_2, \delta_1, r_1). \tag{3}$$

Then it follows from backward induction that at the beginning of the process, a decision δ_1 should be chosen for which the following expression is maximized:

$$\int_\Phi \int_\Omega \int_R u_1(r \mid \theta) dP(r \mid \phi, \delta_1) d\xi_1(\theta) d\xi_2(\phi)$$

$$+ \int_\Phi \int_R \int_\Omega \int_X U_2(\delta_1, r_1, x) dF(x \mid \theta) d\xi_1(\theta) dP(r_1 \mid \phi, \delta_1) d\xi_2(\phi) \, . \tag{4}$$

The important feature of this result from our present point of view is that when the decision maker chooses θ_1, he or she must consider the full range of possible new expected utility functions $v_2(r \mid x)$ that might be obtained from the observation x. It should be noted that both δ_1 and δ_2 will be different from the decisions that would be optimal in traditional theory. The optimal decisions in traditional theory would be based solely on the available information about ϕ. It is clear that the optimal δ_2 in our approach will be different from the one in the traditional theory because of the new information about θ that becomes available from x. It should be emphasized, moreover, that even though the decision maker has no control over the information about θ that will be generated in the first period, the optimal δ_1 in our approach will also be different from the one in the traditional theory.

In a more general problem, the space R_i of possible consequences in period i, the space of Δ_i of possible decisions in period i, and the distribution $P_i(r_i \mid \delta_i, \phi)$ induced on R_i by each decision $\delta_i \in \Delta_i$ can depend on the decisions that were chosen in preceding periods and on the consequences that were observed in those periods. Also, the total utility over the n periods can be an arbitrary function $U(r_1, \ldots, r_n \mid \theta)$ of the entire observed sequence of consequences. An optimal sequence of decisions that takes into account the adaptive nature of the utility functions can again be determined by backward induction.

Utility Effects in Demand Theory

Demand theory is an area for which adaptive utility has important implications. Although the standard analysis of consumption in terms of indifference curves is general enough to admit changes in the utility function, these changes have typically been ignored. Since change in the utility function is an integral part of our approach, we shall demonstrate how the standard analysis can include such changes.

Consider the choices of two commodities made by a particular household or individual. Let M denote the income of the household in a given period, let p and q denote the prices of the two commodities in that period, and let x and y denote the amounts of the commodities that are consumed in that same period. The values of x and y will be chosen to maximize the household's utility function $U(x,y)$ subject to the budget constraint $px + qy = M$.

The standard economic analysis (Cohen and Cyert 1975) proceeds as follows: The utility function U determines a family of nonintersecting indifference curves in the xy-plane. In figure 9.1, two of these indifference curves are denoted I_1 and I_2. In that figure, the line AB represents the budget constraint $px + qy = M$. The amounts x and y to be consumed are specified by the point $F = (x_1,y_1)$ at which the line AB is tangent to the indifference curve I_1.

Now suppose that the household's utility function changes from U to a different function U^*. The new utility function U^* will determine a new family of indifference curves. In figure 9.1, the curve I_1^* represents one of the new indifference curves. In particular, I_1^* is the new indifference curve that is tangent to the line AB. Thus, the consumption of the household will shift from the values x_1 and y_1 to the values x_1^* and y_1^* which are the coordinates of the point F^*.

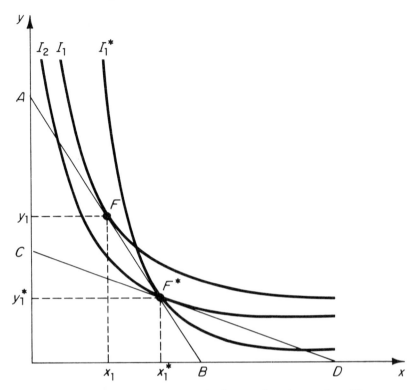

Figure 9.1 Price-income equivalence of a change in utility

It is also shown in figure 9.1 that the *utility effect,* which results from changing the utility function from U to U^*, is equivalent to the effect of changing prices and income while retaining the original utility function. As indicated in the figure, among the original family of indifference curves, the curve I_2 passes through the point F^* and the line CD is tangent to the curve I_2 at the point F^*. Therefore, if the household retained its original indifference curves and its consumption had to satisfy the budget constraint represented by the line CD, then the household would consume the amounts x_1^* and y_1^* specified by the point F^*. It follows that changing the utility function from U to U^* is equivalent to retaining the original utility function and changing the income and prices to new values M^*, p^*, and q^* such that $M^*/p^* = C$ and $M^*/q^* = D$. Clearly, there are an infinite number of different sets of values of M^*, p^*, and q^* which satisfy these two equations.

Another way to think of the utility effect is illustrated in figure 9.2. The curves I_1 and I_1^*, and the points F and F^*, are as before. The curve I_2^* is the indifference curve in the new family which contains the point F. Since both the points F and G lie on the curve I_2^*, the household is

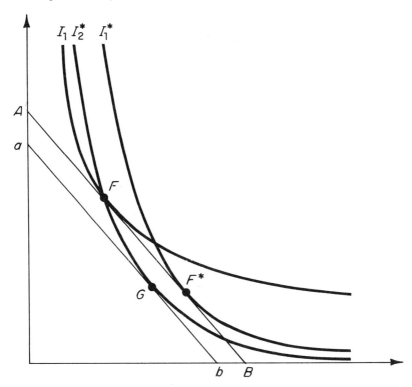

Figure 9.2 The income effect of a change in utility

now indifferent between these points. The line *ab* is parallel to *AB* and tangent to the curve I_2^*. The point of tangency is denoted by *G*. Therefore, if the income of the household were reduced from *M* to the amount represented by the budget constraint *ab*, the household could still attain a consumption *G* equivalent to its original consumption *F*. Thus, from the point of view of the household, this income difference $p(A - a)$, or equivalently $q(B - b)$, can be regarded as the *income effect* of the change in utility.

By analogy with the traditional economic analysis, we can say that we have represented the utility effect, which induces the change in consumption from *F* to *F**, as the sum of the following two effects: (1) a substitution effect which induces the change from *F* to *G* along the curve I_2^*, and (2) the income effect which induces the change from *G* to *F**.

It should be noted that since both the points *F* and *F** satisfy the budget constraint, and income and prices are held fixed, the point *F** must always yield a higher level of utility than *F* in the new family of indifference curves; and it must always yield a lower level of utility in the old family of indifference curves. Therefore, the income effect as defined here resulting from a change in utility must always be positive.

The adaptive utility approach distinguishes between the actual utility and the expected utility functions. The curves drawn in figures 9.1 and 9.2 are based on the expected utility function. The change from F to F^* results from updating the expected utility function in light of the experienced utility at the point (x_1,y_1).

Extension to k Commodities

Consider now the choices of k commodities ($k \geq 2$) made by a particular household or individual. Let M again denote the income of the household in a given period, let $p_1, \ldots, p_k$ denote the prices of the commodities in that period, and let $x_1, \ldots, x_k$ denote the amounts of the commodities that are consumed in that period. The values of $x_1, \ldots, x_k$ will be chosen to maximize the household's utility function $U(x_1, \ldots, x_k)$ subject to the budget constraint $\sum_{i=1}^{n} p_i x_i = M$.

Suppose now that the household changes its consumption from $x_1, \ldots, x_k$ to $x_1^*, \ldots, x_k^*$. This change could be the result of a change in income, a change in the price of at least one of the n commodities, or a change in the household's utility function. It is well known (Slutsky 1915) that under standard regularity conditions, the choices $x_1, \ldots, x_k$ of the household will satisfy the following relations, as well as the budget constraint:

$$\frac{U_1}{p_1} = \frac{U_2}{p_2} = \ldots = \frac{U_k}{p_k}, \tag{5}$$

where $U_i = \partial U / \partial x_i$. Thus, there is typically a wide class of combinations of income, prices, and utility that will result in a particular set of values of $x_1, \ldots, x_k$.

For example, suppose that the values of $x_1, \ldots, x_k$ must be positive and that

$$U(x_1, \ldots, x_k) = \sum_{i=1}^{k} \alpha_i \log x_i, \tag{6}$$

where $\alpha_i > 0$ for $i = 1, \ldots, k$ and $\sum_{i=1}^{k} \alpha_i = 1$. It is easily found that the optimal choices of $x_1, \ldots, x_k$, subject to the constraint $\sum_{i=1}^{k} p_i x_i = M$ are

$$x_i = M \frac{\alpha_i}{p_i} \quad \text{for } i = 1, \ldots, k. \tag{7}$$

A change in the value of x_i means that there must have been a change in the value of M, p_i, or α_i. From the point of view of the consumer, a change from $\alpha_1, \ldots, \alpha_k$ to $\alpha_1^*, \ldots, \alpha_k^*$ in the utility function is equivalent to a change in prices from $p_1, \ldots, p_k$ to $p_1^*, \ldots, p_k^*$, where $p_i^* = p_i\alpha_i/\alpha_i^*$ for $i = 1, \ldots, k$, and income M is held fixed. More generally, the change from $\alpha_1, \ldots, \alpha_k$ to $\alpha_1^*, \ldots, \alpha_k^*$ is equivalent to any change in prices from $p_1, \ldots, p_k$ to $p_1^*, \ldots, p_k^*$ and in income from M to M^* that satisfies the following relations:

$$\frac{p_i^*}{M^*} = \frac{p_i\alpha_i}{M\alpha_i^*} \qquad \text{for } i = 1, \ldots, k.$$

On the other hand, a change in prices from $p_1, \ldots, p_k$ to a new set $p_1^*, \ldots, p_k^*$ is equivalent uniquely to a change in income from M to $M^* = M \sum_{i=1}^{k} \alpha_i p_i/p_i^*$ accompanied by a change in weights from $\alpha_1, \ldots, \alpha_k$ to

$$\alpha_i^* = \frac{M}{M^*}\frac{p_i}{p_i^*}\alpha_i \qquad \text{for } i = 1, \ldots, k.$$

Changes in the weights $\alpha_1, \ldots, \alpha_k$ represent the adaptation of the utility function to information obtained from experiencing consequences in a sequential process. Thus, we have demonstrated that the concept of adaptive utility can be analyzed by standard methods in the case of k commodities.

Learning about Utilities by a Bayesian Process

In this section we show in a demand-theory context how utility functions are learned through Bayesian analysis. Consider two commodities with prices p and q and consumption x and y. Let the utility function be

$$U(x,y \mid \alpha) = \alpha \log x + (1 - \alpha) \log y, \tag{8}$$

where $0 < \alpha < 1$. Suppose that the consumer is uncertain about the exact value of α and assigns a prior distribution to this value represented by a p.d.f. $\xi(\alpha)$. Thus, we are assuming that the learning process we have described has resulted in the consumer's knowledge of the general form of his or her utility function but not the exact weights.

If the consumer is going to choose x and y in only a single period, then values should be chosen for which the expected utility $E[U(x,y \mid \alpha)]$ is a maximum. Since

$$E[U(x,y \mid \alpha)] = E(\alpha)\log x + [1 - E(\alpha)]\log y, \tag{9}$$

the consumer can simply replace the uncertain value of α in the utility function (8) by its expectation $E(\alpha)$. The optimal choices of x and y would, therefore, be

$$x = \frac{E(\alpha)}{p}M \text{ and } y = \frac{1 - E(\alpha)}{q} \tag{10}$$

We shall now consider a process with more than one period. After the consumer chooses the values of x and y in a given period and consumes those amounts of the two commodities, this experience will lead to the formulation of a new posterior p.d.f. of α. The consumer should realize that the more quickly the precise value of α can be learned, the greater will be the utility that can be attained from the choices of x and y in each period. Because of this learning process, it will not be optimal in general to choose x and y in each period in accordance with (10), but rather to choose x and y to increase the rate of learning in order to maximize the total utility to be attained from the entire multiperiod process. We shall now present two examples based on two different models for the learning process. In the first example, the optimal choices of x and y in each period can be made in accordance with (10), and in the second example they cannot.

Example 1: At the beginning of each period, the consumer has an expectation $E(\alpha)$ for α. Therefore, after the values of x and y to be used in a given period have been chosen, the expectation $E[U(x,y|\alpha)]$ for the utility that will be realized in that period is given by (9). We shall assume that after consuming the amounts x and y, the consumer can determine whether the realized utility is larger than, smaller than, or equal to the expected utility given by (9).

The actual utility $U(x,y|\alpha)$ is given by (8). Therefore, we are assuming that at the end of the given period, the consumer can determine which one of the following three relations is correct:

(i) $U(x,y|\alpha) > E[U(x,y|\alpha)]$,
(ii) $U(x,y|\alpha) < E[U(x,y|\alpha)]$,
(iii) $U(x,y|\alpha) = E[U(x,y|\alpha)]$.

It follows from (8) and (9) that these three relations are equivalent, respectively, to the following three relations:

(i) $[\alpha - E(\alpha)] (\log x - \log y) > 0$,
(ii) $[\alpha - E(\alpha)] (\log x - \log y) < 0$,
(iii) $[\alpha - E(\alpha)] (\log x - \log y) = 0$.

If $x \neq y$, then determining which one of these three relations is correct is equivalent to determining whether $\alpha > E(\alpha)$, $\alpha < E(\alpha)$, or $\alpha = E(\alpha)$.

Therefore, if the amounts x and y consumed in a given period are not equal, the consumer will be able to determine whether the actual value of α is greater than, less than, or equal to the expectation $E(\alpha)$ held at the beginning of the period.

Suppose now that $x = y$ in a given period. In this case, it follows from (8) and (9) that

$$U(x,y \,|\, \alpha) = E[U(x,y \,|\, \alpha)] = \log x. \tag{11}$$

Therefore, the consumer will not gain any information about the value of α from the realized utility, knowing in advance that the realized utility will be equal to the expected utility.

The essential feature of this example is that the information that the consumer learns about α in any period does not depend on the values of x and y chosen in that period, provided that $x \neq y$. Therefore, it will be optimal to proceed by choosing x and y in each period to maximize the expected utility in that period, in accordance with (10), provided that (10) does not yield $x = y$. If (10) does specify that $x = y$ in a given period, then strictly speaking there will be no optimal values of x and y in that period. The values $x = y$ will yield the maximum expected utility for that period but will yield no information whatsoever about the value of α. A procedure that will be almost optimal in this situation will be to choose x and y slightly different from each other. With such values for x and y, the expected utility in the given period will be close to the maximum expected utility that could be obtained by choosing $x = y$ and, in addition, the consumer will learn whether the actual value of α is greater than, less than, or equal to $E(\alpha)$.

Example 2: We shall continue to assume that the utility function has the form given in (8). However, suppose now that instead of the special form for the learning process that we have just considered, we assume that this process has the following alternative form: After consuming any particular amounts x and y in a given period, the consumer can determine whether there is a preference for a slightly larger value of x and a slightly smaller value of y, or a slightly smaller value of x and a slightly larger value of y. In more precise terms, we shall assume that the consumer can determine whether the derivative $\partial U(x,y \,|\, \alpha)/\partial x$ of his or her utility function, evaluated at the particular values of x and y consumed in the given period, is positive, negative, or zero. We shall now derive some implications of this assumption.

The amounts x and y consumed in any period satisfy the relation

$$y = \frac{1}{q}(M - px). \tag{12}$$

Therefore, it follows from (8) that

$$\frac{\partial U(x,y \mid \alpha)}{\partial x} = \frac{\alpha}{x} + \left(\frac{1-\alpha}{y}\right)\frac{\partial y}{\partial x}$$

$$= \frac{\alpha}{x} - \left(\frac{1-\alpha}{y}\right)\frac{p}{q} \qquad (13)$$

$$= p\left(\frac{\alpha}{px} - \frac{1-\alpha}{qy}\right).$$

It can be seen from (12) and (13) that the three relations

(i) $\dfrac{\partial U(x,y \mid \alpha)}{\partial x} > 0,$

(ii) $\dfrac{\partial U(x,y \mid \alpha)}{\partial x} < 0,$

(iii) $\dfrac{\partial U(x,y \mid \alpha)}{\partial x} = 0,$

are equivalent, respectively, to the following three relations:

(i) $\alpha > \dfrac{px}{M},$

(ii) $\alpha < \dfrac{px}{M},$

(iii) $\alpha = \dfrac{px}{M}.$

Hence, in this process, the consumer can determine which one of these relations is correct.

In a problem with n periods, a sequence of optimal decisions for the consumer can be found by backward induction. Since the information about α which the consumer gains in each period depends on the choice of x (and y) in that period, the optimal values of x and y in a given period will not typically be the values given by (10).

Conclusions

This chapter introduces an important topic. The concept of a well-defined utility function is central to most theories of decision making. At the same time the empirical work on decision making indicates that human decision makers do not have well-defined utility functions (Becker, DeGroot, and Marschak 1963). The adaptive utility approach uses the utility concept in a manner that is closer to actual behavior by removing the requirement that decision makers have complete knowledge of their utility functions. In adaptive utility theory, the individual is assumed to be capable of determining an expected utility for the consequences of some event and to be capable of comparing the expected value with the actual value when the consequences are experienced. The importance of adaptive utility is underscored for empirical work by the fact that some of the population being studied at any given time will be in the process of learning their utility functions. Furthermore, individuals are always seeking new experiences as part of their nature. Knight (1935) has referred to this aspect as "explorative activity." Adaptive utility incorporates this activity in a formal way by utilizing a random variable in the utility function.

We can summarize our argument to this point. First, it is assumed that a consumer does not know his or her utility function and must learn about it through experience. Second, the determination of this function is a problem of decision making under uncertainty. Thus, Bayesian theory and methodology are appropriate tools for the analysis. Third, the problem should be perceived as an investment problem in which consumption is an investment in information. Fourth, the problem is a multiperiod problem; the more quickly one learns about his or her actual utility function, the greater will be the utility enjoyed over the remaining periods.

10

Some Examples of Adaptive Utility

We have seen that, in general, the concept of adaptive utility is useful when uncertainty exists and the individual is operating in a multiperiod framework. It is the investment in information that characterizes the adaptive utility function in the setting of sequential decision problems. The individual is trying to determine his or her preferences by gaining more information through consuming different commodities or different brands of the same commodity. In this fashion, the consumer will usually be able to determine his or her utility function with a high degree of precision. Typically as more money or time or effort is invested, the uncertainty about the utility function will be decreased. Also, the greater the investment in the early periods, the sooner the form of the utility function can be determined. This exploratory activity is a form of investment that has a payoff in information (see also Kihlstrom 1974).

Income Allocation with an Uncertain Utility Function

Individuals have an interesting investment problem (March 1978). They must decide how much money to invest at present, and in future periods, to gain information about their utility functions. This approach has implications for the allocation of income by a consumer. The consumer has both a consumption and an investment problem. The latter decision is ignored in conventional theory because of the assumption that the utility function is known.

Recognizing that investment is an important part of the consumer's problem, we shall reconsider the problem in which a consumer must allocate income M in a given period among k commodities. Let $x_1, \ldots, x_k$ denote the quantities of the k commodities to be consumed in a given period. Then the consumer must choose the values of $x_1, \ldots, x_k$ subject to the income constraint $\sum_{i=1}^{k} p_i x_i = M$, where $p_1, \ldots, p_k$ and M are fixed, positive constants.

Suppose first that the allocation is to be made for just one period, that

144

the consumer knows his or her utility function $U(x_1, \ldots, x_k)$ exactly, and that the optimal values $x_1, \ldots, x_k$ can be determined as solutions of the first-order conditions as given in equation (5) of chapter 9. Suppose now that the consumer is uncertain about his or her utility function, and let $V(x_1, \ldots, x_k) = E[U(x_1, \ldots, x_k)]$ denote the consumer's expected utility for any quantities $x_1, \ldots, x_k$, where the expectation is calculated with respect to the consumer's prior distribution for his or her utility function. Then again, under the usual regularity conditions, the optimal values of $x_1, \ldots, x_k$ will satisfy (5) in chapter 9 with U_i replaced by V_i.

However, if the consumer must allocate income M among these k commodities in future periods as well as in the given period, then the situation changes. Let $V(x_1, \ldots, x_k)$ again denote the expected utility in the first period, and let $V^*(x_1, \ldots, x_k)$ denote the expected utility in future periods if $x_1, \ldots, x_k$ are consumed in the first period and optimal allocations are made thereafter based on the information gained from the consumption in the first period. We shall assume that the total expected utility over the entire process is

$$V(x_1, \ldots, x_k) + V^*(x_1, \ldots, x_k).$$

The function $V^*(x_1, \ldots, x_k)$ will typically be determined as follows: For any chosen values of $x_1, \ldots, x_k$ in the first period, there could be a variety of different outcomes r that the consumer might realize from the first-period consumption. There will be learning about which of these commodities are liked and which are disliked, and the intensity of these preferences. Each leads to a different posterior distribution ξ_r for the consumer's utility funciton. The consumer can in principle calculate the expected utility V_r^* if optimal choices are made over the entire future with respect to the posterior distribution ξ_r. Furthermore, for any given values of $x_1, \ldots, x_k$, the consumer's prior distribution for his or her utility function will induce a probability distribution for the outcome r, which in turn will induce a probability distribution $P(x_1, \ldots, x_k)$ for the posterior distribution ξ_r. The consumer can, therefore, calculate the expected utility function

$$V^*(x_1, \ldots, x_k) = E[V_r^* | P(x_1, \ldots, x_k)].$$

The consumer must choose an allocation $x_1, \ldots, x_k$ for which $V(x_1, \ldots, x_k) + V^*(x_1, \ldots, x_k)$ is maximized, subject to the constraint $\sum_{i=1}^{k} p_i x_i = M$. Therefore, at the optimal values, equation (5) of chapter 9 will again be satisfied with U_i replaced by

$$\frac{\partial V}{\partial x_i} + \frac{\partial V^*}{\partial x_i}.$$

We shall now investigate the way in which V^* depends on the initial choices $x_1, \ldots, x_k$.

Suppose for simplicity that $k = 2$. Without loss of generality, we can choose the units of measurement so that $p_1 = p_2 = M = 1$. Suppose that (1) the consumer knows his or her preferences in regard to the first commodity (perhaps because the commodity has been consumed often in the past) but is uncertain about his or her preferences in regard to the second commodity. Furthermore, suppose that (2) the information the consumer obtains about the second commodity is an increasing function of the amount x_2 consumed in the first period. Increased information enables the consumer to be more certain about his or her utility function and as a result utility will be larger in future periods; hence, the expected utility in future periods will also be an increasing function of x_2.

Symbolically, the assumption (1) that the consumer does not gain any information from consumption of the first commodity means that for any given value of x_2, $V^*(x_1, x_2) = V^*(x_1', x_2)$ for all values of x_1 and x_1'. The assumption (2) that larger values of x_2 yield more information than smaller values means that $V^*(x_1, x_2)$ is an increasing function of x_2 for any fixed value of x_1.

Now consider any two numbers $0 < x < y \leq 1$, and the following two possible allocations in the first period: (i) $x_1 = x$ and $x_2 = 1 - x$, and (ii) $x_1 = y$ and $x_2 = 1 - y$. It follows from assumptions (1) and (2) that $V^*(x, 1 - x) = V^*(y, 1 - x) > V^*(y, 1 - y)$. In other words, to achieve a greater expected utility in future periods, the consumer should allocate a larger value of x_2 and a smaller value of x_1 in the first period. To explicate this proposition we will compare the optimal allocation in a one-period problem with the optimal allocation in the first period of a multiperiod problem. Let

$$V_i(x, 1 - x) = \frac{\partial V(x_1, x_2)}{\partial x_i} \Bigg|_{x_1 = x, \, x_2 = 1 - x} \qquad (1)$$

and let $V_i^*(x, 1 - x)$ be defined analogously. As mentioned previously, in a single-period problem, the consumer will choose x such that

$$V_1(x, 1 - x) = V_2(x, 1 - x). \qquad (2)$$

Let $x = a$ $(0 < a < 1)$ denote the solution of (2). It follows, in accordance with the usual assumptions of decreasing marginal utility, that

$$V_1(x, 1 - x) > V_2(x, 1 - x) \text{ for } x < a$$

and

$$V_1(x, 1 - x) < V_2(x, 1 - x) \text{ for } x > a.$$

In a multiperiod problem, the consumer will choose x such that

$$V_1(x, 1 - x) + V_1^*(x, 1 - x) = V_2(x, 1 - x) + V_2^*(x, 1 - x). \qquad (3)$$

However, it follows from assumption (1) that $V_1^*(x, 1 - x) = 0$ and from assumption (2) that $V_2^*(x, 1 - x) > 0$. Thus, if $x = b$ denotes the solution to equation (3), then it will be true that $V_1(b, 1 - b) > V_2(b, 1 - b)$ and, hence, that $b < a$. In other words, in the first period of a multiperiod problem, the consumer will consume less of the known commodity and more of the commodity about which there is uncertainty than would be consumed in a one-period problem. It is obvious that $V(a, 1 - a) - V(b, 1 - b) > 0$. This difference is a measure of the investment in information in the first period of the multiperiod process.

An example of the type of model we have been discussing in the context of the theory of the firm is provided by the following problem of sequential investment, which is similar to those developed in the next chapter. Suppose that in each period of a multiperiod process, a firm must allocate a fixed amount of funds between a risky investment project for which the probability distribution of the return depends on an unknown parameter θ and some alternative use of the funds for which the distribution of the returns is completely known. It is assumed that in each period, the firm must decide on the fraction of its funds that it wishes to invest in the project. For larger values of this fraction, the firm risks more money if the resulting investment is bad, but gains more information about θ for its use in future periods.

Trial Offers

We shall now consider a different type of example of adaptive utility, in which a firm recognizes that the demand function for a product is determined in part by the fact that consumers are uncertain about their utility functions (Kirman 1975). From time to time, a firm will offer a product for sale significantly below its usual price and presumably below its per-unit cost. One interpretation of such behavior is that the firm is trying to increase, on a relatively permanent basis, the sales of the product. In other words, the firm is bearing the cost of a trial offer in order to give more potential customers an opportunity to learn about the product (Dixit and Norman 1978). If firms believed in fixed and known utility functions, such behavior would be irrational. In accordance with our argument for adaptive utility functions, it is possible to develop an analytic model for the introduction of a trial offer.

Assume that each consumer x in the population has a utility function that induces a maximum price $y(x)$ that the consumer would pay for the product in each period. For simplicity, we shall assume that one unit of the product is purchased by a consumer in each period. Suppose that the current price of the product is p_0. Those consumers who currently buy the product at this price have obviously tried it and know that their maximum price $y(x)$ is above p_0. Other consumers do not buy the product because, although they are not sure of their values of $y(x)$, they think that $y(x)$ is probably below p_0 and it is not worthwhile for them to experiment. A third group of consumers does not buy the product because they have tried it and know that their values of $y(x)$ are below p_0.

We assume that any consumer who tries the product once, will learn his or her value of $y(x)$. Suppose that if the product is tried and the consumer learns that $y(x) > p_0$, he or she will continue to purchase it at the price p_0 in future periods and will realize a gain in utility of

$$\sum_{i=0}^{\infty} \beta^i [y(x) - p_0] = \frac{y(x) - p_0}{1 - \beta},$$

where β is a discount factor $(0 < \beta < 1)$.

On the other hand, suppose that if the consumer learns that $y(x) < p_0$, he or she turns away from the product with a loss in utility of $p_0 - y(x)$. Presumably the consumer is able to find a satisfactory substitute or is otherwise able to live without consuming the product.

Suppose that a consumer x, who has never tried the product, assigns the subjective p.d.f. $f(y|x)$ to the value of $y(x)$. Then the consumer will try the product if

$$\int_{p_0}^{\infty} \frac{y - p_0}{1 - \beta} f(y|x)dy - \int_0^{p_0} (p_0 - y)f(y|x)dx \geq 0. \tag{4}$$

In other words, the consumer will try the product if

$$p_0 - E(y|x) \leq \beta \int_0^{p_0} (p_0 - y)f(y|x)dy. \tag{5}$$

and will not try it if

$$p_0 - E(y|x) > \beta \int_0^{p_0} (p_0 - y)f(y|x)dy. \tag{6}$$

Thus, the consumer will try the product at price p_0 if $E(y|x)$ is not too far below p_0 and will always try it if $E(y|x) \geq p_0$.

The manufacturer who is considering lowering the price, at least for one period and perhaps longer, can divide the total population of all possible consumers into the three groups mentioned earlier:

Group G_1:   Those who are now purchasers at price p_0.
Group G_2:   Those who have tried the product and learned that $y(x) < p_0$. If the price were lowered to p, the product would be purchased by all those for whom $p < y(x) < p_0$.

Group G_3: Those who have not tried the product because (6) is satisfied. If the price were lowered to p, the product would be purchased at least once by all those for whom (5) is satisfied when p_0 is replaced by p.

Let α_i denote the proportion of the total population of consumers that belong to group G_i. Then $\alpha_i > 0$ ($i = 1, 2, 3$) and $\alpha_1 + \alpha_2 + \alpha_3 = 1$.

Let $g_2(y)$ denote the p.d.f. of the values $y(x)$ over all the consumers $x \in G_2$. For each price $p \le p_0$, let

$$\gamma_2(p) = \int_0^p g_2(y)dy.$$

For each consumer $x \in G_3$, let $f(y|x)$ denote the p.d.f. of the value of $y(x)$. Each of these p.d.f.'s satisfies (6). Also, for each $x \in G_3$, let $\Pi(x)$ denote the largest value of p_0 for which (5) is satisfied. Finally, for each price $p \le p_0$ let $\gamma_3(p)$ denote the proportion of the consumers $x \in G_3$ for which $\Pi(x) \ge p$. Thus, $\gamma_3(p)$ denotes the proportion of consumers in G_3 who will purchase the product at least once at the price p.

Now suppose that if the firm sells the product at the price p in a given period, its profit in that period will be of the form $Np\gamma(p) - C(p)$, where N is the size of the total population, $\gamma(p)$ is the proportion of the total population that will purchase the product at the price p, and $C(p)$ is the total production cost. Note that

$$\gamma(p) = \alpha_1 + \alpha_2\gamma_2(p) + \alpha_3\gamma_3(p).$$

Suppose that the firm were going to change the price to p and then hold it at p throughout all the remaining periods. Then the proportion $\gamma(p)$ will purchase the product in the first period. Furthermore, of the proportion $\gamma_3(p)$ of the consumers in G_3 who purchase the product, we expect a certain fraction $\delta_3(p)$ of these consumers x to learn that $y(x) \ge p$ and we expect the remaining fraction $1 - \delta_3(p)$ to learn that $y(x) < p$. Hence, the expected proportion of consumers in G_3 who will continue to buy the product at price p is $\delta_3(p)\gamma_3(p)$.

If the firm uses a discount factor β, the expected discounted profit of the firm over the whole process will be

$$Np[\alpha_1 + \alpha_2\gamma_2(p) + \alpha_3\gamma_3(p)] - C(p)$$

$$+ \sum_{i=1}^{\infty} \beta^i \{Np[\alpha_1 + \alpha_2\gamma_2(p) + \alpha_3\delta_3(p)\gamma_3(p)] - C(p)\} \tag{7}$$

$$= \frac{Np\gamma(p) - C(p)}{1 - \beta} - \frac{\beta}{1 - \beta} Np\alpha_3[1 - \delta_3(p)]\gamma_3(p).$$

The firm will choose p to maximize this value, assuming that the expected discounted profit function is the firm's utility function.

Now let us return to the more interesting strategy where the firm lowers the price to p for one period only, and then changes it to p_1 for the remainder of the process. Here, p_1 would typically be larger than p but in general it could be larger than, smaller than, or equal to p_0. We consider first the following problem: The firm announces in advance that it will lower the price to p for one period and will then raise it to p_1 for the remainder of the process. What are the optimal values of p and p_1 that the firm should announce?

Consider any given values of p and p_1. Among the proportion $\gamma_3'(p, p_1)$ of consumers in G_3 who purchase the product in the first period, we expect a certain fraction $\delta_3(p, p_1)$ to learn that $y(x) \geq p_1$. Since we assume that $p_1 \geq p$, it follows that among the proportion $1 - \gamma_3'(p, p_1)$ of consumers in G_3 who do not purchase the product in the first period, there are none who will subsequently try it—that is, for whom (5) will be satisfied with p_0 replaced by p_1.

Thus, for any fixed value of p in the first period, the firm's expected discounted profit will be

$$Np[\alpha_1\gamma_1(p) + \alpha_2\gamma_2(p) + \alpha_3\gamma_3'(p, p_1)] - C(p)$$

$$+ \frac{\beta}{1 - \beta} \{Np_1[\alpha_1\gamma_1(p_1) + \alpha_2\gamma_2(p_1) \qquad (8)$$

$$+ \alpha_3\gamma_3'(p, p_1)\,\delta_3(p, p_1)] - C(p_1)\},$$

where $\gamma_1(p)$ and $\gamma_2(p)$ are the proportions of the consumers in G_1 and G_2 respectively for whom $y(x) > p$. It should be noted that the proportion $\gamma_3'(p, p_1)$ of consumers in G_3 who purchase the product in the first period depends not only on the price p in the first period but on the price p_1 that the firm is going to charge in future periods. In other words, a consumer may not try the product in the first period, even though the price p is low, if it is known that the firm is going to raise the price to a high level p_1 in all future periods. In principle, for each pair of prices (p, p_1), the firm can determine the function $\gamma_3'(p, p_1)$, and can therefore determine the values of p and p_1 that maximize (8). These will be the optimal prices from the standpoint of the firm.

The problem of setting the price in a trial offer is an example of one type of problem that faces the firm when the consumers are characterized by adaptive utility functions. Clearly there are other implications for microeconomic theory, since the adaptive utility approach introduces uncertainty into the demand (see DeGroot 1983 for other types of examples). More generally, however, the concept of adaptation has significance for understanding many aspects of human behavior besides economic behavior. The ways in which human beings within firms adapt to cues from the environment and the ways in which the firms modify price and output policies are material for economic and social models. Adaptive behavior involves learning and requires discrimination among sources of information and the construction of appropriate responses to relevant information. Rather than assume complete knowledge as has been usual in economic models, it is more desirable, in terms of explaining actual behavior, to study the process of adaptation. Some of the fundamental problems of adaptive or sequential decision making involve optimal search procedures and optimal stopping rules.

11

Sequential Investment Decisions

Management must regularly make decisions under conditions of uncertainty that exist because of an inability to forecast the future accurately. More specifically, a firm may be unable to determine the level of demand for some product in the future; it may be unable to predict rivals' reactions to some particular action of its own; or it may be unable to estimate costs satisfactorily. These conditions of uncertainty are particularly critical when the firm is contemplating an investment in a fixed asset. Therefore, the organizational unit responsible for the original definition of the project may be able to estimate profit potential only within a wide range. In addition, the personnel who provide the impetus necessary to have the project considered may tend to understate certain perceived risks in order to obtain funding. In this institutional context, the top management must face the problem of making a decision on a large investment without adequate knowledge. The most promising approach to decision making in these circumstances is a sequential approach in which the decision in each phase is designed to gather information that is useful for subsequent decisions (Harpaz and Thomadakis 1982).

The firm may be able to divide a large, fixed investment into parts and thus reduce the risk inherent in a major financial commitment (Prastacos 1983). This "module" system would enable a firm to begin production on a small scale and expand if the operation is profitable. If investments can be made sequentially, the information obtained from initial operations may have a significant impact on subsequent decisions. The problem is especially interesting when a greater level of investment can be expected to provide more precise information about the profitability of the investment activity. This experimental aspect of investment is central to the models that will be considered in this chapter.

Formulation of the Problem in Modular Form

Suppose that the investment project consists of a number of modules,

152

each of which constitutes a fraction of the total possible investment. In any period of time, the firm must decide which investments to make. That is, the firm can initially invest in a small fraction of the project and thus reduce its financial exposure. This ability to reduce the size of the maximum loss which can occur in the initial period can be important if the management is sensitive to the "downside risk." In subsequent periods, the firm has the option of expanding the investment, holding it at the same level, or abandoning the project entirely. A model along these lines for a marketing problem has been described by Rutenberg (1982, chapter 8).

We will assume that the probability distribution of profit from the investment depends on an unknown parameter θ. The management's knowledge about θ will be based on the profitability estimates contained in the funding proposal and on the credibility of the division making the proposal. (This topic will be discussed in the next chapter.) We assume that the management processes information according to Bayes' rule. Initially it assigns a prior distribution to θ, and then calculates a posterior distribution for θ after it has observed the results at the end of the period. The subsequent investment decision is based on the revised information about θ. For simplicity, it is assumed that θ does not change over time, although it would be possible to build a model in which the probability distribution of investment returns changes from period to period in accordance with a time series model.

If the distribution that the firm assigns to θ is such that there are likely to be significant positive gains from investing in a large fraction of the project, then the decision problem for the firm is easy. A large investment will simultaneously provide a high expected gain in the period of investment and also generate a large amount of information about θ.

The firm's decision, however, is more difficult when the prior distribution for θ is such that an investment in a large fraction of the modules might result in a major loss. In this situation, the firm can avoid high risk by investing in only a few modules so that the gains or losses are likely to be relatively small. On the other hand, the management must consider the advantage of making an investment large enough to provide relatively precise information about θ.

Suppose that the given project comprises k modules. Let the fraction of the total investment corresponding to the ith module be P_i, where $P_i > 0$ for $i = 1, \ldots, k$ and $\sum_{i=1}^{k} P_i = 1$. Also, let X_{it} be the profit (or loss if $X_{it} < 0$) attributed to the ith module in period t. Therefore, the total profit is

$$\sum_{i \in I_t} X_{it},$$

where I_t is the set of modules which are operational in period t. We assume that the modules are homogeneous in the sense that the probability distribution of X_{it} is normal with mean $P_i\theta$ and variance $P_i\sigma^2$, where σ^2 is a known number and θ and σ^2 are the same for each module. We assume also that the profits $X_{1t}, \ldots, X_{kt}$ in the k modules are independent, given θ. Then for any given value of θ, the profit in period t, denoted T_t, will have a normal distribution with mean

$$\left(\sum_{i \in I_t} P_i\right)\theta,$$

and variance

$$\left(\sum_{i \in I_t} P_i\right)\sigma^2.$$

In particular, the total profit for the entire investment will have a normal distribution with mean θ and variance σ^2.

The fact that there is a finite number of modules and that each of them represents a nonnegligible part of the total project leads to certain computational difficulties which are more or less incidental to the problem with which we are mainly concerned. Therefore, we shall assume that each of the modules can be subdivided into arbitrarily small investment projects and that the firm might undertake any group of these small investments. In this way, we replace the notion of a finite number of discrete projects with the notion of a total investment which is continuously divisible into projects of arbitrary size. We shall let P_t $(0 \leq P_t \leq 1)$ represent the proportion of the entire project in which the firm has invested during period t. In analogy with the discussion we have given for discrete projects, if the proportion of the firm's investment is P_t, then its total profit T_t has a normal distribution with mean $P_t\theta$ and variance $P_t\sigma^2$. As P_t increases, the variance $P_t\sigma^2$ increases and, hence, there is more uncertainty about the profit.

It should be noted that the assumption that σ^2 is known, as we specified in the description of the discrete case, is not restrictive in the continuous case. Since each module can be divided into infinitesimally small investments, it follows that σ^2 can be determined exactly from any investment, no matter how small. In other words, because each investment can be subdivided continuously, we can regard the investment as providing an infinite sample of independent observations for estimating σ^2. This concept of subdivision does not help in estimating θ. The difference is due to the fact that the sufficient statistic for estimating θ is the sum of the observations on the subdivisions which is merely the profit from the initial investment itself. This result is analogous to the notion of estimating the variance of a Wiener process exactly from observing the process over an arbitrarily small period of time (Dvoretzky, Kiefer, and Wolfowitz 1953).

For any choice of P_1, the statistic T_t/P_t can be analyzed to determine the effect of the investment on information about θ. It follows from the distribution of T_t that this statistic is normally distributed with mean θ and variance σ^2/P_t. Thus, a larger investment will reduce the variance and provide a more precise estimate of θ.

A Two-Period Model

If the firm's objective is to maximize the expected value of discounted profit over an n-period horizon, then the optimal investment strategy can in principle be determined by backward induction. The essential features of this problem are contained in the special case of a two-period planning horizon with the addition of a cost for adjusting the capital stock. In each period the adjustment cost is assumed to be proportional to the size of the change in the investment. Let c be the cost of a unit increase in the level of investment and a the cost of a unit decrease, so that the adjustment cost in period t is

$$(P_t - P_{t-1})c \text{ if } P_t > P_{t-1},$$

$$(P_{t-1} - P_t)a \text{ if } P_t < P_{t-1}.$$

The cost factor c for new investment will generally differ from the cost factor a for abandonment.

Let the firm's prior distribution for θ at the beginning of the first period be normal, with mean m and precision τ. In the first period, the firm chooses an investment proportion P_1, incurs a cost of $P_1 c$, and receives a profit T_1. Since T_1 has a normal distribution with mean $P_1\theta$ and variance $P_1\sigma^2$, it can be shown from proposition 2 of chapter 2 that the posterior distribution of θ at the end of the first period will be normal with mean

$$m' = \frac{\tau\sigma^2 m + T_1}{\tau\sigma^2 + P_1}$$

and precision

$$\tau' = \tau + \frac{P_1}{\sigma^2}.$$

In the second period, the firm has three options with respect to the size of its investment: It can reduce the size, keep it at the same level, or increase it. It is optimal to abandon the project entirely if the posterior

Table 11.1 Optimal Decision Criteria

Posterior Mean	Decision	Expected Profit in Period 2	Adjustment Cost
$m' < -a$	Abandon ($P_2=0$)	0	$P_1 a$
$-a \leq m' \leq c$	Maintain ($P_2=P_1$)	$P_1 m'$	0
$m' > c$	Expand ($P_2=1$)	m'	$(1 - P_1)c$

mean m' is sufficiently negative so that $P_1 m'$, the expected loss in period 2 from the initial investment, is worse (more negative) than the abandonment loss of $-P_1 a$. On the other hand, the initial investment is retained and possibly expanded if $m' > -a$. This investment should be expanded to a proportion $P_2 > P_1$ only if the expected gain from the expansion exceeds the expected cost, that is, if $(P_2 - P_1)m' > (P_2 - P_1)c$. If $m' > c$ and it is optimal to expand, then it is optimal to invest in the complete project ($P_2 = 1$). However, if $-a < m' < c$, then the management's prior beliefs in period 2 are not optimistic enough to warrant new investment, nor are they pessimistic enough for a shutdown. The optimal decision for each case with the consequent adjustment cost is summarized in table 11.1.

For any value of P_1, let $\pi(P_1)$ denote the expected total discounted profit minus the adjustment cost over the two periods when an optimal level is chosen in the second period in accordance with table 11.1. The basic problem is to determine the proportion P_1 that will maximize $\pi(P_1)$.

Let

$$s = \left[\tau\left(\frac{\tau\sigma^2}{P_1} + 1\right)\right]^{1/2} \tag{1}$$

and define the function Ψ as

$$\Psi(x) = \int_x^\infty (y - x)\phi(y)dy$$
$$= \phi(x) - x[1 - \Phi(x)] \quad \text{for } -\infty < x < \infty, \tag{2}$$

where $\phi(\cdot)$ and $\Phi(\cdot)$ are the p.d.f. and d.f. respectively of the standard normal distribution. Properties of the function Ψ are described in DeGroot (1970, section 11.9). Further, let δ ($0 < \delta < 1$) be the discount factor used to derive the present value of the second-period profit. Then it is

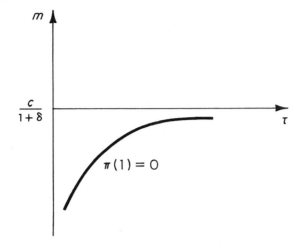

Figure 11.1. Investment criteria in the (τ, m) plane

shown in Appendix A at the end of this chapter that

$$\pi(P_1) = P_1(m - c - \delta a) + \delta P_1 \frac{\Psi[-s(a + m)]}{s}$$

$$+ \delta(1 - P_1) \frac{\Psi[s(c - m)]}{s}. \quad (3)$$

Properties of the Optimal P_1

Assume for the moment that the firm must maintain its first-period investment in the second period also—that is, $P_2 = P_1$. Then the expected discounted profit for the two periods is $P_1(m + \delta m - c)$. Thus, it can be seen that the optimal investment rule is $P_1 = 1$ if $m > c/(1 + \delta)$ and $P_1 = 0$ if $m < c/(1 + \delta)$.

The firm's knowledge about θ is characterized by the mean m and precision τ of the firm's prior normal distribution. Each possible prior distribution corresponds to a point in the (τ, m) plane in figure 11.1. When this point lies above the line $m = c/(1 + \delta)$, then the full investment $P_1 = 1$ is optimal. When the point lies below the line, then no investment ($P_1 = 0$) is optimal. It should be noted that the optimal decision is independent of the prior precision τ.

Now let us change the assumption and revert back to the true sequential problem. Since learning can occur, the initial investment decision will be related to the prior uncertainty about θ. A relatively small prior precision τ indicates that additional information about θ will be valuable and management should make an investment. Specifically, we now show that for any fixed value of m, a full investment $(P_1 = 1)$ is always preferred to no investment $(P_1 = 0)$ if τ is sufficiently small.

The proof of this proposition is as follows: When $P_1 = 1$, it follows from (1) that $s = (\tau^2\sigma^2 + \tau)^{1/2}$ and from (3) that $\pi(P_1)$ reduces to

$$\pi(1) = m - c - \delta a + \frac{\delta \Psi[-s(a + m)]}{s}. \tag{4}$$

As $\tau \to 0$, it follows that $s \to 0$ and $\Psi[-s(a + m)] \to \Psi(0)$, a positive constant. For any given values of a, c, δ, and m, there is a value of τ so small that the expected gain from a full investment in the first period will be positive. (Note that it is possible to change P_2, so that in the second period the investment may be smaller.) Consequently, $P_1 = 1$ is preferred to $P_1 = 0$, which would give a zero profit. The curve in figure 11.1 represents the locus of points (τ,m) that satisfy the equation $\pi(1) = 0$. For any point above the curve, the investment decision $P_1 = 1$ is preferred to $P_1 = 0$. The reverse is true for any point below the curve. For a prior value of $m < c/(1 + \delta)$ and above the curve, some investment would always be optimal, whereas under the constraint $P_2 = P_1$, previously analyzed, a zero investment is optimal.

Partial Investment

We have just established the fact that it may be optimal for the firm to make some investment in the first period under a sequential approach when the optimal investment would be zero under a nonsequential approach. We prove in Appendix B at the end of this chapter that a partial investment $(0 < P_1 < 1)$ in the first period may be optimal under a sequential approach when a full investment would be optimal under a nonsequential approach. Recall that when the prior distribution is represented by a point above the horizontal line in figure 11.1, then the optimal decision under a nonsequential approach is $P_1 = 1$. For these points, when the investment can be made sequentially, we show that a partial investment will be optimal for sufficiently small values of the prior precision τ and sufficiently large values of the abandonment cost a. Furthermore, even when $a = 0$, we show that a partial investment will be optimal if τ is sufficiently small and the prior mean m lies in the interval

$$\left(\frac{1}{1 + \delta}\right)c < m < \left(1 - \frac{\delta}{2}\right)c. \tag{5}$$

In summary, we have in this chapter identified conditions under which some investment is optimal when a sequential approach is followed but no investment would be made under a nonsequential approach. These experimental investments are attractive when the project appears to be uneconomical, but the management's prior knowledge about the profit from the investments is relatively imprecise. In addition we have identified conditions under which partial investment is optimal when a sequential approach is followed but a full investment would be made under a nonsequential approach. These partial investments are optimal when the project appears to be profitable, but again the management's prior knowledge about the profit from the investments is relatively imprecise. In these cases ability to invest sequentially enables the management to avoid making large, potentially unprofitable commitments. Similar sequential decision problems for consumers are studied by Tonks (1984). Sequential models for firms in the presence of a learning curve are developed by Spence (1981).

APPENDIX A:
Derivation of $\pi(P_1)$

In this appendix we will derive the expression for $\pi(P_1)$ given in (3). The expected profit in the second period, calculated at the beginning of the first period, depends on the probability distribution of m' which, in turn, depends on the investment P_1 in period 1. To determine this distribution, recall that the distribution of T_1, given θ, is normal with mean $P_1\theta$ and variance $P_1\sigma^2$, and the prior distribution of θ is normal with mean m and precision τ. It follows that the marginal distribution of T_1 is normal with mean P_1m and variance $P_1[\sigma^2 + (P_1/\tau)]$. For an initial investment of P_1, the firm's distribution of its posterior mean m', prior to the realization of T_1, is normal with mean m and precision $\tau[(\tau\sigma^2/P_1) + 1]$.

Let $F(\cdot)$ be the normal d.f. of m' prior to the realization of T_1. Then it follows from table 11.1 that the expected profit in the second period is

$$\pi_2(P_1) = -aP_1 \int_{-\infty}^{-a} dF(m') + P_1 \int_{-a}^{\infty} m' dF(m') \tag{A1}$$
$$+ (1 - P_1) \int_{c}^{\infty} (m' - c)dF(m').$$

For any d.f. $G(\cdot)$ for which the mean is finite, let the transform $T_G(\cdot)$ be defined as follows (DeGroot 1970, p. 246):

$$T_G(x) = \int_{x}^{\infty} (y - x)dG(y) \quad \text{for } -\infty < x < \infty. \tag{A2}$$

Then $\pi_2(P_1)$ can be expressed as

$$\pi_2(P_1) = -aP_1 + P_1 T_F(-a) + (1 - P_1)T_F(c). \tag{A3}$$

It follows from DeGroot (1970, p. 248) that

$$T_F(x) = \frac{\Psi[s(x - m')]}{s},$$ (A4)

where s and Ψ are defined by (1) and (2). Hence,

$$\pi_2(P_1) = -aP_1 + P_1 \frac{\Psi[(-a - m)s]}{s} + (1 - P_1) \frac{\Psi[(c - m)s]}{s}.$$ (A5)

The firm's expected profit in the first period minus the initial setup cost is

$$E(T_1) - P_1 c = P_1(m - c).$$ (A6)

For the discount factor δ, it follows that the expected profit $\pi(P_1)$ over the two periods is given by (3).

APPENDIX B:
Conditions under Which Partial Investment Is Optimal

The derivative with respect to P_1 of the expected profit $\pi(P_1)$ given by equation (3), evaluated at the point $P_1 = 1$, is

$$\pi'(1) = m - c - \delta a + \frac{1}{s}[\delta\Psi(-as - ms) - \delta\Psi(cs - ms)]$$
$$+ \frac{d}{dP_1}\left[\frac{\delta\Psi(-as - ms)}{s}\right],$$ (B1)

where s is given by (1) and Ψ by (2). It can be shown that the derivative of Ψ has the properties

$$\frac{d\Psi(x)}{dx} = \Phi(x) - 1,$$ (B2)

$$\frac{d}{dx}\left[\frac{\Psi(kx)}{x}\right] = \frac{-\phi(kx)}{x^2} \quad \text{for any constant } k.$$ (B3)

Hence,

$$\frac{d}{dP_1}\left[\frac{\Psi(ks)}{s}\right] = \frac{-\phi(ks)}{s^2}\left(\frac{ds}{dP_1}\right) = \frac{-\phi(ks)\tau^{1/2}\sigma^2}{2P_1^2[(\tau\sigma^2/P_1) + 1]^{3/2}}$$ (B4)

and

$$\lim_{\tau \to 0} \frac{d}{dP_1}\left[\frac{\Psi(ks)}{s}\right] = 0.$$ (B5)

It follows from (B5) that the limit as $\tau \to 0$ of the final term on the right-hand side of (B1) is 0. Furthermore, by using L'Hospital's rule, one can show that

$$\lim_{\tau \to 0} \frac{1}{s} [\Psi(-as - ms) - \Psi(cs - ms)] = \frac{a + c}{2}. \tag{B6}$$

Therefore,

$$\lim_{\tau \to 0} \pi'(1) = m - \left(1 - \frac{\delta}{2}\right) c - \frac{\delta}{2} a. \tag{B7}$$

For any fixed values of m, c, and δ, (B7) will be negative for sufficiently large values of a. It follows from these conditions that there is some value of $P_1 < 1$ that is preferred to the value $P_1 = 1$. We have already shown that for any point above the curve in figure 11.1, the value $P_1 = 1$ is preferred to $P_1 = 0$. Hence, for sufficiently small values of τ the optimal choice is a partial investment $0 < P_1 < 1$, not only for points above the horizontal line but also for points above the curve in figure 11.1.

Furthermore, if $a = 0$, then (B7) will be negative for any value of m satisfying (5). Hence, under these conditions, the optimal choice will again be a partial investment for sufficiently small values of τ.

12

Capital Allocation within Firms

This chapter is concerned with decisions involving the allocation of resources for capital expenditures by a firm. Such capital investment is crucial for a firm since the amount of the investment determines in the long run whether the firm is expanding or contracting. The process has been studied extensively by economists with the objective of deriving an investment function for the economy as a whole under the assumption that management is making decisions in accordance with a profit-maximizing model. One exception to this statement is the book by Bower (1970), which contains an empirical study of the allocation of resources to capital expenditures within firms.

Our analysis will focus on the process used to determine the allocation of funds for capital expenditures in large, multidivisional firms. Capital expenditures include (1) the replacement of fixed assets, such as buildings and equipment; (2) the investment in new fixed assets in order to expand the productive capacity of the firm's current operations; (3) the purchase of some items that are not directly related to the production process but that are large enough to warrant capitalization rather than expensing, such as the purchase of snow removal equipment or the construction of a new parking lot for employees; and (4) the investment in new projects, including the acquisition of other firms. Expenditures in category (4) are the riskiest and require the most analysis.

The type of firm we have in mind is a large, decentralized organization in which each division is a profit center. The manager responsible for each division is judged by the division's contribution to the firm's total profit. In this type of firm each division may be in a different market or industry. The markets are generally oligopolistic, and the firm's market share will be different for each division. These elements characterize most of the firms in the *Fortune* 500 listing, and thus our analysis includes most of the investment made in the economy.

Initial Budget Allocation

The actual allocation process of the firm has generally been ignored by economists in the belief that external market considerations dominate internal decisions (Cyert and March 1963). Market considerations are clearly important, but so is an understanding of the internal process.

The firm starts the process of capital allocation by determining in its budget the amount that will be allocated within the firm to capital expenditures. The size of the allocation will be related to the rate of growth desired by the firm. With constant demand conditions and a zero rate of inflation, the reinvestment of depreciation generated annually would keep the firm at the same size and with the same product composition. With inflation the firm must invest some or all of its retained earnings in addition to depreciation in order to maintain its size. If depreciation plus retained earnings and deferred taxes do not allow the achievement of the firm's growth goal, the firm must borrow funds. Ultimately, it will probably be necessary to raise more equity capital, but that decision depends upon the amount of leverage that the firm is willing to use. Most firms have a debt-to-equity limit imposed by the board of directors that constrains the amount of the debt in the capital structure.

The pool of internal funds available for capital expenditures (that is, the sum of depreciation, retained earnings, and deferred taxes) represents the cash flow of the business. The firm will generally tend to budget this amount, and will budget some other amount only if it wishes to grow at a faster rate than is consistent with the amount of funds available or to reduce its capital base or capacity. Once this pool is established, the firm's management must allocate the funds to the divisions. The first step in the allocation process is to get a "wish list" from each division manager. The manager is requested to submit a list of projects for which capital is needed and an estimate of the amount necessary for each project. The tentative budget allocation among the divisions is influenced by these submissions. If the total amount requested by all the managers does not exceed the available pool of funds, then each manager will usually receive the amount requested. If the amount requested is larger than the pool of funds available, the appropriation committee will screen the proposed projects and eliminate enough to make the total requested equal to the amount available. At this stage projects are eliminated primarily on the basis of the committee's knowledge of the various projects and their view of the likely payoffs.

However, the allocation may also be modified by strategic considerations such as management's desire to increase the rate of growth of a particular division. In addition, there can be organizational considerations that will affect the budget allocation and the final approval process. For example, the central management may want to encourage the manager of a division that generates a large proportion of the capital being allocated. Division managers will resent a budget allocation that is considerably below the division's contribution to profit. Incentives must be maintained and stimulated. When a division manager receives less capital than requested and less than the division generates, there can be a significant reduction in incentive in the division.

The Actual Appropriation Process

Once the capital budget is established and the fiscal year is begun, division managers prepare proposals to get the actual funds that have been budgeted. Projects that are relatively small can be approved by the division manager; very large projects require the approval of the board of directors. Requests greater than the amount which the division manager can approve and less than the amount required for approval by the board are submitted to a capital allocation committee. This committee includes the major operating officers at the central office, such as the chief financial officer, perhaps legal counsel, some group vice-presidents, and others at a similar level. The division manager, a central committee, and the board of directors are the three sources of approval, depending upon the size of the capital appropriation request. These details may vary from firm to firm, but the basic procedure described here is generally followed.

The project proposals must be the same as those on the "wish list" that were approved for budgeting purposes. As projects are evaluated, the divisional management must decide whether the project should be recommended and submitted to the approprations committee. It should be noted that divisions are not in direct competition with each other. The objective of the analysis is to convince the appropriations committee that the project should be funded. If the project is large enough to require board approval, the committee can send it to the board with a recommendation for approval. If a project fails to gain the approval of the committee, the appropriation is not allocated to another division. It is perfectly proper for the firm to underspend the budget. If a promising new project, one not in the budget, is found, it may be financed from the unspent funds. However, if there were no unspent funds, the firm would borrow to finance the new project. The committee neither follows a deliberate strategy of trying to underspend the budget for general purposes nor, surprisingly, does it reject a project because it knows a new one with better financial prospects has appeared. In other words, the projects budgeted have first priority because they have passed the planning and analysis process. However, we shall see later that the committee, under certain conditions, has the power to make the criteria stiffer and thus eliminate some budgeted projects.

Decision Criteria

Some distinction should be made among types of investments because the decision criteria vary with the type. The most straightforward type is equipment replacement. The committee usually routinely approves a request to replace equipment unless it believes the firm should consider leaving the business. Typically, the request is approved on grounds that the replacement is necessary if the firm is to stay in the business. A second type of investment occurs when a new technology has been discovered. If competitors have not already adopted the new technology, a proposal for investment is examined carefully because adoption of the new technology will generally mean that some equipment which is not completely depreciated will have to be abandoned. However, if the competitors have already adopted the new technology or the probability is perceived as high that they will adopt it, the situation changes. Since new technology generally results in either lower costs or an improved product, the firm will be forced to follow its competitors or leave that industry.

Investments in new projects or in the expansion of an existing plant or project must meet two criteria. These criteria are a minimum rate of return on investment before taxes and a specific payback period. A large number of firms in a variety of industries use a five-year average return of 25 percent before taxes and a payback period of three to five years. The division manager making the request must give estimates of revenue, costs, and profits for five years. In this analysis trends are important. A project with strong long-term prospects may be funded if the return for the fifth year meets the criterion but the five-year average does not. The firm can reduce risk on new investments by following a sequential procedure whenever possible, as we have discussed in chapter 11.

The appropriations committee selects the projects that will be submitted to the board. In general, the committee is careful about the documentation and the positive arguments for projects that it sends to the board. It does not want to embarrass the chairman or the president of the firm by having the board refuse to fund a project that has been recommended by the committee and, therefore, by the management. For the most part, however, the board follows the recommendations of the committee. The management knows more about the projects than the directors, and the board will rarely attempt to kill a proposed project. At worst, considerations may be raised that will force management to delay a project temporarily while a new analysis is made.

From the point of view of the appropriations committee, the sponsor of a project is the manager who makes the primary recommendation. Thus, the sponsor is held responsible, and the eventual success or failure of the project may affect the sponsor's status in the organization. In evaluating a proposal, the committee must consider both the credibility of the sponsor and the ability of the sponsor's division to generate profitable projects. At the "wish list" stage, prior to receiving a careful project evaluation, the committee's beliefs about the profitability of a project will be influenced by past rates of return on projects in the sponsor's division. These prior beliefs will be modified if a strong case has been made for the project in the proposal. However, even the amount of useful information in the proposal depends in part on the credibility of the sponsor. Thus, the committee's evaluation will depend heavily on past experience with the sponsor.

At the same time it must be recognized that it is difficult to analyze past results because it is difficult to separate the effects on profits of recent investments from the many other changes that take place over a period of time. Nevertheless, post-audits of the results of projects are made and reported to the committee and the board. These audits give a measure of the ability of managers to estimate rates of return accurately. In turn, approval of new proposals will tend to be influenced by the committee's perception of the ability of the individual sponsors to make good estimates. Similarly, at the next level, the board's decision is based on its confidence that the management's recommendations are good. Again, this confidence will presumably evolve from past results. Thus, at each stage of the allocation process, the sponsor's recommendations must be evaluated by the committee or the board in the context of previous experience with the sponsor.

Rejection of Projects and the Role of Uncertainty

The major cause for the elimination of projects that have been put into the budget is the inability of the division to demonstrate that the project meets the payback and rate of return criteria. In addition, however, from time to time the firm will arbitrarily raise the criteria so that some of the projects will be rejected by the new, higher criteria and the total amount of funds allocated for capital expenditures will not be spent.

This approach is a way of dealing with uncertainty. It is an option that central management retains when it makes the initial budget. The budget will be made for a year and will probably be completed three months or so before the start of the fiscal year. Thus an event that was not taken into account during the planning, or was not given a high enough probability of occurrence to incorporate into the planning, can result in a relative shortage of cash. For example, during the year the firm may get the opportunity to make a desirable acquisition that requires some cash, and one way to get the cash is to reduce capital expenditures by raising the criteria.

The interest rate enters the capital expenditure process in essentially the same way. As the interest rate increases, cash becomes more expensive. Those projects that may not have a cash return—building a driveway, installing a lounge, building a new office building—will tend to be postponed. The interest rate also affects the two decision criteria directly. Increases in working capital must come from essentially the same sources of funds as the capital expenditure funds—depreciation, retained earnings, deferred taxes, and borrowing. As the short-term interest rate rises, it is highly likely that the firm will tend to reduce its interest expense by using internal funds. To make these funds available the firm will raise the return-on-investment criterion and shorten the payback period and thus reduce capital expenditures. Conversely, when the interest rate falls, the firm will tend to put more of its internal funds into capital expenditures.

This common method of dealing with uncertainty is consistent with the general sequential approach to decision-making we have stressed in this book. The method might be characterized as one in which a decision is made, but options are retained that may be exercised when more information becomes available. Since the division manager knows that the criteria might be changed in midstream, it might be assumed that managers adjust by raising their estimates to meet the new criteria. There is, however, a cost to such an approach, as we shall now discuss.

Credibility

Each capital proposal specifies both the total funding requested A and a vector r of various estimates of rates of return. The components of r are estimates of the rates of return for a period of years under different economic conditions. The amount that is actually awarded will depend on A, r, and the credibility of the manager making the proposal. If the estimated rates of return have been consistently higher than the division's actual rate of return, the committee will deflate estimates, and the sponsor will lose credibility in the process. This possibility is clearly stated in an interview with a manager as reported by Bower (1970, p. 59):

> What it really comes down to is your batting average. Obviously anything cooked up, I have to sell and approve. My contribution is more in the area of deciding how much confidence we have in things. The whole thing—the size, the sales estimate, the return, is based on judgment. I can kill or expand a project based on my judgment. I decide the degree of optimism incorporated into the estimates. You know your numbers change depending on how you feel. The key question is "How much confidence has the management built up over the years in my judgment?" A guy in

my position must think this way. He loses his usefulness when he loses
the confidence of higher executives in the company. Otherwise his ideas
won't be accepted when he goes up.

For any given vector **r**, the committee's beliefs about the actual rate
of return ρ for the proposed project can be represented conceptually by
a conditional probability distribution $F(\rho \mid \mathbf{r})$ which will have evolved
from previous experience both with the particular manager and with managers in general. The manager's credibility with the committee is summarized by this distribution. If the manager has tended to overestimate
rates of return on previous projects, then the committee will assign a
significant probability to the occurrence of returns substantially smaller
than those specified by **r**. Since management is generally sensitive to
"downside risk," the probability of a major loss will tend to offset an
equal or greater probability of a signficant profit. Thus the committee in
these circumstances will tend to reject the project even though the expected value of net profit meets the criterion. In other words the committee operates as if it has a risk-averse utility function.

In summary, after a request is submitted, the actual level of funding
will depend on the amount requested and on the committee's distribution
$F(\rho \mid \mathbf{r})$. If the probability of high returns is large relative to the downside
risk, the project is likely to be funded, at least partially. The committee
does *not* auction off capital to the highest bidder, but rather allocates
capital to acceptable projects as they arise. When an acceptable project
is encountered, it is either fully or partially funded, depending on its profit
potential.

Relation to Previous Literature

In the capital budgeting literature, the firm is often advised to determine
the internal rate of return on each possible investment. Prospective investments are to be ranked on the basis of their internal rates of return,
and the firm is advised to approve each investment that has a rate of return
greater than its cost of capital. This simultaneous ranking of projects implies that the cost of capital is an increasing function of the total amount
of investment (Dean 1951, 1967). As we have shown, however, the firm
does not and cannot operate this way. Proposals come in from the divisions in a nonsystematic fashion and each proposal is considered on its
own merits in the order in which it is submitted. The committee or the
board, depending on the size of the proposed project, approves or dis-
approves the proposal at its regular meeting without rankings or comparisons of projects.

In addition, the process as outlined in the literature may not be appropriate when there are significant uncertainties. For example, there are

uncertainties involved in estimating revenue. The total amount of sales stemming from a proposed project is uncertain, and sales revenue will depend upon the status of the economy and other factors. The usual approach in predicting revenue is to extrapolate in a linear fashion from the data of past periods, although this approach may be modified when some synergistic factor justifies anticipating an increase in revenue. There is generally no attempt to make estimates in a statistically justifiable manner since the uncertainty is believed to be so great that statistical estimates will have large variances. Therefore, with or without statistical estimates, the firm will have to rely on the personal judgments of its knowledgeable managers.

There may be an additional source of uncertainty from the allocation committee's point of view. Given the desire for capital and the advantage of firsthand knowledge, there may be a tendency for the division manager to bias estimates upward to guarantee approval. For example, the division management will know where there are uncertainties in the estimates but could suppress this information rather than pass it on to the committee. This phenomenon is known as uncertainty absorption (March and Simon 1958, p. 165). Thus, estimates which are presented to the committee on the request forms must be carefully evaluated.

If the project involves a demonstration of cost savings, it is also possible to bias the information in a manner favorable to the project. Cyert, Simon, and Trow (1956) studied a firm making a decision on whether or not to buy a computer. The proponents of the computer system showed that it produced greater cost savings than an alternative system by monetizing the intangible benefits. Their analysis demonstrates a biasing process resulting from the overemphasis of intangibles in relation to tangible considerations. These factors—great uncertainty in predicting the future, uncertainty absorption in estimation, and the extent to which intangible considerations are monetized—make the actual allocation process significantly different from the normative process described in the literature (Cyert and Simon 1983).

There are other and more fundamental differences between the description of the allocation process here and models presented in the literature of economics and management. We have argued in this chapter that capital investment is determined to a significant extent by the pool of funds available for capital expenditures—depreciation expense plus retained earnings plus deferred taxes. In other words, the investment process as we have described it is best explained by a liquidity theory. Some economists feel that other variables are more important. For example, Jorgenson and Siebert (1968) compare five different models including a liquidity model that is similar to the one we have proposed, using data from standard accounting reports (10K's). They report:

We have compared alternative theories of investment behavior with regard to their ability to explain corporate investment behavior. Although the relative performance of the alternative theories may be measured in a number of ways, the three measures of relative performance we have used—proportion of correct turning points, standard error of the regression, number of changes in desired capital entering the fitted distributed lag function—produce an almost identical ordering of alternative theories of investment behavior: (1) Neoclassical I; (2) Neoclassical II; (3) Expected Profits; (4) Accelerator; and (5) Liquidity. Our tests discriminate sharply among the Neoclassical theories and the Expected Profits and Accelerator theories and between these theories and the Liquidity theory. [pages 706–7]

Their rejection of the liquidity theory has been criticized in detail (Cyert, DeGroot, and Holt 1979).

The investment function is complex, and we do not believe that the evidence presented by Jorgenson and Siebert warrants their conclusion ". . . that the liquidity theory of investment can be dismissed from serious consideration as an explanation of corporate investment behavior" (page 705). The following assessment given by Meyer and Kuh (1957) is consistent with the thrust of this chapter:

An alternative theory, highly eclectic in nature, has been proposed in this concluding chapter. In this formulation the investment decision is explained within the framework of a modern industrial economy typified by oligopolistic markets, large corporations distinctly separated in management and ownership, and highly imperfect equity and monetary markets. Under such circumstances, the investment outlay on fixed and working capital seems, in the short run, most plausibly treated as a residual defined to be the difference between the total net flow of funds realized from current operations less the established or conventional dividend payments. This equality is, of course, only a first approximation: Investment will often exceed or fall short of this residual. [pages 204–5]

In the investment process there are a large number of variables involved, and the resulting behavior is too complex to be explained by standard statistical models. The approach we have taken gives insight into the investment behavior of the firm. We believe that an accurate theory of investment will be derived ultimately from studies that go inside the firm to obtain the data appropriate for a behavioral model (Carter 1974; Lioukas 1983).

13

Rational Expectations

The concept of rational expectations was introduced in an important article by Muth (1961) and has been extensively developed since then (Lucas and Sargent 1981). Muth's hypothesis was that the mean expectation of firms with respect to some phenomenon, say price, was equal to the prediction that would be made by the relevant economic theory. Muth gives his reasons for believing in the hypothesis, proceeds to develop it further, and does some testing as to the general consistency of the hypothesis. Our objective in this chapter is to build on Muth's basic concept by providing some insight into the process by which the equilibrium assumed by the rational-expectations hypothesis can, in fact, be realized. We will introduce the concept of Bayesian learning into expectations and then demonstrate for three different models how this learning might work in achieving a market equilibrium. Our third model leads to an alternative meaning of the term rational expectations.

The Process of Generating Rational Expectations

Muth sees his hypothesis developing out of a process in which each economic actor (he generally uses firms) has an expectation (prediction) about the value of some economic variable. He makes it clear that each expectation is not perfect (in the sense of being accurate), nor are all the expectations the same. Out of this process Muth hypothesizes that the arithmetic mean of these expectations is equal to the prediction of the relevant economic model, generally the equilibrium value of the model. It is our view that a model of the process by which rational expectations evolve must be developed if the rational-expectations hypothesis is to have a scientific basis. Without well-developed process models, the concept of rational expectations is essentially a black box (Turnovsky 1969; Townsend 1978, 1983; Frydman 1982).

Muth assumes that the predictions made by the firms are stochastically independent. Empirically, however, it is more reasonable to assume that the predictions are correlated. The management of each firm in a given market operates in essentially the same kind of environment and has much the same kind of information. In most cases, the managers have also experienced the same set of historical inputs from having been in the particular industry for some time. Therefore, even if all firms did not initially have the same prior distributions for the market variable being predicted, the feedback from the market would tend to modify the priors to the extent that similarity becomes a reasonable assumption at some point. *For this reason, we will postulate the same prior probability distributions for the decision makers in our models.*

Initially, Muth makes the assumption of independent shocks within his model. He assumes that the error term is randomly distributed, with no serial correlation. This model always leads to the trivial conclusion that the mean expectation is equal to the equilibrium value. Thus, the existence of a cobweb is antithetical to Muth's notion, and in his paper he argues that the cobweb model is not a good description of the data (Shonkwiler 1982). As an alternative explanation, Muth has recourse to the fact that a dynamic system hit with random shocks exhibits cycles with a stable period. Process models such as we will develop may be a middle ground for explaining the phenomena. To develop these models, we do not have to assume irrationality and a lack of learning, as is true of the traditional cobweb model, or to rely solely on random processes for an explanation of the real world.

Muth himself recognizes the fact that a model assuming rational expectations does not accommodate a dynamic process showing the path to equilibrium. He attempts to accommodate such a process by introducing the notion of serially correlated disturbances. He assumes that these disturbances can be represented as linear combinations of normally and independently distributed random variables and that both the actual price and the expected price can also be represented as linear combinations of these independent variables with appropriate weights. This approach gives Muth's work greater flexibility. However, in applications, the notion of independently and identically distributed disturbances is, for a variety of reasons, the most generally used. As a result, most models incorporating rational expectations move directly to the equilibrium value of the model without specifying an adequate process to produce the result. Simon (1978b) presents an excellent analysis of this issue.

Learning and Uncertainty

The model that we will follow will utilize Bayesian learning in describing the process by which expectations, once formed, lead to an equilibrium (Grossman 1975; Lewis 1981; Swamy, Barth, and Tinsley 1982). Rather than assume that market expectations lead directly to the equilibrium value, we will assume that learning takes place in the market and that this learning has the effect of continually modifying the prior probability distribution with which the firms start. Through this process we will show that the market will typically converge to an equilibrium.

The learning in our analysis comes from the feedback resulting from the actions taken by the firm. If a firm has a prior distribution for a particular price and supplies the appropriate quantity, its prior will be modified and a new expectation formed when it observes the results in the market. The new prior in turn leads to another decision. The form of learning that takes place is learning about the unknown values of the parameters in the particular market in which the firm is operating. The first step is the formation of a prior probability distribution about the values of the important parameters in the market. The learning process then continues through feedback from the market and continuing modification of the prior.

We propose to deal with models in which there is uncertainty. However, the term "uncertainty" takes on a completely different meaning when one moves from classical statistics to a Bayesian approach. Uncertainty has been generally used to describe a situation in which the outcome of a decision maker's action is not precisely predictable because of the existence either of parameters with unknown values or of random error terms. The traditional approach for analyzing uncertainty has been to assume a probability distribution for the error term but not for the unknown values of the parameters. This procedure leads ultimately to the need for some choice criterion such as the minimax or Neyman-Pearson approach (see chapter 2). When we move into the Bayesian world, these choice criteria no longer have relevance. To the Bayesian, as described in chapter 2, all uncertainty can be represented by probability distributions. Thus, the approach is to assign a prior distribution to the unknown values of all the parameters wherever they appear in the model. Learning then takes the form of changing conditional distributions for the outcomes in future periods on the basis of past outcomes. The structure of the changes will vary depending on whether they arise from updating the posterior distributions of parameters or from serially correlated error terms. The only conditions under which the learning process described in the preceding paragraph is not present are represented by models that consist of error terms independently distributed over time and no other parameters. Our models will consist of both unknown values of parameters and independently distributed error terms. The kind of learning we have described will be possible in these models. In fact, as we shall now discuss, this kind of learning is possible even when the form of the model is unknown to the economic agents.

An Inconsistent Model

We classify the first model that will be discussed as an inconsistent model because the firms do not know the form of the model of the process determining the price and, in fact, base their decision on an incorrect model (Brock 1972; DeCanio 1979). Through learning from the feedback of market information, it is possible for the firms to reach an equilibrium even though they have the wrong model (Arrow and Green 1973; Bray 1982). However, since the model that the firm is using is incorrect, this process may at times converge only slowly or may not converge at all. We shall present numerical examples illustrating the various possibilities.

This first model involves a parameter whose exact value is unknown to the firm. The firm assigns a prior distribution to the value of the parameter, and after the price in each period is observed, the firm updates this distribution in accordance with Bayes' theorem. However, since the price in each period is influenced by the firm's expectations, and these expectations are at least partly incorrect, the time series of prices that are generated could be highly unstable, even though other conditions of the model indicate that a convergence to equilibrium should prevail.

Assume that the firm's model for the price p_{t+1} in period $t + 1$, given the price p_t in period t, is of the following form:

$$p_{t+1} = ap_t + v_{t+1}, \quad t = 0, 1, 2, \ldots \tag{1}$$

Here the value of the coefficient a is fixed throughout the process but is unknown, and $v_1, v_2, \ldots$ form a sequence of independent and identically distributed random error terms. Suppose also that the firm believes that the common distribution of each of the error terms is normal with mean 0 and known precision r.

If the firm has a given posterior distribution for the value of a after it has observed the price p_t, then this distribution becomes the new prior and the firm can apply Bayes' theorem to determine the posterior distribution of a after the price p_{t+1} has been observed. In particular, it follows that if the posterior distribution of a at the end of period t is normal with mean m_t and precision h_t, then the posterior distribution at the end of period $t + 1$ will be normal with mean m_{t+1} and precision h_{t+1}, where

$$m_{t+1} = \frac{h_t m_t + r p_t p_{t+1}}{h_t + r p_t^2} \tag{2}$$

and

$$h_{t+1} = h_t + r p_t^2. \tag{3}$$

It follows from these relations that at the end of period t, the firm's expectation $E_t(p_{t+1})$ of the price in period $t + 1$ will be

$$E_t(p_{t+1}) = E_t(a)p_t + E_t(v_{t+1}) - m_tp_t, \tag{4}$$

since

$$E_t(a) = m_t \text{ and } E_t(v_{t+1}) = 0.$$

We shall assume that in fact, however, the actual price p_{t+1} depends on the firm's expectation $E_t(p_{t+1}) = m_tp_t$. Specifically, we shall assume that the market equations take the following form in any period t:

$C_t = d_1 - \beta p_t,$	(demand)	(5)
$Q_t = d_2 + \gamma E_{t-1}(p_t) + u_t,$	(supply)	(6)
$Q_t = C_t.$	(market equilibrium)	(7)

In these relations, Q_t is the number of units produced in period t, C_t is the amount consumed in that period, and u_t is a random variable representing the uncontrollable factors which affect the amount produced in period t. It is assumed that d_1, d_2, β, and γ are given constants. It should be noted that the existence of a random variable in the supply implies a random variable in the production function of the individual firms. However, the existence of a random variable in the production function does not in any sense imply that the firms are not attempting to maximize profits. It does mean that the firms must make their production decisions under uncertainty. We are assuming that they do this in an optimum fashion, and that (6) is the aggregate result of such decisions. We have taken the same model as Muth to facilitate comparisons between his results and ours.

By solving the market equations, we obtain the relation

$$p_t = \frac{d_1 - d_2}{\beta} - \frac{\gamma}{\beta} E_{t-1}(p_t) - \frac{1}{\beta} u_t. \tag{8}$$

We shall assume for simplicity, as did Muth, that $d_1 = d_2$ (so that the equilibrium price is 0), and we shall let $v_t = -(1/\beta)u_t$. Then we have

$$p_t = -\frac{\gamma}{\beta} E_{t-1}(p_t) + v_t. \tag{9}$$

Thus, the price p_{t+1} is actually determined by the relation

$$p_{t+1} = -\frac{\gamma}{\beta} E_t(p_{t+1}) + v_{t+1}, \tag{10}$$

or equivalently

$$p_{t+1} = -\frac{\gamma}{\beta} m_tp_t + v_{t+1}. \tag{11}$$

It is again assumed that $v_1, v_2, \ldots$ are independent and identically distributed, each having a normal distribution with mean 0 and precision r.

Thus, although the firm believes that prices are determined in accordance with (1), and forms its expectations about the value of a in accordance with (2), prices are actually determined in accordance with (11). We have, therefore, a relatively sophisticated cobweb process. As in other economic processes, the model becomes consistent at equilibrium. Thus, if the firm becomes convinced that $a = 0$, so that $m_t = 0$, then the model is no longer inconsistent, because equations (1) and (11) become identical, p_{t+1} becoming equal to the error term v_{t+1}.

In the conventional cobweb analysis, the attainment of equilibrium is dependent on the relative slopes of the demand and supply curves. In terms of the parameters of our model, in which the slope of the demand curve is $-(1/\beta)$ and the slope of the supply curve is $1/\gamma$, the conventional conditions become

$\beta > \gamma$: convergence, (a)

$\beta = \gamma$: oscillation, (b)

$\beta < \gamma$: divergence. (c)

However, these conditions do not hold for our model. It can be seen from equation (11) that the condition for convergence is that $(\gamma/\beta)|m_t|$ ultimately becomes less than 1.

Numerical Results

To give a better understanding of the operation of the model, we present the results of several Monte Carlo runs. A given run was carried out by specifying the values of γ/β and r to be used throughout the run, as well as the initial price p_0, the mean m_0, and precision h_0 of the prior distribution of a; generating a sequence $v_1, v_2, \ldots, v_n$ of independent and identically distributed errors for a fixed number of periods n; and computing the corresponding sequence $p_1, p_2, \ldots, p_n$ of prices.

All of the runs were made using the value $h_0 = 0$. That is, it was assumed that the prior distribution of a was an improper, diffuse prior over the real line, although in order to determine the price p_1, it was still necessary to specify the value of m_0.

As a first example, for $\gamma/\beta = r = p_0 = m_0 = 1$, the sequence given in table 13.1 was generated for a process of $n = 100$ periods. As can be seen from table 13.1, the value of m_t is close to 0 after 100 periods, and the prices p_t, therefore, tend to differ little from the random error terms v_t. It seems noteworthy, however, that even at $t = 100$, the values of m_t are still exhibiting small fluctuations. In a second example, the initial price was changed to $p_0 = 10$, and the process was again followed for

Table 13.1   Initial Conditions: $p_0 = m_0 = r = \dfrac{\gamma}{\beta} = 1$

t	m_t	h_t	p_t	$E_{t-1}(p_t)$	v_t
1	−.539	1.000	−.539	1.000	.461
2	.566	1.290	.355	.290	.645
3	−.198	1.416	1.267	−.201	1.066
4	−.043	3.021	.119	−.250	−.132
5	−.050	3.035	−.177	−.005	−.182
•	•	•	•	•	•
•	•	•	•	•	•
•	•	•	•	•	•
96	.084	76.458	.101	.031	.132
97	.085	76.468	.695	.008	.703
98	.085	76.951	.063	.059	.122
99	.083	76.955	−1.618	.005	−1.612
100	.054	79.572	1.309	−.135	1.174

100 periods using the same values of the random errors v_t. The value of m_t fluctuated near -0.03 after 100 periods, and thus again p_t differed little from the random error terms.

It is of particular interest that we are getting convergence in two cases that the conventional analysis classifies as oscillating. This effect comes from the Bayesian learning built into the model. The strength of the firms' beliefs in the correctness of their expectations can be seen in the growth of the precision h_t in table 13.1. (In the second example $h_t = 336$ after 100 periods.) The large values of h_t indicate that the variance of the posterior distribution is very small. The firms are beginning to treat their expectations as being based on essentially certain knowledge of the value of a.

These results derive from single runs of the process and therefore do not necessarily represent average behavior of the process. In table 13.2 the results of 10 independent runs for $p_0 = m_0 = r = 1$ and $\gamma/\beta = 0.1$ are given, and in every run the model behaves as would be expected from conventional analysis. As the value of γ/β is increased beyond 1, and the values of the other parameters remain the same, the model produces an increased number of explosive solutions. For $\gamma/\beta = 1.2$, we got convergence in each of 10 independent runs. For $\gamma/\beta = 1.5$, however, 5 out of 10 runs diverged in the sense that the price p_t began oscillating wildly, being positive for two periods, then negative for two periods, as its absolute value increased. Essentially the same kind of re-

Table 13.2   Initial Conditions: $p_0 = m_0 = r = 1;\ \dfrac{\gamma}{\beta} = 0.1.$

Ten Runs of 100 Periods

Run	m_{100}	h_{100}	p_{100}	$E_{99}(p_{100})$
1	.046	76.307	1.186	−.119
2	.030	105.143	−2.054	−.010
3	−.174	104.052	−.598	−.071
4	−.094	97.170	2.160	−.021
5	.125	104.670	−1.969	−.032
6	−.004	100.390	−1.049	.003
7	−.005	92.691	−.969	.016
8	−.081	80.874	−.473	.036
9	−.017	95.349	−.136	−.010
10	−.028	104.113	−.397	.001

sult prevails for different initial values of p_0 and m_0. For example, with $p_0 = 10$, $m_0 = 1$, and $\gamma/\beta = 1.5$, we got convergence for each of 10 runs in contrast to the previous result for $p_0 = m_0 = 1$, but $\gamma/\beta = 1.75$ led to each of 10 runs exploding.

An analytic study of the convergence or divergence of this process appears to be difficult. In order to gain a better understanding of the Monte Carlo runs just described and to convey the essential nature of the process, we shall eliminate all stochastic elements by taking the error term v_t in (11) to be 0 in every period. When $\gamma/\beta = 1$, it is found that the price p_t converges quickly to 0 for each of the following three sets of initial values: (1) $p_0 = m_0 = 1$; (2) $p_0 = 10$, $m_0 = 1$; (3) $p_0 = m_0 = 2$. When $\gamma/\beta = 1$ and the initial values are $p_0 = m_0 = 10$, the results are as shown in table 13.3. This process appears to be exploding during the first 30 periods. The price p_t spirals wildly outward, and again it is positive for two periods, then negative for two periods, as its absolute value increases. The absolute value reaches a maximum of 2.684×10^{24} at period $t = 30$. After that period, however, the price p_t moves rapidly toward 0 and the process converges.

To assess the significance of the error term in this process, a Monte Carlo run was also carried out for these same initial values $p_0 = m_0 = 10$ and $\gamma/\beta = r = 1$, but with the error terms v_t again included in (11). Even with these error terms present, the process was found to behave similarly to the process represented in table 13.3. The price p_t reached its maximum absolute value of 1.60×10^{24} in period $t = 20$ and then began to decrease in magnitude. When $t = 29$, the values of m_t and h_t were found to be

Table 13.3 **Initial Conditions:**

$$p_0 = m_0 = 10, r = \frac{\gamma}{\beta} = 1, v_t = 0$$

t	m_t	h_t	p_t
1	-10	10^2	-10^2
2	9.802	1.010×10^4	-10^3
3	-9.606	1.010×10^6	9.802×10^3
4	9.406	9.709×10^7	9.416×10^4
5	-9.203	8.963×10^9	-8.857×10^5
10	8.115	3.085×10^{19}	-4.601×10^{10}
15	-6.873	2.810×10^{28}	1.185×10^{15}
20	5.422	4.334×10^{36}	1.177×10^{19}
25	-3.584	4.823×10^{43}	-2.702×10^{22}
30	0.9246	3.732×10^{48}	-2.684×10^{24}
35	-0.0773	1.761×10^{49}	3.556×10^{20}
40	-0.0773	1.761×10^{49}	9.817×10^{14}
45	-0.0773	1.761×10^{49}	2.709×10^9
50	-0.0773	1.761×10^{49}	7.475×10^3
55	-0.0773	1.761×10^{49}	0.0206
60	-0.0773	1.761×10^{49}	0.0000

$m_t = 0.771$ and $h_t = 1.67 \times 10^{48}$. All these values are in approximate agreement with the values given in table 13.3.

Our conclusion is that the expectational model brings the market to equilibrium under varying initial values, including some values when the constraints on the slope condition derived from conventional analysis indicate that divergence will occur. It is clear that, if a mechanism were built into the model to allow the firm to modify its expectational models when they were clearly wrong, convergence could be attained with large ratios of γ/β and at a faster rate than we have observed in the current model. Thus, one approach to further research of this kind (utilizing simulation) is to find learning mechanisms that will allow the economic units to change expectational models in a rational fashion. The construction of inconsistent models is not the most fruitful way to progress in this field. If the firms have models that diverge drastically from reality, it seems reasonable to assume that the management would recognize this condition and change the model. Firms would continue searching for a model that produced predictions that coincided more closely with actual observations. In fact, the term "rational expectations" coined by Muth actually describes models that are consistent. We shall investigate such models in the next section.

A Consistent Model

We will continue to work with the market equations described by (5)–(7), and we will now derive analytic solutions for a model that is free of any of the inconsistencies previously discussed. We will assume that the values of some or all of the parameters d_1, d_2, β, and γ appearing in the demand and supply equations are unknown. Moreover, the distribution of u_t may involve other parameters with unknown values.

A consistent model means that the firm's expectations are based on the correct model, in this case (5)–(7) (Kihlstrom and Mirman 1975; Blume and Easley 1982). Therefore, we can derive an explicit expression for these expectations by taking the expected value of both sides of (8). Thus,

$$E_{t-1}(p_t) = E_{t-1}\left(\frac{d_1 - d_2}{\beta}\right) - E_{t-1}\left(\frac{\gamma}{\beta}\right) E_{t-1}(p_t) - E_{t-1}\left(\frac{1}{\beta} u_t\right). \tag{12}$$

It then follows from this relation that

$$E_{t-1}(p_t) = \frac{E_{t-1}[(d_1 - d_2)/\beta] - E_{t-1}[(1/\beta)u_t]}{1 + E_{t-1}(\gamma/\beta)}. \tag{13}$$

Equation (13) represents the actual expectations of the firm in the market. The market price will differ from this price because of the firm's incomplete knowledge of the values of the relevant parameters and random terms.

The economic process will evolve as follows: In each period, the firms form their expectation of the price in the next period from (13). The actual price is then generated in accordance with (8). The observed actual price leads the firms to change their expectations of the values of the parameters in (13) and, hence, to change their expectation of the price in the following period. The next price is then generated from (8), and the process continues in this way.

As a simple example, suppose that in the market equations (5)–(7) the values of β and γ are known but that the value of $D = d_1 - d_2$ is not known with certainty. Suppose also that the random variables u_t are independent from period to period and that each u_t has a normal distribution with mean 0 and known precision τ. (This assumption of known τ can be relaxed by the introduction of a prior distribution for τ when its value is unknown.) It follows from (13) that

$$E_{t-1}(p_t) = \frac{E_{t-1}(D)}{\beta + \gamma}. \tag{14}$$

Suppose now that the posterior distribution of D at the end of period $t - 1$ is normal with mean m_{t-1} and precision h_{t-1}. Then $E_{t-1}(p_t) = m_{t-1}/(\beta + \gamma)$. Furthermore, (8) can be rewritten in the form

$$\beta p_t + \gamma E_{t-1}(p_t) = D - u_t. \tag{15}$$

Therefore, it follows from Bayes' theorem that the posterior distribution of D at the end of period t will be a normal distribution with mean

$$m_t = \frac{h_{t-1} m_{t-1} + \tau[\beta p_t + \gamma E_{t-1}(p_t)]}{h_{t-1} + \tau}, \tag{16}$$

and precision $h_t = h_{t-1} + \tau$. Substituting (14) into (16), we get

$$m_t = \frac{\{h_{t-1} + [\tau\gamma/(\beta + \gamma)]\}m_{t-1} + \tau\beta p_t}{h_{t-1} + \tau}. \tag{17}$$

It can be shown from these relations that

$$\plim_{t \to \infty} m_t = D,$$

and, hence,

$$\plim_{t \to \infty} E_{t-1}(p_t) = \frac{D}{\beta + \gamma}. \tag{18}$$

Therefore, as $t \to \infty$, the expected price in each period becomes stabilized at the value $D/(\beta + \gamma)$. It follows from (8) that the distribution of the actual price in each period also becomes stabilized as a normal distribution with mean $D/(\beta + \gamma)$ and precision $\beta^2\tau$.

Muth distinguishes between two concepts, the prediction of the model (theory) $E_{t-1}(p_t)$ and the aggregate expectation of the firms p_t^e. It is necessary for him to make the special assumption that $E_{t-1}(p_t) = p_t^e$, which he calls the hypothesis of rational expectations. In our model and from the Bayesian point of view, this relation arises naturally and is nothing more than a necessary condition for the internal consistency of the model we have presented here. In the above example, it is an immediate consequence of the hypothesis of rational expectations that $E_{t-1}(p_t) = p_t^e = D/(\beta + \gamma)$. In contrast, the consistent model we have presented shows the process leading to (18). If the firm is using a correct model, incorporating as many unknown parameters as might be needed, then (12) and (13) must be satisfied. Indeed, it can be seen in (12) and (13) that it is in the Bayesian framework that the rational-expectations approach finds its natural setting.

Sequences and Expectations

Up to this point we have dealt with the problem of rational expectations essentially in the way that Muth posed it. The essential characteristic of that problem is that the firms are attempting to find the equilibrium output at every decision point. Another, and more sophisticated, approach to the problem is to view the firms in the market as attempting to reach equilibrium in a specified number of stages or time periods. The logic of moving in a sequence of stages stems from the fact that large and rapid changes in output are costly and, therefore, a smooth adjustment is sought. Posing the problem in this way enables us to utilize control theory and, thereby, to determine the optimum output the firms should produce at each point. These outputs then play the role of the equilibrium output in Muth's definition of rational expectations. In this formulation, a rational sequence of expectations leads to the optimum sequence of outputs as determined from control theory.

The Control Model

In order to illustrate these ideas, we will work with the competitive model and will assume that all but one of the firms is operating at the long-run equilibrium price. The lone firm not yet in equilibrium can be viewed as a new entrant or a firm that has been badly managed and has new management. It is operating in a market with a fixed price, the long-run equilibrium price, and is attempting to maximize profits in reaching the long-run equilibrium output.

It is assumed that at the beginning of the process, the firm's output is at a certain given level q_0. Then for $j = 1, \ldots, n$,

$$q_j = q_{j-1} + u_j + e_j, \tag{19}$$

where u_j is the adjustment that the firm makes to its output q_{j-1} when moving into period j, and e_j is a random factor affecting the output q_j with mean 0 and variance σ_j^2 It is assumed that the random factors $e_1, \ldots, e_n$ are independent. If there is no random factor in any particular period, then $\sigma_j^2 = 0$ for that period.

In a general formulation there would be a specific sequence of targets or goals $q_1^*, \ldots, q_n^*$ with the property that the firm would like to have its output q_j in period j close to the target q_j^*. The cost of being away from the target in period j is assumed to be $\alpha_j(q_j - q_j^*)^2$, and the cost of making an adjustment u_j in the output when moving into period j is assumed to be $\beta_j u_j^2$, where $\alpha_j \geq 0$ and $\beta_j \geq 0$ are given constants.

In our particular example the targets $q_1^*, \ldots, {}_n^*$ are all equal to the same value q^*, which is the long-run equilibrium output for this industry.

The cost $\alpha_j(q_j - q^*)^2$ reflects the distance of the firm's output in a given period from q^* and includes the usual costs of production. The cost $\beta_j u_j^2$ reflects such items as hiring and firing costs, overtime pay, supervision cost increases, and other such costs not included in the first term. The symmetric quadratic form of these costs provides, under the usual differentiability conditions, an effective second-order approximation to a wide variety of actual cost functions.

Since the two costs we have defined are separate, the total cost in a given period is the sum of the two, and the total cost of the process is the sum of all these costs for $j = 1, \ldots, n$. Since we assume that the firm's utility function is linear, the problem is to choose the sequence of adjustments $u_1, \ldots, u_n$ in order to maximize expected profit. Given the fixed market price, the firm achieves this objective by minimizing the overall expected cost

$$\sum_{j=1}^{n} E[\alpha_j(q_j - q^*)^2 + \beta_j u_j^2]. \tag{20}$$

The optimal sequence of adjustments can be derived in this problem by the method of backward induction and has the following properties: The optimal adjustment u_j in period j is a linear function of the previous output q_{j-1}; that is, $u_j = a_j q_{j-1} + b_j$, where the constants a_j and b_j depend on q^* and the values of $\alpha_j, \ldots, \alpha_n$ and $\beta_j, \ldots, \beta_n$. However, these optimal adjustments do not depend on the variances $\sigma_1^2, \ldots, \sigma_n^2$.

In the problem we are considering, we shall assume that the coefficients α_j and β_j which enter the cost function are of the form $\alpha_j = \alpha\rho^j$ and $\beta_j = \beta\rho^j$, where α and β are given positive constants and ρ is a discount factor $(0 < \rho < 1)$. Thus, the total expected cost of the process is

$$\sum_{j=1}^{n} \rho^j E[\alpha(q_j - q^*)^2 + \beta u_j^2]. \tag{21}$$

It can be shown that if we let the number of periods $n \to \infty$, then the optimal adjustment u_j converges to the following value, for $j = 1, 2, \ldots$:

$$u_j = \gamma(q^* - q_{j-1}), \tag{22}$$

where γ is a certain constant in the interval $0 < \gamma < 1$ specified by the relation

$$\gamma = \frac{[(\alpha + \beta - \rho\beta)^2 + 4\alpha\beta]^{1/2} + \alpha + \rho\beta - \beta}{[(\alpha + \beta - \rho\beta)^2 + 4\alpha\beta]^{1/2} + \alpha + \rho\beta + \beta}. \tag{23}$$

With this choice of the adjustment u_j, the output in period j will be generated by the model

$$q_j = (1-\gamma)q_{j-1} + \gamma q^* + e_j. \tag{24}$$

Thus, with this derivation we can determine the optimal sequence of outputs for the firm to follow in adjusting to its ultimate target q^*. The values $q_1, \ldots, q_n$ determine the least-cost path and help to determine another definition of rational expectations. Thus, since the firm cannot reach the equilibrium value immediately, as is assumed in the Muth formulation, rational expectations in each period should be couched in terms of $q_1, \ldots, q_n$. The firm's expectations about price in each period should lead to the appropriate output in the optimal sequence if the expectations are rational as defined.

Formally, q_j will be a function of $E_{j-1}(p_j)$, the firm's expectation of the price p_j in period j based on all observed prices and outputs up to the end of period $j - 1$. We shall let f denote this function, so that

$$q_j = f[E_{j-1}(p_j)] + e_j, \tag{25}$$

where e_j again denotes a random factor with mean 0 and variance σ_j^2 which affects the output in period j.

We now define the expectation $E_{j-1}(p_j)$ to be *rational* if this expectation yields a model for q_j which agrees with the control theory model that was derived from the optimal sequence of adjustments. In other words, $E_{j-1}(p_j)$ is a *rational expectation* if

$$f[E_{j-1}(p_j)] = (1 + a_j)q_{j-1} + b_j. \tag{26}$$

For the special problem with constant targets, discounted costs, and an infinite number of periods, $E_{j-1}(p_j)$ is a rational expectation if

$$f[E_{j-1}(p_j)] = (1 - \gamma)q_{j-1} + \gamma q^*. \tag{27}$$

For example, suppose as in (6) that f is simply an increasing linear function of $E_{j-1}(p_j)$, as follows:

$$f[E_{j-1}(p_j)] = c_1 E_{j-1}(p_j) + c_2. \tag{28}$$

Then $E_{j-1}(p_j)$ is a rational expectation if and only if

$$E_{j-1}(p_j) = \frac{1}{c_1} [(1 - \gamma)q_{j-1} + \gamma q^* - c_2]. \tag{29}$$

The sequence of expectations generated in this way has the property that the expectation is updated in each period j after the output q_j in that period has been observed or, equivalently, after the price p_j in that period has been observed. This updating is not "Bayesian" in the usual sense of the word, simply because there are no unknown parameters in this model about which the firm must learn. Furthermore, the firm's expectations are not consistent or correct for the cobweb model in our earlier sense, because the actual expected price in period j, given the firm's choice of q_j

as determined by the market equations, will not be equal to $E_{j-1}(p_j)$. In what sense then are these expectations rational? They are rational in the sense that they lead the firm to an optimal output in each period, that is, they lead to a sequence of outputs that minimizes the total expected loss or, equivalently, maximizes the total expected profit.

As a result of the application of control theory, it is possible to extend the definition of rational expectations to a process-oriented model. There is no need to postulate a model in which the equilibrium price is attained by special assumptions about the average expectation. Given the costs of moving to the equilibrium position, it is possible, as demonstrated in this chapter, to determine the points on an optimum path. A set of rational expectations should then lead the firm along this path. The net effect will be to dampen the fluctuation of the cobweb model and carry the firms toward the equilibrium position.

Conclusions

Our basic thrust in this chapter has been the development of models that describe the process by which rational expectations may be developed within a market. We accept the fundamental notion that phenomena based on nonrationality such as those exhibited in the cobweb model cannot exist for any period of significant duration. However, we have also pointed out that no attention is given to the process by which rational expectations may develop in a market. In particular, the learning process has been ignored and we have attempted to remedy this deficiency by introducing the concept of Bayesian learning. We have also added the concept of consistent as well as rational expectations (see also Blume, Bray, and Easley 1982). Finally, we have tackled the problem of expectations under conditions in which the firm cannot immediately move to an equilibrium position. It should be noted that we have retained Muth's approach of defining rational expectation in terms of conditions on just the mean value of a distribution and have attempted to expand the concept as described. Lucas and Prescott (1971) have defined rational expectation of a variable to mean that the actual values and the anticipated values of the variable have the same probability distribution.

The work on expectations has its ultimate significance in its impact on the construction of dynamic models. The development of dynamic models generally hinges on using some form of expectations as the means of enabling the decisions of one period to be made rationally. More generally, expectations in a dynamic model become the basis for relating a current period to future periods. We have indicated in this chapter some new approaches for incorporating expectations in dynamic models involving complex types of adjustments.

14

Epilogue

A major part of this book has relied upon the application of the subjective Bayesian approach to decision-making. We have found this approach to be a convenient way of introducing learning into models of firm behavior and have built into many of these models the capacity of managers to make probability judgments about possible changes in price and output by rival firms. In fact, one of the main contributions of this book is the demonstration that the Bayesian approach is an effective methodology for handling uncertainty in economic theory.

However, much recent work (Kahneman, Slovic, and Tversky 1982) has shown that in the context of psychological experiments, the likelihoods and preferences expressed by subjects do not satisfy the coherence properties that are necessary for the existence of subjective probabilities and utilities. Concern has been expressed (Nelson and Winter 1982, p. 405) that this work has been ignored in economics. Thus, it might be inferred that because these psychological experiments show that Bayes' theorem lacks empirical relevance, Bayesian analysis should not be used in economic theory.

We have examined the evidence in many of these experiments and believe it can be broadly classified into two categories. In the first category (for example, Edwards 1968), subjects followed an updating process akin to that described by Bayes' theorem but did not utilize information that they obtained efficiently. That is, their posterior probabilities differed quantitatively from the probabilities specified by a proper use of Bayes' theorem but were similar in many qualitative aspects. In the second category, the subjects made judgments under certain experimental conditions that violated some of the fundamental properties of the subjective Bayesian theory.

The first category does not pose a challenge to our models. The decision makers whose behavior we are modeling can get the technical help necessary to make any required calculation efficiently. It is the second category that presents the greater challenge. Even here, however, it is difficult to conclude from the experimental evidence that our particular use of Bayesian analysis is unjustified on empirical grounds. Tversky and Kahneman (1974), for example, conclude that "Evidently, people respond differently when given no evidence and when given worthless evidence. When no specific evidence is given, prior probabilities are properly utilized; when worthless evidence is given, prior probabilities are ignored." Later in the same article they conclude that "This article describes three heuristics that are employed in making judgments under uncertainty . . . A better understanding of these heuristics and of the biases to which they lead could improve judgments and decisions in situations of uncertainty." We assume that professional managers will have gained that better understanding in their fields of expertise.

Since we are writing about managers who are relatively expert in making decisions under uncertainty, it does not seem out-of-place to model their thinking with the most efficient technique available. At the same time we recognize that we do not have evidence that the managers about whom we are writing know and use Bayes' theorem. They probably do not. The important point is that managers do somehow make probabilitiy assessments with respect to a rival's behavior and they do make decisions based on these judgments. It is reasonable to conclude that most of the firms that survive in the market have a management coalition that is capable of making decisions under uncertainty in an efficient manner, and therefore we believe that Bayesian analysis functions as a good analogue of the process that actually goes on in the manager's mind.

We have in this book introduced uncertainty into a number of important areas of economic theory and have shown how firms and individuals make decisions in the face of this uncertainty. In taking this approach we have been able to increase the empirical relevance of economic theory.

In duopoly we have shown how firms may reach the monopoly solution without collusion when each firm is uncertain about the willingness of its rival to cooperate. We have achieved this result with a methodology that has a broad significance for economic theory. We utilized multiperiod horizons and concepts such as the coefficients of cooperation and mutually optimal reaction functions in establishing equilibrium points. Most importantly we have been able to develop models that incorporate Bayesian learning so that the managers of the firm behave intelligently with respect to their rivals. Thus economists no longer need to rely on inconsistent models, collusion, or a black box such as rational expectations to justify equilibrium.

Another important theme of this book is the applicability of the concepts of control theory to the theory of the firm. We have developed a model of the firm that weds the behavioral approach with a stochastic control model. The idea of management as a control process is empirically relevant and leads to a model that is closer to the actual behavior of a firm than does the traditional marginal approach.

The inclusion of uncertainty in the utility function has led to the concept of adaptive utility. We reject the standard notion of decision theory that individuals know their utility functions. Instead we adopt the position that individuals gain information about their utility functions by learning from experience. We have shown how adaptive utility functions can modify and fit into the economic theory that incorporates uncertainty.

One of our incentives in carrying out the research on which this book is based was to develop dynamic models in which managers of the firms involved made sequential decisions under uncertainty. Therefore, sequential decision processes are present in almost every chapter and they form the dominant methodology of the book. We have applied such processes to duopoly, the kinked demand curve, adaptive utility, a control theory of the firm, and investment and capital allocation by the firm. The sequential decision process in economics is an idea with a powerful theoretical structure which, at the same time, provides a valid description of empirical decision-making. We believe that it can be the building block for dynamic models that marginalism has been for static models.

References

Allais, M. (1953). Le comportement de l'homme rationnel devant le risque: critique des postulats et l'école Americaine. *Econometrica, 21,* 503–546.

Allais, M., and Hagen, O. (eds.)(1979). *Expected Utility and the Allais Paradox.* Dordrecht, Holland: D. Reidel.

Allen, R. G. D. (1938). *Mathematical Analysis for Economists.* New York: St. Martin's Press.

Anderson, J. (1980). *Cognitive Psychology and Its Implications.* San Francisco, CA: Freeman.

Arrow, K. J., and Green, J. (1973). Notes on expectations equilibria in Bayesian settings. Working Paper No. 33, The Economics Series, Institute for Mathematical Studies in the Social Sciences, Stanford University.

Axelrod, R. (1984). *The Evolution of Cooperation.* New York: Basic Books.

Balch, M., McFadden, D., and Wu, S. (eds.)(1974). *Essays on Economic Behavior under Uncertainty.* Amsterdam: North-Holland.

Becker, G. M., DeGroot, M. H., and Marschak, J. (1963). Stochastic models of choice behavior. *Behavioral Science, 8,* 41–55.

———. (1964). Measuring utility by a single-response sequential method. *Behavioral Science, 9,* 226–232.

Bellman, R. (1957). *Dynamic Programming.* Princeton, NJ: Princeton University Press.

Benhabib, J., and Bull, C. (1983). Job search: the choice of intensity. *Journal of Political Economy, 91,* 747–764.

Bishop, R. L. (1960). Duopoly: collusion or warfare. *American Economic Review, 50,* 933–961.

Blume, L. E., and Easley, D. (1982). Learning to be rational. *Journal of Economic Theory, 26,* 340–351.

Blume, L. E., Bray, M. M., and Easley, D. (1982). Introduction to the stability of rational expectations equilibrium. *Journal of Economic Theory*, **26**, 313–317.

Bornstein, M. (1978). Unemployment in capitalist regulated market economies and socialist centrally planned economies. *American Economic Review*, **68**, 38–43.

Bower, J. L. (1970). *Managing the Resource Allocation Process*. Boston: Harvard Graduate School of Business Administration.

Boyer, M., and Kihlstrom, R. E. (eds.) (1984). *Bayesian Models in Economic Theory*. Amsterdam: North-Holland.

Bray, M. M. (1982). Learning, estimation, and the stability of rational expectations. *Journal of Economic Theory*, **26**, 318–339.

Brock, W. A. (1972). On models of expectations that arise from maximizing behavior of economic agents over time. *Journal of Economic Theory*, **5**, 348–376.

Carter, E. E. (1974). *Portfolio Aspects of Corporate Capital Budgeting*. Lexington, MA: D. C. Heath.

Caves, R. E. (1980). Corporate strategy and structure. *Journal of Economic Literature*, **18**, 64–92.

Chamberlin, E. H. (1946). *The Theory of Monopolistic Competition*. Cambridge, MA: Harvard University Press.

Chandler, A. D., Jr. (1966). *Strategy and Structure*. Garden City, NJ: Doubleday.

Chow, G. C. (1975). *Analysis and Control of Dynamic Economic Systems*. New York: John Wiley.

Cohen, K. J., and Cyert, R. M. (1975). *Theory of the Firm: Resource Allocation in a Market Economy*. Englewood Cliffs, NJ: Prentice-Hall.

Cohen, M. D., and Axelrod, R. (1984). Coping with complexity: the adaptive value of changing utility. *American Economic Review*, **74**, 30–42.

Cournot, A. (1897). *Researches into the Mathematical Principles of the Theory of Wealth* (N. T. Bacon, trans.). New York: Macmillan.

Crawford, R. G. (1973). Implications for learning for economic models of uncertainty. *International Economic Review*, **14**, 587–600.

Cyert, R. M. (1955). Oligopoly price behavior and the business cycle. *Journal of Political Economy*, **63**, 41–51.

Cyert, R. M., DeGroot, M. H., and Holt, C. A. (1979). Capital allocation within a firm. *Behavioral Science*, **24**, 287–295.

Cyert, R. M., and March, J. G. (1955). Organizational structure and pricing behavior in an oligopolistic market. *American Economic Review*, **45**, 129–139.

——— . (1963). *A Behavioral Theory of the Firm*. Englewood Cliffs, NJ: Prentice-Hall.

Cyert, R. M., and Simon, H. A. (1983). The behavioral approach: with emphasis on economics. *Behavioral Science,* **28,** 95–108.

Cyert, R. M., Simon, H. A., and Trow, D. B. (1956). Observation of a business decision. *The Journal of Business,* **29,** 237–248.

Day, R. H., and Groves, T. (eds.)(1975). *Adaptive Economic Models.* New York: Academic Press.

Dean, J. (1951). *Capital Budgeting.* New York: Columbia University Press.

———. (1967). *Managerial Economics.* Englewood Cliffs, NJ: Prentice-Hall.

DeCanio, S. J. (1979). Rational expectations and learning from experience. *Quarterly Journal of Economics,* **93,** 47–57.

Decision Analysis Group, SRI International (1977). *Readings in Decision Analysis.* Menlo Park, CA: Stanford Research Institute.

DeGroot, M. H. (1970). *Optimal Statistical Decisions.* New York: McGraw-Hill.

———. (1980). Improving predictive distributions. *Bayesian Statistics* (J. M. Bernardo et al., eds.), 385–395. Valencia, Spain: University Press.

———. (1983). Decision making with an uncertain utility function. *Foundations of Utility and Risk Theory with Applications.* (B. P. Stigum and F. Wenstop, eds.), 371–384. Dordrecht, Holland: D. Reidel.

DeGroot, M. H., and Kadane, J. B. (1980). Optimal challenges for selection. *Operations Research,* **28,** 952–968.

———. (1983). Optimal sequential decisions in problems involving more than one decision maker. *Recent Advances in Statistics* (M. H. Rizvi, J. S. Rustagi, and D. Siegmund, eds.), 197–210. New York: Academic Press.

Dixit, A., and Norman, V. (1978). Advertising and welfare. *Bell Journal of Economics,* **9,** 1–17.

Dvoretzky, A., Kiefer, J. and Wolfowitz, J. (1953). Sequential decision problems for processes with continuous time parameter. Testing hypotheses. *Annals of Mathematical Statistics,* **24,** 254–264.

Edgeworth, F. Y. (1881). *Mathematical Psychics.* London: C. Kegan Paul & Co.

Edwards, W. (1968). Conservatism in human information processing. *Formal Representation of Human Judgment.* (B. Kleinmuntz, ed.), 17–52. New York: John Wiley.

Efroymsen, C. W. (1955). The kinked oligopoly curve reconsidered. *Quarterly Journal of Economics,* **69,** 119–136.

Fama, E. (1977). Risk-adjusted discount rates and capital budgeting under uncertainty. *Journal of Financial Economics,* **5,** 3–24.

Ferguson, C. E., and Pfouts, R. W. (1962). Learning and expectation in dynamic duopoly behavior. *Behavioral Science,* **7,** 223–237.

Fienberg, S. E., and Zellner, A. (eds.)(1975). *Studies in Bayesian Econo-*

metrics and Statistics. Amsterdam: North-Holland.

Fogelman-Soulie, F., Munier, B., and Shakun, M. F. (1983). Bivariate negotiations as a problem of stochastic terminal control. *Management Science,* **29,** 840–855.

Fried, D. (1984). Incentives for information production and disclosure in a duopolistic environment. *Quarterly Journal of Economics,* **99,** 367–381.

Friedman, A. (1971). *Differential Games.* New York: John Wiley.

Friedman, J. W. (1968). Reaction functions and the theory of duopoly. *Review of Economic Studies,* **35,** 257–272.

———. (1977). *Oligopoly and the Theory of Games.* Amsterdam: North-Holland.

———. (1983). *Oligopoly Theory.* Cambridge: Cambridge University Press.

Frisch, R. (1951). Monopoly-polypoly—the concept of force in the economy (N. Beckerman, trans.). *International Economic Papers* (E. Henderson, ed.), 23–26. New York: Macmillan.

Frydman, R. (1982). Towards an understanding of market processes: individual expectation, learning and convergence to rational expectation equilibrium. *American Economic Review,* **72,** 652–668.

Goel, P. K. (1983). Information measures and Bayesian hierarchical models. *Journal of the American Statistical Association,* **78,** 408–410.

Goel, P. K., and DeGroot, M. H. (1979). Comparison of experiments and information measures. *Annals of Statistics,* **7,** 1066–1077.

Grannick, D. (1967), *Soviet Metal-Fabricating and Economic Development.* Madison: University of Wisconsin Press.

Green, E. J. (1984). Continuum and finite-player noncooperative models of competition. *Econometrica,* **52,** 975–993.

Green, E. J., and Porter, R. H. (1984). Noncooperative collusion under imperfect price information. *Econometrica,* **52,** 87–100.

Grossman, S. J. (1975a). Equilibrium under uncertainty and Bayesian adaptive control theory. *Adaptive Economic Models* (R. H. Day and T. Groves, eds.) 279–308. New York: Academic Press.

———. (1975b). Rational expectation and the econometric modeling of markets subject to uncertainty: a Bayesian approach. *Journal of Econometrics,* **3,** 255–272.

Grossman, S., Kihlstrom, R. E., and Mirman, L. J. (1977). A Bayesian approach to the production of information and learning by doing. *Review of Economic Studies,* **44,** 533–547.

Grossman, S., and Stiglitz, J. (1976). Information and competitive price systems. *American Economic Review,* **66,** 246–253.

Hall, R. L., and Hitch, C. J. (1939). Price-theory and business behavior. *Oxford Economic Papers,* No. 2, 12–45.

Harpaz, G., Lee, Y. W., and Winkler, R. L. (1982). Learning, experimentation, and the optimal output decisions of a competitive firm. *Management Science,* **28,** 589–603.

Harpaz, G., and Thomadakis, S. B. (1982). Systematic risk and the firm's experimental strategy. *Journal of Financial and Quantitative Analysis,* **17,** 363–389.

Harris, M., and Raviv, A. (1978). Some results on incentive contracts with application to education and employment, health insurance, and law enforcement. *American Economic Review,* **68,** 20–30.

Harsanyi, J. C. (1977). *Rational Behavior and Bargaining Equilibrium in Games and Social Situations.* New York: Cambridge University Press.

Hirshleifer, J., and Riley, J. G. (1979). The analytics of uncertainty and information—an expository survey. *Journal of Economic Literature,* **17,** 1375–1417.

Holt, C., Modigliani, F., Muth, J., and Simon, H. (1960). *Planning Production, Inventories, and Work Force.* Englewood Cliffs, NJ: Prentice-Hall.

Holthaus, D. M. (1979). Kinky demand, risk aversion and price leadership. *International Economic Review,* **20,** 341–348.

Jones, A. J. (1980). *Game Theory: Mathematical Models of Conflict.* Chichester: Ellis Horwood Limited.

Jones, M. (1980). Note on oligopoly: rival behavior and efficiency. *Bell Journal of Economics,* **11,** 709–714.

Jorgenson, D. W., and Siebert, C. D. (1968). A comparison of alternative theories of corporate investment behavior. *American Economic Review,* **58,** 681–712.

Kadane, J. B., Dickey, J. M., Winkler, R. L., Smith, W. S., and Peters, S. C. (1980). Interactive elicitation of opinion for a normal linear model. *Journal of the American Statistical Association,* **75,** 845–854.

Kadane, J. B., and Larkey, P. D. (1982). Subjective probability and the theory of games. *Management Science,* **28,** 113–120.

Kahneman, D., Slovic, P., and Tversky, A. (1982). *Judgment under Uncertainty: Heuristics and Biases.* Cambridge: Cambridge University Press.

Kamien, M. I., and Schwartz, N. L. (1971). Limit pricing and uncertain entry. *Econometrica,* **39,** 441–454.

——— . (1983). Conjectural variations. *Canadian Journal of Economics,* **16,** 191–211.

Keeney, R. L., and Raiffa, H. (1976). *Decisions with Multiple Objectives: Preferences and Value Tradeoffs.* New York: John Wiley.

Kihlstrom, R. E. (1974). A Bayesian model of demand for information about product quality. *International Economic Review,* **15,** 99–118.

Kihlstrom, R. E., and Mirman, L. J. (1975). Information and market equilibrium. *Bell Journal of Economics,* **6,** 357–376.

Kirman, A. P. (1975). Learning by firms about demand conditions. *Adaptive Economic Models* (R. H. Day and T. Groves, eds.), 137–156. New York: Academic Press.

Knight, F. (1920). *Risk, Uncertainty, and Profit.* New York: Harper & Row.

Knight, F. H. (1935). *The Ethics of Competition.* New York: Harper & Row.

Krelle, W. (1973). Dynamics of the utility function. *Carl Menger and the Austrian School of Economics* (ed. by J. R. Hicks and W. Weber), Oxford: Clarendon Press.

Kreps, D. M., and Wilson, R. (1982). Sequential equilibria. *Econometrica,* **50,** 863–894.

Laitner, J. (1980). "Rational" duopoly equilibria. *Quarterly Journal of Economics,* **95,** 641–662.

Lewis, G. (1981). The Phillips curve and Bayesian learning. *Journal of Economic Theory,* **24,** 240–264.

Lindley, D. V., Tversky, A., and Brown, R. V. (1979). On the reconciliation of probability assessments. *Journal of the Royal Statistical Society, Series A,* **142,** 146–180.

Lioukas, S. K. (1983). Investment behaviour in a nationalized industry. *Applied Economics,* **15,** 665–679.

Lippman, S. A., and McCall, J. J. (1976). The economics of job search: a survey. *Economic Inquiry,* **14,** 155–189.

——— . (1981). The economics of uncertainty: selected topics and probabilistic methods. *Handbook of Mathematical Economics* (K. J. Arrow and M. D. Intriligator, eds.) 211–284. Amsterdam: North-Holland.

Long, N. V., and Manning, R. (1976). Adaptive demand theory: the case with a linear utility function. Unpublished report, School of Economics, University of New South Wales.

Lucas, R. E., Jr. and Prescott, E. C. (1971). Investment under uncertainty. *Econometrica,* **39,** 659–681.

Lucas, R. E., Jr. and Sargent, T. J. (eds.)(1981). *Rational Expectations and Econometric Practice.* Minneapolis: University of Minnesota Press.

Luce, R. D., and Raiffa, H. (1957). *Games and Decisions.* New York: John Wiley.

Luce, R. D., and Suppes, P. (1965). Preference, utility, and subjective probability. *Handbook of Mathematical Psychology* (R. D. Luce, R. R. Bush, and E. Galanter, eds.), Vol. 3, 249–410. New York: John Wiley.

Machina, M. J. (1982). "Expected utility" analysis without the independence axiom. *Econometrica,* **50,** 277–323.

Manning, R. (1978). Resource use when demand is interdependent over time. *Economic Record,* **54,** 72–77.

Manski, C. F., and McFadden, D. (eds.)(1981). *Structural Analysis of Discrete Data with Econometric Applications.* Cambridge, MA: MIT Press.

March, J. G. (1978). Bounded rationality, ambiguity and the engineering of choice. *Bell Journal of Economics,* **9,** 587–608.

March, J. G., and Simon, H. A. (1958). *Organizations.* New York: John Wiley.

Marschak, J., and Radner, R. (1972). *The Economic Theory of Teams.* New Haven: Yale University Press.

Marschak, T. A. (1978). On the study of taste changing policies. *American Economic Review,* **68,** 386–391.

McKinney, S. (1984). Public good producers and spillovers: an analysis of duopoly behavior. *Public Finance Quarterly,* **12,** 97–116.

McLennan, A. (1985). Justifiable beliefs in sequential equilibrium. *Econometrica,* **53,** 889–904.

Meyer, J. R., and Kuh, E. (1957). *The Investment Decision.* Cambridge, MA: Harvard University Press.

Milgrom, P., and Roberts, J. (1982). Limit pricing and entry under incomplete information: an equilibrium analysis. *Econometrica,* **50,** 443–459.

Muth, J. F. (1961). Rational expectations and the theory of price movements. *Econometrica,* **29,** 315–335.

Nakagome, M. (1982). Learning behavior in non-Walrasian economy. *Journal of Economic Theory,* **26,** 171–182.

Nelson, R., and Winter, S. (1982). *An Evolutionary Theory of Economic Change.* Cambridge, MA: The Belknap Press.

Nguyen, D. (1984). The monopolistic firm, random demand, and Bayesian learning. *Operations Research,* **32,** 1038–1051.

Novick, M. R., and Lindley, D. V. (1979). Fixed-state assessment of utility functions. *Journal of the American Statistical Association,* **74,** 306–311.

Novshek, W., and Sonnenschein, H. (1982). Fulfilled expectations Cournot duopoly with information acquisition and release. *Bell Journal of Economics,* **13,** 214–218.

Palfrey, T. R. (1982). Risk advantages and information acquisition. *Bell Journal of Economics,* **13,** 219–224.

———— . (1985). Uncertainty resolution, private information aggregation and the Cournot competitive limit. *Review of Economic Studies,* **52,** 69–83.

Pessemier, E. A. (1978). Stochastic properties of changing preferences. *American Economic Review,* **68,** 380–385.

Peston, M. H. (1967). Changing utility functions. *Essays in Mathemat-*

ical Economics in Honor of Oskar Morgenstern (ed. by M. Shubik), 233–236. Princeton, NJ: Princeton University Press.

Pollak, R. A. (1978). Endogenous tastes in demand and welfare analysis. *American Economic Review*, **68**, 374–379.

Prastacos, G. P. (1983). Optimal sequential investment decisions under conditions of uncertainty. *Management Science*, **29**, 118–134.

Prescott, E. C. (1972). The multi-period control problem under uncertainty. *Econometrica*, **40**, 1043–1058.

Prescott, E. C., and Townsend, R. M. (1980). Equilibrium under uncertainty: multiagent statistical decision theory. *Bayesian Analysis in Econometrics and Statistics* (A. Zellner, ed.), 169–194. Amsterdam: North-Holland.

Radner, R. (1975). A behavioral model of cost reduction. *Bell Journal of Economics*, **6**, 196–215.

Raiffa, H. (1968). *Decision Analysis*. Reading, MA: Addison-Wesley.

Raiffa, H., and Schlaifer, R. (1961). *Applied Statistical Decision Theory*. Boston: Division of Research, Graduate School of Business Administration, Harvard University.

Rao, R. C., and Rutenberg, D. P. (1979). Preempting an alert rival: strategic timing of the first plant by analysis of sophisticated rivalry. *Bell Journal of Economics*, **10**, 412–428.

Rutenberg, D. (1982). *Multinational Management*. Boston: Little, Brown.

Savage, L. J. (1954). *The Foundations of Statistics*. New York: John Wiley.

Shapira, Z., and Venezia, I. (1981). Optional stopping on nonstationary series. *Organizational Behavior and Human Performance*, **27**, 32–49.

Shapiro, L. (1980). Decentralized dynamics in duopoly with Pareto optimal outcomes. *Bell Journal of Economics*, **11**, 730–744.

Sharpe, W. (1964). Capital asset prices: a theory of market equilibrium under conditions of risk. *Journal of Finance*, **19**, 425–442.

Shonkwiler, J. S. (1982). An empirical comparison of agricultural supply response mechanisms. *Applied Economics*, **14**, 183–194.

Shubik, M. (1959). *Strategy and Market Structure*. New York: John Wiley.

Simon, H. A. (1955). A behavioral model of rational choice. *Quarterly Journal of Economics*, **69**, 99–118.

――― . (1956). Dynamic programming under uncertainty with a quadratic criterion function. *Econometrica*, **24**, 74–81.

――― . (1957). *Models of Man*. New York: John Wiley.

――― . (1959). Theories of decision making in economics and behavioral science. *American Economic Review*, **49**, 253–283.

――― . (1976). From substantive to procedural rationality. *Method and Appraisal in Economics* (S. J. Latsis, ed.), Cambridge: Cambridge University Press.

———— . (1978a). On how to decide what to do. *Bell Journal of Economics*, **9**, 494–507.

———— . (1978b). Rationality as process and as product of thought. *American Economic Review*, **68**, 1–16.

———— . (1979). Rational decison making in business organizations. *American Economic Review*, **69**, 493–513.

Simon, J. L., Puig, C. M., and Aschoff, J. (1973). A duopoly simulation and richer theory: an end to Cournot. *Review of Economic Studies*, **40**, 353–366.

Slutsky, E. E. (1915). On the theory of the budget of the consumer. *Giornale degli Economisti*, **51**, 1–26. Reprinted in *Readings in Price Theory* (G. J. Stigler and K. Boulding, eds.), 27–56. Chicago: Richard D. Irwin, 1952.

Smithies, A., and Savage, L. J. (1940). A dynamic problem in duopoly. *Econometrica*, **8**, 130–143.

Spence, A. M. (1981). The learning curve and competition. *Bell Journal of Economics*, **12**, 49–70.

Stackelberg, H. v. (1952). *The Theory of the Market Economy* (A. J. Peacock, trans.). New York: Oxford University Press.

Stigler, G. J. (1940). Notes on the theory of duopoly. *Journal of Political Economy*, **48**, 521–541.

———— . (1947). The kinky oligopoly demand curve and rigid prices. *Journal of Political Economy*, **55**, 432–449.

———— . (1961). The economics of information. *Journal of Political Economy*, **69**, 213–225.

———— . (1962). Information in the labor market. *Journal of Political Economy*, **70**, 94–105.

———— . (1978). The literature of economics: the case of the kinked oligopoly demand curve. *Economic Inquiry*, **16**, 185–204.

Stigler, G. J., and Becker, G. S. (1977). De gustibus non est disputandum. *American Economic Review*, **67**, 76–90.

Swamy, P. A. V. B., Barth, J. R., and Tinsley, P. A. (1982). The rational expectations approach to economic modelling. *Journal of Economic Dynamics and Control*, **4**, 125–147.

Sweezy, P. M. (1939). Demand under conditions of oligopoly. *Journal of Political Economy*, **47**, 568–573.

Tonks, I. (1984). A Bayesian approach to the production of information with a linear utility function. *Review of Economic Studies*, **51**, 521–527.

Townsend, R. M. (1978). Market anticipations, rational expectations, and Bayesian analysis. *International Economic Review*, **19**, 481–494.

———— . (1983). Forecasting the forecasts of others. *Journal of Political Economy*, **91**, 546–588.

Turnovsky, S. J. (1969). A Bayesian approach to the theory of expectation. *Journal of Economic Theory,* **1,** 220–227.

Tversky, A., and Kahneman, D. (1974). Judgment under uncertainty: heuristics and biases. *Science,* **185,** 1124–1131.

von Neumann, J., and Morgenstern, O. (1947). *Theory of Games and Economic Behavior.* Second Edition. Princeton, NJ: Princeton University Press.

Wald, A. (1950). *Statistical Decision Functions.* New York: John Wiley.

Weerahandi, S., and Zidek, J. V. (1981). Multi-Bayesian statistical decision theory. *Journal of the Royal Statistical Society, Series A,* **144,** 85–93.

———— . (1983). Elements of multi-Bayesian decision theory. *Annals of Statistics,* **11,** 1032–1046.

White, C. C., III (1984). Sequential decision making under uncertain future preferences. *Operations Research,* **32,** 148–168.

Whittle, P. (1982). *Optimization over Time.* New York: John Wiley.

Williamson, O. E. (1975). *Markets and Hierarchies: Analysis and Antitrust Implications.* New York: Free Press.

Witsenhausen, H. S. (1974). On the uncertainty of future preferences. *Annals of Economics and Social Measurement,* **3,** 91–94.

Zellner, A. (1971). *An Introduction to Bayesian Inference in Econometrics.* New York: John Wiley.

———— , (ed.)(1980). *Bayesian Analysis in Econometrics and Statistics.* Amsterdam: North-Holland.

———— . (1985). Bayesian econometrics. *Econometrica,* **53,** 253–270.

Author Index

Subject Index